SILENT THUNDER

SILENT THUNDER

THE HIDDEN VOICE OF ELEPHANTS

Katy Payne

Weidenfeld & Nicolson

LONDON

First published in Great Britain in 1998
by Weidenfeld & Nicolson

A CIP catalogue record for this book is available
from the British Library.

ISBN 0 297 84265 X

Printed in Great Britain by Clays Ltd, St Ives plc

Weidenfeld & Nicolson

The Orion Publishing Group Ltd
Orion House
5 Upper Saint Martin's Lane
London WC2H 9EA

TESE

which in Shona means

FOR ALL OF US

CONTENTS

PREFACE

The dozen and one years that followed May 1, 1984, are strange years to recall. The thread that ties them together is a scientific effort to learn how elephants communicate with each other and to gather evidence about the social processes that endow elephant societies with their integrity. The effort has led to some knowledge we didn't have before and to many questions, some of which are new and some of which cannot be addressed by science.

Too much happened for me to relate it all. It happened in two zoos, one circus, five nations, three deserts and a forest, several tents and offices and laboratories and a thinking cabin, and it transformed my life into a landslide of notebooks, recordings, photographs, disks, tapes, books, articles, reports, files, and correspondence, all on the subject of elephants. My research partners and I extracted information from the landslide and constructed of it a few scientific papers for the high shelves of libraries. But my personal notebooks were not emptied by the extraction—they remained almost unchanged from their state on the last day of each expedition, when I tenderly wrapped them in the exhausted shreds of my towels, sleeping bag, and clothes and packed them in a battered crate that had served as pantry and table. They were hardly shrunk by the removal of what we had come to gather. And after a time I realized that all kinds of things were moving out of the notebooks and taking up residence in the corners and on the rafters of my house and cabin. These were the memories.

They are memories of living elephants who were not dissected into parts for analysis but were so deeply a part of their larger families, and the families so deeply a part of their societies, and each society so fully embedded in its own land, and each land so defined by the journeys and bonding calls of elephants, that nothing less than the whole is real. They are memories, too, of people strange to one another whom I came to know through elephants—people dispersed by different ideas as inevitably as seeds are dispersed by different winds.

There are also memories of dreams, which arrived unexpectedly, in shocking contrast to other things that were going on. They affected the course of events. Not that they contained answers—on the contrary, they opened up questions and made things harder. In telling my story I offer the dreams as a reminder that there is no such thing as an indifferent observer. "The water tastes of the pipes," as the Quakers say, so you may as well know a few things about the pipes.

It was only after many changes of heart that I decided to reveal the pipes so openly. In the end, what clinched the decision was a conversation with a friend in Zimbabwe. In the research institute where we both worked, he was a truck driver, a botanist, a radio operator, and an assistant to foreign researchers. At home, he was a revered elder in an Ndebele community. I asked him, "How do you tell people about things that happen that are far from their experience?" He answered me emphatically. "You just tell what happened! You just tell what you saw—only God knows what it means." I saw that he was right, and started writing this book in accordance with his advice.

1

A THROBBING IN THE AIR

"Meet Rosy, the matriarch," says Jay Haight, from inside a cage in the elephant house in the Washington Park Zoo in
Portland, Oregon. The Asian elephant looms above him as they
walk toward the thick vertical bars that separate them from me.
Jay's shoulder is level with the bottom of Rosy's right ear, which,
like her forehead and trunk, is pink-bordered with delicate pale
tan and gray spots. The spots are denser at the bottom than at the
top, as if they were particles slowly sliding down a liquid poured
from the top of her forehead. Her body rises and sinks hugely
with each step. One shoulder at a time shifts upward and bulges;
one knee at a time straightens and accepts weight; underneath
the vast belly the opposite leg moves forward; the broad toe-
nailed foot swings forward just above the concrete floor, sets itself down, and splays out. Steadily, the feet, legs, and shoulders
shift, muscles alternating, bulk flowing forward, huge and slow.
The eyes are looking down; the speckled ears are waving slowly
and symmetrically in and out; the face—well, to call it a face . . .

"A-l-l right," says Jay, and the feet and shoulders and belly and back come to a rest, sinking a little. I look up at an immense gray forehead. At its base the forehead gives way to the broad top of the freckled trunk, larger in girth than my girth, longer than I am tall, on each side a gray cheek wider than my torso. From a wrinkled leather pocket on the forward side of the left cheek a patient amber eye looks down. I can see that eye but not the other. Raising myself on tiptoes and leaning close to pat Rosy's forehead, I can't see either one. Her mouth is hidden, too, under her trunk. The dry soft leather of her forehead is warm, warmer than my hand. I slide my hand down the wall of the forehead to the top of the trunk and then down the trunk, passing it over row upon row of thick warm wrinkles. All the time the trunk is moving, its tip searching and reaching this way and that, hovering, whiffing, eventually reaching tentatively through the bars and approaching my other hand, which I hold open and still.

"Hello, Rosy," I say in a low voice, and under the hand that is still stroking the trunk I feel a shiver.

"A-l-l right," says Jay to Rosy, and to me, "Meet her son Rama. Thirteen months old. HEY there, Rama, watch out!"

Out of the top of Rama's head and along his back spring wiry orange and black hairs. He looks up from below me with a full face, two wild eyes visible at once. The whites of the eyes show; he looks surprised, and I respond with a smile. Pressing against his mother, Rama stretches his short, stubby trunk through the bars next to Rosy's long, supple one, and the open tip of each is pink and flexible, cool and wet as it gropes and sniffs my hand.

"This one is Hanako. GET OVER HERE, HANAKO! BACK UP, ROSE. BACK, RAMA! BACK!! Hanako's big boy here is our first grandchild. He's nineteen months old. Git over, Look-Chai, meet Katy."

"Ah!" I hold out my hand, but it is my sandaled feet that the elephants' trunks are delicately exploring, tickling them with breath.

A tall, quiet keeper named Jim Spenser now joins Jay in the cage: he's brought a wheelbarrow and two shovels. The two men fill the barrow with elephant dung. The elephants seem glad that Jim has come: I notice the gladness as a relaxation, and I feel a faint thrill in the air and hear a gentle rumble as he strokes Rosy's trunk between her eyes. The men stand together, each rubbing a different elephant. The elephants' trunks reach around the men's bodies, sniffing.

The keepers ask me what inspired me to come for this visit. I tell them I'm an acoustic biologist from Cornell University, and I've been wondering what kinds of sounds elephants make. I've spent the last fifteen years studying the songs of whales, which are long and complex, and change continuously and progressively. Last week some colleagues who also study culture (learned behavior) in animals invited me to California so we could compare our findings. That brought me within reach of this zoo, with its eleven elephants. I called Warren Iliff, the zoo's director, and he said sure, come ahead, you can spend the first week in May with our elephants if you like.

Jim and Jay tell me about Look-Chai's heritage and the circumstances of his birth. His grandmother, old Tuy Hoa from Vietnam, was the zoo's first elephant. She gave birth to Hanako in 1963. Hanako grew up in the zoo and in her nineteen years gave birth four times; but of her calves only Look-Chai has survived.

Tuy Hoa was old and arthritic during Hanako's fourth pregnancy. The vet decided not to risk having her present at the birth, for even standing up was harmful to her. But they moved Hanako into an adjacent cage where the mother and daughter would be able to smell and hear each other, for a grandmother elephant would naturally assist in birthing. Hanako labored for two days without giving birth. At last, exhausted and worried, the vet and keepers opened the gate connecting the cages. As Hanako ran to her mother both elephants bellowed, rumbled, trumpeted, and screamed, and from other elephant cages farther back in the building came answering rumbles, trumpets, and screams. Then Hanako dropped Look-Chai onto the floor beside his grandmother.

Within two weeks an extraordinary thing happened. Milk formed in the old grandmother's breasts, although she had not had a calf of her own for several years. Along with Hanako, Tuy Hoa nursed the last of her descendants to be born in her lifetime.

"This one is Pet," says Jay. "GET BACK, LOOK-CHAI! Pet's the bottom of the social heap. She'll do anything to stay subordinate—you'll see." Pet's yearling daughter, Sunshine, is pushing forward to join her, and now six trunks are hovering and gliding a few inches from my feet, legs, hands, and belly.

Suddenly Jay makes a decision: no more trunks allowed on my side of the bars. He shouts a volley of commands, and swats each reaching trunk with the flat side of an elephant hook until they reluctantly withdraw.

"And don't you let them sniff you if we're not here," says Jay to me.

Rama starts to break the rule. "No, Rama," I say.

"But *you* should not discipline them," says Jay, quickly. "GET BACK, RAMA! The only people who should try to establish discipline are the ones who will enforce it. We'll tell you stories . . . " And they did. Only a fool attempts to read the mind of an elephant, and I heard about quantities of fools. Each of them had been a fool at least once. Fools had been kneeled on and pressed against concrete walls; some had died. "You'll be noodles if they drag you through the bars," the men warned me.

They finished cleaning the cage, ordered the elephants to stay away from me, and left for lunch.

The indoor air was chilly and dank, and I was tired. I leaned my head against one of the bars, thinking how to begin, and closed my eyes. But a sudden feeling of warmth on my left shoulder caused me to open them again. The radiator was Rosy's body–she had moved up against the bars as close to me as she could get, beginning a process that was repeated each time the keepers left, a slow, gradual migration of all the elephants in my direction. Six trunks reached slightly through the bars, gently surrounding me with whiffing as the elephants decided, more deliberately than before, who I was.

Thus began my first week in a matriarchy. A calm, pervasive discipline regulated the elephants' behavior, for the three adults, born on separate continents and thrown together in captivity, had established a dynamic order among themselves. Rosy, though smaller than Hanako, was the eldest, and whenever no keepers were present her authority was supreme.

It was an authority that extended to and included me. I thought about that as I listened to the whiffing, the inhaling of my smell along with the smells of one another's dung and urine and flesh along with the hay and fruit and nuts on the cage floor. Of what did the authority consist, and how was it communicated among the elephants? I sensed a comprehensive but relaxed mutual attention. Rosy was granting her herd the privilege of exploring my smell carefully. She was granting me the privilege of being carefully smelled. She growled when a calf became too inquisitive, and the little trunk hastily withdrew. Not sure how to keep my end of the bargain, I stayed quiet and kept my hands still, without hiding my interest. When an adult moved in close to the bars I looked up into the hazy dark pupil of her solemn eye. The pupil was so large that I never felt our eyes really met: I didn't know whether I was in or out of focus.

I wished that I had a hovering and whiffing trunk of my own so I could learn the same things about the elephants that they were learning about me.

The square, burly babies moved on to nurse and explore with their supple trunks. Scooping up, sucking in, puffing, sniffing, blowing out, they took in every detail of the floors and walls. In a burst of vertical curiosity all trunks lifted at once, and for a minute or two the three little elephants walked about exploring smells high over their heads. Encountering one another, they entwined trunks, putting the tips in one another's mouths or ears and sniffing. They invented strategy upon strategy for picking things up, with mixed success. Their fuzzy heads were littered with bits of slung hay. They groomed one another and put what they found in their mouths or ears, or poofed the scraps into the corners of the stall. They galloped stiff-legged, heads high, trunks surging, feet loose and floppy, foreheads wrinkled up and eyes wide. At a certain level of abandon, the mothers subdued and separated them. In this they reminded me of the mother right whales that Roger, my husband, and I had watched a decade earlier from the cliffs of the Peninsula Valdés in Argentina. When the whales subdued and separated their calves, we had surmised that the mothers were saving their collective metabolic energy for the long migration across the South Atlantic Ocean to South Georgia and back.

In the back room, our feet up on desks, their hooks laid down and my pencil taken up, the keepers and I compared experiences. They wanted to know what whales were like. I told them about watching the sea hour after hour through binoculars, searching for distant dark shapes—teardrops and exclamation points—which were the caps of whales' backs visible on the surface on a clear and calm day. There were lucky hours when a group of whales would come so close under our cliff that we could identify them as individuals; then for the rest of the day we'd watch them slide away across the silver sea to line up parallel and slip down under, perhaps to rise again a half mile farther out, and be joined by others, and line up parallel, and disappear again, heading for the mouth of the Golfo San José, from which if you go due east, the first land you will strike is New Zealand.

They told me about one swaying elephant belly at a time. About elephants' knees in their faces. About dangerous, affectionate, and often inscrutable individuals. The elephants they knew were as full of quirks and idiosyncrasies as an assortment of very weird people. The confinement and echoing walls of the elephant house amplified whatever propensities each captive animal and each keeper had for dominance, retribution, compassion, and caregiving. These exaggerated personalities were the basis of the relationships that developed within the walls.

Except for an occasional break to run down a path through a forest just below the zoo, and then up again, I spent the whole of every day in the elephant house. Elephants may not have been the only interesting animals in the zoo, but I had eyes, or ears, only for them. At the end of the week I boarded a plane and started the journey home. My ears and the back of my neck were itchy with pins and needles of straw and hay and other zoo frass. I tucked a plastic bag into the overhead bin—my barn jacket, bagged to preserve its smell. I sighed to think that the warm beings who had taken such an interest in *my* smell would become a fading memory as I got back to normal life.

The sigh acknowledged a slight failure as well as sadness. I would have liked to learn something new, but it seemed that the time was not ripe. I closed my eyes to review the happenings I'd witnessed in the zoo. I would glean them, and then say good-bye.

Here stood Pet in the back corner, the end of her trunk moving over the floor like a squeegee, collecting together a few last stems and scraps in the hour before feeding time. Here came

Hanako and Rama sauntering in her direction. Were they coming to visit her, or to deprive her of what she had gathered? The latter, I decided, and I watched carefully, thinking of Jay's comment that Pet would do anything to stay on the bottom of the hierarchy. I heard a faint rumble and the animals shifted, but Pet held her own. The air thrilled a little: I felt happy for Pet.

Here came Jim with the grain and hay. All the elephants moved to greet him, and I enjoyed his gentle voice, and again sensed a kind of thrill in the air.

Here stood little Sunshine reaching toward me through the bars; behind her, her mother standing by, to "turn me into noodles" should I prove untrustworthy. The airplane throbbed, reminding me of the faint throbbing, or thrilling, or shuddering I'd felt at that moment. It had been like the feeling of thunder but there'd been no thunder. There had been no loud sound at all, just throbbing and then nothing.

Now a recollection from more than thirty years earlier joined the first. I was thirteen years old, and I was standing not in a zoo but in Sage Chapel at Cornell University in Ithaca, New York. And what I was hearing was not silence but enormous chords from a pipe organ that was accompanying singers, and I was one of the singers. My mother was across the room in the alto section. The organist and conductor were lit by lamps that illuminated their music. The little circles of yellow light from the lamps were framed by the darkness of early evening inside a vast building. High up in the space a series of round stained-glass windows, still receiving light from the sky, glowed down on us.

The organ was alive. In a powerful combination of voices it was introducing the great chorus that opens the second half of Bach's *Passion According to St Matthew*; we were drawing breath to sing, "Oh man, bewail thy grievous sin." The organist pulled out the great stop and the air around me began to shudder and throb. The bass notes descended in a scale. The deeper they went, the slower the shuddering became. The pitch grew indistinct and muffled, yet the shuddering got stronger. I felt what I could not hear. My ears were approaching the lower limit of their ability to perceive vibrations as sound.

Is that what I was feeling as I sat beside the elephant cage? Sound too low for me to hear, yet so powerful it caused the air to throb? Were the elephants calling to each other in infrasound?

Earthquakes, volcanic eruptions, wind, thunder, and ocean storms—gigantic motions of earth, air, fire, and water—these are the main sources of infrasound, sound below the range of human hearing, which travels huge distances though rock, water, and air. Among animals only the great fin and blue whales were known to make powerful infrasonic calls. No land animal approached the mass or power of these great mammals of the sea, but now I wondered: might elephants, too, be using infrasound in communication?

Once home, I called Carl Hopkins and Bob Capranica, acoustic biologists at Cornell whom I'd known slightly for a long time. Without a moment of hesitation they offered to loan me equipment that could record and measure infrasound, and challenged me to go back to the zoo and find out what was going on.

Four months later I returned to the zoo with the borrowed equipment and two old friends, Bill Langbauer, a biologist whose doctoral research had been a study of captive dolphins, and Elizabeth Marshall Thomas, like myself an unquenchable observer. John McIlhenny, a generous friend with a long-held interest in zoos and elephants, gave us plane tickets. Another friend, Loki Osborn, organized free meals for us at Lewis and Clark College, where he was a student, and got us the laundry room floor in a dormitory as a place to sleep, joining us whenever his own work allowed.

With the help of the keepers, we recorded everything any of us thought might be interesting. We ran the tape recorder at its slowest speed so that in playing back the tapes we could speed them up, raising the pitch of all recorded sounds and bringing the lowest sounds into the range of human hearing. Hoping to learn the meanings of particular calls, we kept written notes, mapped the elephants' movements, and used a mechanical event recorder to time the changes in behavior we noticed.

The elephants had been rearranged since I'd visited them in May. Rama and Look-Chai had been sold and trucked away, and Hanako had been moved to another cage. Now there were just four residents in the big exhibit hall—Pet, Sunshine, Rosy, and Rosy's daughter Metu. In this grouping Rosy was again the oldest, and the undisputed matriarch.

As we recorded, a strange saga unfolded. Metu, who had recently lost a calf in a zoo accident, wanted to adopt Pet's calf, Sunshine. Pet was a dedicated mother, but she was also Metu's subordinate. Rosy was indifferent to the contest between the young adults, but she, too, was partial to the calf. Only Pet had milk for Sunshine, but everyone had a belly she might sleep under. Sunshine liked all the adults and wandered unperturbed between her mother, her adoptive aunt, and her adoptive grandmother. But signs of fatigue in Sunshine led to signs of strain between Pet and Metu as each one jockeyed for the privilege of standing over the sleeping baby. One night, unable to resolve their struggle for custody, they settled for standing side by side facing Sunshine, with their two trunks laid side by side over her back as it rose and fell in the slow breathing of sleep.

In the cold yellow-green fluorescent light, we watched, reminded of the biblical women who, each claiming to be the mother of the same child, had sought King Solomon's advice; and King Solomon had laid his sword, as they were laying their trunks, in such a way that it suggested a fair division of the child into two pieces. What stirred in Pet but motherhood? What stirred in Metu but longing for her own calf? What stirred in them both were feelings so akin to feelings we all recognized that no translation was required. This was a vigil, this was a contest, fueled by the same energies that fuel human contests.

Metu started swaying, as animals often do in zoos, bumping Pet's shoulder or leaning heavily against her at the end of each sway. This caused Pet to shuffle slightly to the side. With every bump she moved a little nearer to her calf's tail. Metu's sways became more and more exaggerated until they were preposterous. There was no question that she intended to displace Pet, and indeed, shuffle by reluctant shuffle, inch by inch, Pet was relinquishing her position. Eventually she gave up and retired to the back of the stall, where she flung hay against the wall, coughing loudly. Metu immediately stepped into the position she had won. A sleeping baby lay in the center of the rectangle made by her four feet. There she stood for hours without moving, a happy, fulfilled four-poster bed.

In the morning, Sunshine woke feeling fine and entertained herself with a heap of lettuce. She flung lettuce leaves onto her back, she skated on whole lettuces, she slipped on them, slid down onto her front knees, then onto her back knees, than stiffened her front legs and pressed lettuce into the floor with her forehead. She rubbed lettuce on a part of her leg that had been irritated by a chain. She put lettuce in the water trough, drank messily, and poured gallons of water onto the floor with her trunk. So began the day. But when evening came, she chose to sleep under Rosy. Protected by the matriarch's dominance, she averted the contest between her mother and Metu, and everybody slept better.

One day, Sunshine and her mother were taken into an

adjacent cage so that Pet's feet could be cleaned and medicated. In their absence Metu bellowed, slammed her body against the wall, then stood on her hind legs, reaching her trunk over it to sniff the chamber that contained the object of her desire. On the other side of the wall, Sunshine was ripping around in circles with her eyes rolled up white, squealing. When the great hydraulic door between the two chambers opened, Sunshine rushed to greet Metu amid screaming and rumbling from all three animals. Then she rushed back to her mother, Pet, and nursed from one of the two plump, humanlike breasts that hung full of milk between her front legs. Metu reached with her trunk to pull at her own barren nipples, then quickly stepped beside Pet and reached her trunk to Pet's right breast. She returned her trunk, now milky, to her own breast, which she coated with Pet's milk.

The adult elephants competed less dramatically for hay and space, for it was a foregone conclusion that Pet's share would be less than Metu's and Metu's share would be less than Rosy's, and every elephant would hold her peace. As for Sunshine, she was welcome to go wherever and eat whatever she wished.

Pet had a special skill, an adjunct to her poverty. She spent hours of every day gleaning—using her trunk as a blower to gather into piles the little bits of hay that remained after the other elephants had fed. She would slowly rotate the tip of her trunk in a circle with a two-foot diameter, focusing it always toward the center. When the crumbs were consolidated she would carefully lift them with the tip of her trunk and place them on her tongue. No other elephant had such a mastery of this art. For all her effort, however, she remained the thinnest member of the herd.

Metu also had a feeding specialty. She would store hay in her lower lip while eating from the upper. Then she would move the stored pile to the upper lip and refill the lower. None of the other elephants did this.

So Metu was a hoarder and Pet a gleaner. Except in relation to Sunshine, there seemed to be a general good-naturedness about the unequal division of property. As Jay had pointed out, Pet insisted on her place at the bottom of the social ladder just as the other adults insisted on their places higher up. Dominance hierarchies, although established through competition, are ultimately the result of a collaborative effort.

Outside in a large sand yard, a male elephant named Tunga was living a miserable existence, trapped in an uncomfortable state called musth. Musth is the condition in which mature males appear to do their most successful mating. Tunga's body was charged with testosterone, which made him aggressive, restless, and inconsolable in his solitary confinement. He paced around his yard, throwing water and dirt clods at visiting people, being shouted at by his keepers, eating almost nothing, and losing weight. His hormones would not let him rest, and the abnormal proximity to the zoo's two other males would not let his hormones rest—this at least is my interpretation, since musth acts, among other things, as a spacing mechanism. He had been in musth for six months and had lost over 1,100 pounds. He was an enormous, unhappy bag of bones.

In his contentious frame of mind Tunga had bitten off the end of another elephant's trunk during a period when both were in musth. Poor Hugo was the loser. It had happened in the aftermath of bad behavior from the zoo's largest and third male, Pachy. Pachy didn't appreciate confinement—he used to slam his cage till our ears rang and teeth rattled—and on this day he had beaten down the door of his cage. While the keepers repaired the broken door, they had no choice but to move two of the bulls into adjacent cages. Hugo and Tunga seemed the least fractious, but the move was no sooner accomplished than Hugo

reached his trunk around to explore the smell of Tunga's cage—
and lost the organ of exploration.*

There was no way to see natural male behavior in this environment. We could only move from cage to cage, recording the
sounds, locations, movements, and actions of the elephants in
them. In moments of excitement we heard high-pitched chirps
and barks from females and calves. We heard, and some of us
felt, low rumbles, and were aware that these were contagious,
sometimes spreading from one cage to another. It seemed that
most of the calls were made by females. But in the wee hours of
the morning, when the adult elephants would lie down, we
heard males and females alike snoring, with long, slow strains of
sound that varied from individual to individual. Tunga's snores
were sonorous and drawn out, like chords from an organ. They
conveyed to my ears a noble peace that contrasted with his miserable waking life. I was moved to hear them and made a long
recording one night to remember him by, and to think about
what he might have been as a free bull in a world large enough
to hold him.

Some nights Liz, Loki, Bill, and I worked around the clock,
taking turns recording, observing, and resting. We rested in the
back of the barn below a towering stack of hay bales; hung on
the walls were huge shovels and many-tined pitchforks, huge
chains, black slickers, and two girths, like horses' girths. There
was a grimy desk in a back corner on which we piled our grimy
belongings and our peanut butter, raisins, apples, and cheese,
next to a grimy coffee machine and a grimy telephone. Above
these hung huge cylindrical heating pipes, from which were sus-

*Perhaps Hugo blew into Tunga's trunk. During musth, an elephant's breath, like his
urine and temporal gland secretions, is charged with pheromones that cause other
musth elephants to react aggressively. This is a recent finding of L. E. L. Rasmussen
of the Oregon Graduate Institute.

pended a filthy blue inflated plastic elephant and enormous lights that illuminated a set of ancient and magnificently gross spiderwebs, layer draped from layer. It was a wonderful room, sneezy with the smell of hay and alive with the quiet movements of sleepy animals. Remembering the atmosphere in the barn in my farming childhood, I felt comfortable there.

During our hours of recording, Liz and I felt throbbing in the air every now and then when we heard nothing. We kept notes on the timing of these events. Bill felt nothing, and said we must not be disappointed if all we managed to do was to record the calls we could hear and link them to behavior. We continued to collect our recordings in such a way that infrasound, if it was present, would also be documented. But for reasons that perhaps stemmed from Bill's doubts, and perhaps from our desire to use all our time and battery power recording, none of us listened to the tapes during our month together. When we dispersed, Bill to New York City, Liz to Peterborough, New Hampshire, and I to Ithaca, we did not know what I was carrying in my briefcase.

It was the eve of Thanksgiving when I opened it. Carl Hopkins was working in his Cornell lab on that evening, and was not too busy to receive a visitor. He rigged the recorder to a machine of his own invention, which displayed a sequence of sounds as dots on a screen, while I selected a tape from a period when Liz and I had felt shuddering in the air. Rosy had just walked to the end of the spacious exhibition cage, and was standing alone facing its thick outer concrete wall. Liz, whispering "I feel it!" had run outdoors to look in the large sand yard for Tunga. She had found him opposite Rosy and almost touching the same wall that Rosy was facing from the inside. Their heads were within three feet of each other, and if the wall had been removed they would have been face-to-face.

The flickering dots of light on the screen of Carl's machine, and the crisscrossing black curves printed on the page, revealed a complex array of overlapping animal calls that none of us had heard in the zoo. With the tape running ten times its usual speed, we heard the calls, condensed and nearly three octaves too high—a little like the mooing of cows. The loudest calls coincided with a period when Liz and I had both sensed throbbing. Two animals had been carrying on an extensive and animated conversation below the range of human hearing. I suppose that they were Rosy and Tunga, calling to each other through the wall.

I looked up as the tape ended and saw a funny quizzical expression on Carl's face. "Goddamned infrasound," he mumbled, and I laughed. Goddamned infrasound, you were a mode of airborne communication all these years while Carl was teaching the sensory world to cohort after cohort of students, and you didn't show your face. Slowly, he began to smile the smile of a contented philosopher. "Infrasound," he mused, with his eyes still on the spectrogram. Then he looked up at me kindly, a hint of paternal worry in his eyes. "If I were you," he said, "I wouldn't tell anybody about this just yet."

I went home and tumbled into bed. Immediately I received a dream.

I was lying in a deep, damp, warm grassy sward in the faint light of predawn. Close, in fact looming over me, was a swaying, silent circle of elephants. They were large and small, and several were reaching out with their trunks to sniff me where I lay, tiny and helpless. They swayed hugely, breathing over me for a long time, and then the largest female spoke in a voice that I heard the way you can sometimes hear in a dream, without vocal features, language, or sound. "We did not reveal this to you so you would tell other people."

I lay silent, holding my breath, waiting for more. But there was only the sound of the elephants' breathing and their strange eyes looking down, down, and down at me, me at the very bottom of all those trunks and all those gazes, with the serious, inscrutable expression that I associate uniquely with elephants.

Gradually the image faded, and I woke in the predawn of Thanksgiving Day. At six o'clock the Ithaca Quakers (Friends) would gather in a silent meeting to bring in the dawn. I rose and put on warm clothes, boots, mittens, and a coat, climbed into the car, and drove through darkness over snow to the old meetinghouse in the country.

Seven Friends were there ahead of me. The woodstove in the middle of the dark old wooden room had been lit, and its warmth was just beginning to push back the chill. The flickering of flames inside the stove sent erratic flashes out through the vent. This and a candle were the only sources of light. I did not know whose lumpy, blanket-wrapped forms surrounded me on the benches facing the stove. We settled, each into our own mound of blankets and our own reverence, or thought, or nothingness.

Inside me, the dream was drumming on my heart. From somewhere outside myself I saw myself stand up between two of the shapes on the benches. The gathered Friends listened as people do when sound comes out of deep silence. I did not hear my own voice, but in the gray light now entering the room through the clear glass of tall windows, I saw tears running down the cheeks of a woman I did not know. I sat down. We remained in silence until the end of the hour. Then, taking our blankets, we dispersed to celebrate the day, each in our own form of thanksgiving.

2

THANKSGIVING

MIST WAS RISING IN WISPS THROUGH THE WHEAT AND CORN stubble on the two sides of the road that led beyond the meetinghouse. Soon after leaving the company of the Friends, I stopped the car to fill my lungs with the clean, sweet smell of the countryside.

I smelled snow-spread cow manure from a distant field, and the smell reminded me of home, for just a few miles over the hills, out by Taughannock Creek, lay the farm where I had spent my childhood. The manure smelled much like the dung of the elephants I'd recently left: I closed my eyes. "Elephants, if you did reveal this to me . . .

"Anyway," I said. "Thanks."

The road descended for several miles and ran along a cliff top beside a lake blue with winter. A few miles farther on, it entered Ithaca, a small city built on a hill and divided by three deep gorges. In the middle of town I looked over the edge of a bridge to a creek about a hundred feet down. An uprising gust lifted the fragrance of the gorge's shale walls and turbulent water: this, too, was a smell of home. And five minutes later, I walked into my parents' embrace, and it was Thanksgiving morning.

Mary and Damon, as I called them—my mother and my father—were no longer young enough to stride across the hills as we used to do; we spent all day inside their little house. Although not the old farm I'd grown up in, it was a house we loved. It had belonged to my mother's ancestors, who went by the name of Fuertes, which means strong in the plural. When Mary was a little girl, her father, an artist, had built it to be his studio, and he had painted his delicate, lifelike watercolors of birds on a drawing table under the same north window where we now sat peeling apples and talking.

We talked in tones of celebration, for I had come home to stay after twenty-five years away. Of the marital failure that lay behind my return we would not speak. With help from my former husband, my parents, and a local bank, I had bought a small stone house not far from the Cornell campus. Its swampy wooded land, in a glacial valley alive with deer, beavers, frogs, and ferns, interested me. I was invited to use an office in a Cornell-owned barn next to the Laboratory of Ornithology for research on animal sounds. The laboratory, the libraries, and an occasional course would help me fill the gaping holes in my unconventional education. I would have colleagues and music. I would be near two of my four children—my daughters, Holly and Laura, who were both Cornell students—and near my parents in their oncoming old age.

The words I wrote in my journal that night remind me of the day:

Mary and Damon—the three of us together with
pomegranates; jokes about a broken mailbox; talk about

farming, the great loss that is the loss of farming families. . . .
Putting up storm windows (Damon needing a stepladder
and not finding one: "I think I can use the wheelbarrow.")
. . . Abundant company, we filled the house and it
overflowed.

We ourselves were farmers during the first seventeen years
of my life. Damon was also a professor of agriculture at Cornell,
but about that I only knew that we often ate apples, strawberries, and peaches that we hadn't grown ourselves. Of the farm I
knew our sixty-six acres of thin stony soil, half in crops and half
in poorly fenced pastures; our shifting assortment of farm animals; our small shed and huge, weak old barn. In August, I
knew the dense honey-manure smell of buckwheat wafting into
our dining room window while its little white flowers fluttered
in the side field. In the front field the corn grew dark green and
tall until I could hardly reach the tassles; up the road the pale
blue-green of oat fields vibrated against the adjacent glowing orange of wheat. There were gone-wild crops as well—walnuts, inside soft shells that dyed our hands dark brown; pears from two
trees, one yielding gritty and the other smooth fruits; tiny wild
strawberries that Mary made into sun-cooked jam.

During the Second World War, we had a full acre in vegeta-
bles, a Victory Garden—or it had us: my brother commented re-
sentfully that the price of victory included child labor. In the fall,
the kitchen was a steam bath smelling of tomatoes and pears, including the gritty ones Louis and I didn't like, and in the winter, it was the place where Mary baked the best apple pies in the
world. Parsnips, which only Damon liked but we all ate, were
also cooked there. On the days before the Tompkins County
fair I filled the kitchen with pumpkins, and one of mine won a
blue ribbon, as did my pig named Hoggy, two noisy, dusty
lanes over and four booths down.

Damon had a thousand red-eyed White Leghorn hens. They were skittery and ugly but productive. My dozen Rhode Island Reds, which I kept separately in the shed, laid few eggs but were beautiful and friendly, purring and squatting to have their shoulders stroked. But in the depth of winter it was all I could do to carry their water in pails from the kitchen to the shed, grasping the handles in my two mittened hands and straining to lift each pail above the crust of deep snow while groping with my feet for the footprints Damon had made on his way to the barn.

We had a pair of pigs and sixteen sheep, a recalcitrant pony, and one year a pair of long-horned cattle from the Wild West who leaped over our fences as if they didn't exist. To contain all our animals within the farm fences would have taken something we lacked, so we chased and tracked and searched and got to know the land from the point of view of the escapees. Before I was ten I wrote my first book, and called it *My True Animal Chases*.

Many wild animals lived among us, indoors and out. My north bedroom window looked into a hole high up in a great oak tree; every spring a new family of baby red squirrels peered and crept out of the hole and learned to climb before my eyes. At the supper table I would give out the news. "The babies are climbing up and they don't know how to go down again. The mother is frantic." "They're okay, Kate," my brother would answer, shrugging his shoulders. "They're heading for the attic."

A farm is an unlimited undertaking, in many senses a labor of love. Even as Damon would mend and build here, something over there would be escaping or falling apart. He rigged our huge, wobbly old barn with a web of ropes that ran from corner to corner, to keep it from falling onto its knees in our wild winter storms. Their tension adjusted with block and tackle, the ropes were so placed that they might send an unaware worker in the hayloft headlong to the main floor three stories down. One day Mary asked Damon to adjust the rig, but he'd no sooner done so than he built a vertical wooden chute from the loft into the big chicken room on the ground floor. Unaware of it while sliding in the hay, I shot down the chute. I'll never forget the dust and feathers, the terrified birds plastered against walls and nest boxes and our combined screeching, all of us appalled by my sudden arrival.

By the time of my earliest memory, the farming adventures had given rise to a family saga called the Johnny Possum stories. Damon invented these on Sunday mornings when Louis and I got into our parents' bed before Damon got out of it. Mary would lie among us to hear what our father had been brooding over, for he was spare with words and there were times when only the possum brought him out.

Johnny was a sluggish, ornery being with possum habits and a maverick farmer's concerns. "Johnny O'Possum—long ago his family came across the ocean from a little town in Ireland"—so began the last story, the only one from which I remember a direct quote. Johnny was always sleepy. He would half awaken in his burrow deep under a snowdrift with a problem that was slow to emerge because of the brain-slowness that afflicts a creature in winter. He'd try to remember an urgent farm task that would come only haltingly as he struggled to wake up, or to overcome his resistance. He would lie procrastinating with an invention on his mind, a snow-defeating vehicle perhaps to be made out of pieces that might still be heaped in a corner of the barn, if the barn was still there.

In 1947–48, a year of endless blizzards, we had sixteen sheep that, for some reason, Damon decided to sell in the depth of winter. He transported them to the buyer's truck by tying their legs together and strapping them, one by one, to a toboggan that he dragged from the barn nearly half a mile to the road over deep, fluffy, unplowed snow. Mary groaned at the folly of the enterprise: it was with shovels and the muscles of their backs, later, that he and Louis cleared our quarter-mile driveway. The next Sunday morning, resting his back, Damon engaged us all with stories. First he dissolved Louis and me in giggles over Johnny and his livestock, then he illustrated for Mary the psychology of a possum's relations with ropes, ladders, toboggans, wheelbarrows, and a possum's love for short-cuts, the sum of which always forced the poor creature to failure. Feeling the bed shake we looked through the pillows to see Mary, too, in giggles, tears pouring down her cheeks.

Mary's days, unlike Damon's, had time in them. She played the piano modestly and loved the music of Bach immodestly. She almost always had a tune in her head, and could whistle and sing at the same time. We'd hear her doing duets, often two parts (any two) of a Bach chorale. Before I was born, she'd been a scholar of literature in the university, and had much of Aesop and Homer, Virgil, and parts of the Bible by heart, and words from Dante, Shakespeare, Milton, Keats, and Wordsworth. Words played in her head just as music did, and she taught some of them to us. All these things were as alive to her as we were, and as were the frosty blue harebells and the red-and-yellow columbines that trembled in the crevices of Taughannock gorge, where she often took us children and her books for long days of pleasure.

One winter morning, a month after I turned seven, she gave birth to a baby, and named her Mia. While Mary and Damon were away at the hospital getting Mia, Louis and I had our own adventure, for that night the tamest of our ewes gave birth to twins. Damon brought Mary and Mia home and put them in the Johnny Possum bed together. I carried the twin lambs up to join them, and we compared babies. Mary's was helpless and pink, while mine were fully covered with crinkly pure-white coats, their bright black eyes and pink ears alert, their sharp little hooves ready to gambol. After we'd admired everyone born on March 13, 1944, I took the lambs back out to the sheep pen and my mother sang to her new baby,

> I love a lassie, a bonny bonny lassie,
> she's as sweet as the heather on the hill.
> She's my own true lassie, my bonny bonny lassie,
> she's my lassie, my Scotch bluebell.

Louis and I helped Mary wash Mia's diapers in our old half-automatic Water Witch, and we wrung the water out of them using an electric wringer that could also catch and wring your arm if you weren't careful. We hung them between two pear trees to dry. On winter days when the clothes were half dry we would take them off the line and snap them, one by one. If it was sunny, ice crystals would fly into the air, twinkling and disappearing as if by magic, in a transformation whose name, Mary told us, was "sublimation." Then we'd pin everything onto the line again and retrieve them at sundown. But if it was cloudy or snowing, we'd snap them and then carry the straw basket, one child on each handle, into the warm kitchen, where they'd hang until suppertime on rope lines between the stove and the table.

On many evenings, Mary or Damon read aloud, instilling images that would occupy our minds for the rest of our lives. For Mia they read Laura Ingalls Wilder's pioneer stories, sinking into the long winters and fiddle tunes that once filled little houses in the big woods and on the prairie all across this young land. For Louis they read *The Wind in the Willows*: Mr. Toad's passion for motorized vehicles echoed Louis's identical passion. For me the same book was about something entirely different— a mole and a water rat who watched together through Midsummer Night and heard the Piper at the Gates of Dawn. He was Pan, the pagan god of nature, and his worshippers were animals.

My lifelong fantasy was expressed in certain stories in *The Jungle Book*s. These were the stories containing the password that enabled the boy Mowgli to understand and be understood by the wild animals in the jungle. I read those stories so many times and at so many ages that I came to regard them almost as autobiography. I practiced the password in its English translation, for the pleasure of hearing it. "We be of one blood, thou and I."

Mary had lost her father before we were born. Damon had escaped with his mother from a broken family to the farm where he learned his love of farming. Later he made another escape, from a ship that was torpedoed off the coast of England in the Second World War. After that his longing for peace was palpable; it shaped his melancholy and the quality of love he felt for us, his family who survived. Though American and with the privilege of education, my parents were aware of survival. Neither was sure of the benevolence of the universe. What they had was each other and us, our farm and our books.

We got our first six years of public education in the one-room Willow Creek School, where Damon was both the sole trustee and the janitor. He would light the potbellied stove before dawn on his wintry drive to Cornell. Louis and I would walk to school later, sometimes with gentle Skeeter Hovenkamp and sometimes with wild Billy Wolf, boys who lived down the road beyond us. We were a dozen students, more or fewer in different years, huddling around the stove in the first morning hours. The smell of burning wool and the pain of little blue-white fingers and toes regaining sensation are part of my association with school.

On the way to school in early spring, Louis and I would dip our fingers into the maple buckets hanging from trees bordering the road. After Louis graduated to Trumansburg Junior High, I had no walking companion, so I set up an experiment for myself: could I tell the trees apart by taste? I began getting to school very late—two hours late on the day Mary heard about it. The next morning she woke and dressed me before sunrise, so I could sample sap from all the buckets and still arrive with the other students.

By the time Mia turned six, and I thirteen, the local community had grown so large that twenty students were enrolled in the school. A group of parents built a second room onto the century-old schoolhouse. Then Mary became one of its two teachers. Willow Creek School was the institution that got the greatest benefit from her fine education.

Or maybe I did, for before she taught the school, Mary had taught me. I was a scrawny child, and much at home during my first ten years. Maybe I had a touch of polio or meningitis—both were around and incurable in those days—but nobody admitted more than a little worry. Mary read to me out of her wonderful books and taught me quiet ways to entertain myself. If the day was cold or wet she'd write and I'd read and draw, or gaze for long periods at my grandfather's sketches, which hung in simple frames on the wall—a skunk, a weasel, an owl so true to life you felt the living creatures in the room. If the day was fine she'd open the door and send me out with boots on and no limit as to where I could go or when I should return.

I remember my first encounter with myself, on a high day in late summer. Standing alone in a field where wildness crowded up yellow and green against our garden and house, I said out loud, "This is the happiest day of my life and I'm eleven." I raised my skinny arms to the blue sky and noticed them, and my ragged cuffs, and a mass of golden flowers that was hanging over me. Their color against the sky made my heart leap. Since then I have seen the same yellows, green, and

blue in Van Gogh's harvest paintings and heard the same hurrahing in Hopkins's harvest poem, but my hurrahing, that made
me inside out with exuberance, was for wildness.

My relationships with the wild creatures that surrounded us
were different from those with the domestic ones. The idea that
I was a caretaker or steward of wild nature never crossed my
mind. I was only a creature listening for the passwords of the
others. Once I was surprised by a voice from a tiny black-eyed
salamander, brilliant orange with minute round red spots
ringed with fine black circles, its belly fat and lithe—a newt in the
stage called "eft." I'd been wandering down our home creek,
daydreaming and playing from one waterfall to the next, and it
was a lovely day when every pool was enchanting and every
bend in the view ahead an invitation. I turned over a stone in
the black crushed shale at the edge of the stream and there it
was. I was overcome by desire to feel its cool, soft belly and admire its fine jointed fingers on my hand, but a sensation almost
like a shock from an electric fence stopped me: I thought the eft
said, in a little sharp voice, *No!* I moved quickly away, not looking back. I mustn't offend it. When I got home I made a map of
the stream, with its five waterfalls tumbling down over four
miles to the lake. Between the second and third falls I drew a
tiny orange salamander with an irregular circle around it, the
area I thought the eft was guarding. Nowadays I would call it the
eft's home range.

Afterward, it seemed that it was not the eft who had
screamed, but something else. In later life I have had the sensation on several other occasions: each time I felt I was breaking
a law of nature. One of my scholarly friends tells me that
Socrates reported a similar restraining voice in himself, which
he received as an indication of his guiding principles. "This sign
I have had ever since I was a child. The sign is a voice which
comes to me and always forbids me to do something which I

am going to do, but never commands me to do anything."*
Well, I'm not Socrates, but it seems I have a similar experience.

I was seventeen when my family experienced the loss of our
farm. We moved into town so Mary could teach, and I be a student, at Cornell. The move went against a powerful wish in my
soul. Although I loved what I then learned—I studied music—I
only vaguely remember the house to which we moved, and the
walk I took two, four times a day for four years between that
house and the Cornell campus. For my family was no longer the
"we" we'd been. We'd become "I" and "you" and "he" and
"she," divided by occupation; and we never heard from Johnny
Possum again.

I had lost both farm and childhood in a single move. But for
Damon, farming had been more than a personal passion.
Shortly after I left home, he and Mary moved to Costa Rica and
thence to Peru, where for almost two decades he worked with
small farmers to preserve the indigenous knowledge of which
they were the only reservoir. He had seen the cost the Green
Revolution would exact of the land and the cultures it displaced, even as it promised vast increases in world food production. When, on Thanksgiving Day, he mentioned the loss of
farming families, I suppose he meant the loss to the world of
people who have known and felt and done what farming families have to know and feel and do in order to survive.

At the end of Thanksgiving Day, I told my parents about the
elephants. We looked at each other in astonishment, mine refreshed by theirs. But our hearts and minds were already over-
full, so we said no more. We walked outside together. At a curve
in the path to the driveway I looked back and saw them on the

---

* Plato, *Apology*, in *The Works of Plato*, vol. 3, translated by B. Jowett (Franklin Center,
Pa.: Franklin Library, 1979), pp. 120–21.

porch of my grandfather's studio, framed by the yellow pillars that supported its roof. They were holding hands as they watched me go.

Bill, Liz, and I met for a weekend at Liz's house in Peterborough, New Hampshire. We talked and feasted and heaped wood into a big old kitchen stove, and roared with laughter. We must have gotten to work, too, for our report entitled "Infrasonic Sounds of Asian Elephants" was soon published in the journal *Behavioral Ecology and Sociobiology.* Before it came out, an eight-column article entitled "Secret Language Found in Elephants" had appeared in *The New York Times.*

I glued the articles into my journal not far from each other, a few pages after my summary of the dream in which the elephant said to me, "We did not reveal this to you so you would tell other people." There they remain, three responses to the same event. The articles announce a discovery in which Bill, Liz, and I are agents and the elephants are objects. The dream announces a revelation in which elephants are agents and I am a receiver. The articles refer to a world in which animals and people are separate and secret from each other, poorly acquainted and without common birthright. The dream refers to a world where we are of one blood—where you know a tree by its sap, and have a possum for a father and a bluebell for a sister, and the Piper waits at the Gates of Dawn. In such a world animals reveal things to each other, and even occasionally to people like me: their attention to us is commensurate with ours to them.

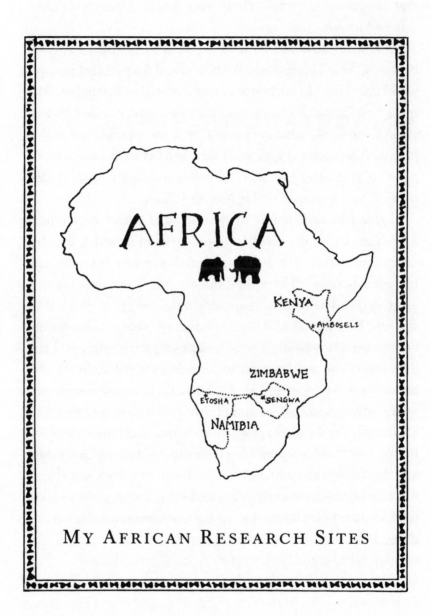

AFRICA

KENYA

*AMBOSELI

ZIMBABWE

ETOSHA *SENGWA

NAMIBIA

MY AFRICAN RESEARCH SITES

3

MATRIARCHS, SISTERS, AND BABY-SITTERS

THE FIELD BIOLOGISTS IN AFRICA HAD SEEN INDICATIONS that elephants communicate with one another over inexplicably long distances. In Tanzania, Iain Douglas-Hamilton had wondered about the ability of elephants to silently organize themselves when no organizing cue was visible or audible. Laughingly, he'd suggested they had extrasensory perception. In Kenya, Cynthia Moss and Joyce Poole had wondered how male and female elephants, living separately and sometimes far apart, were finding each other during the brief and unpredictable windows of time when both were available for breeding. Joyce had marveled that "twelve-thousand-pound males were making aggressive calls I could barely hear!" Cynthia had proposed, without testing for it, that there was sound below human hearing. In Zimbabwe, Rowan Martin had radio-tracked female elephants from different families for several years. He'd wondered how these animals, separated by miles of forest, were coordinating their movements with each other for days and sometimes weeks at a time without meeting. And in India, where elephants had been beasts of burden for three thousand years, the folklore was rich in references to their relation to clouds and thunder, and to their uncanny abilities. Then in 1972 the naturalist M. Krishnan remarked on the possibility that elephants might communicate using sound frequencies not fully audible to humans. No one who knew elephants was entirely surprised by our discovery. "Of course!" they all said.

It also happened that another researcher, Judith Berg in the San Diego Zoo, had reported infrasonic frequencies in the calls of elephants before us. Our findings were complementary. Berg's recorder wasn't designed for sound outside the range of human hearing, so she had not realized that the low-frequency energy was sufficient to be the basis of a long-distance system. It was we who had made that connection, mentally and technically, but we'd recorded Asian elephants while Berg had recorded African elephants. Much work lay ahead for us all, and many questions remained.

The distance a sound travels depends on the medium it passes through, on the strength of the sound, and on its frequency. High sounds travel in short waves that lose energy quickly, for they are deflected by grasses, trees, and other obstacles, and dissipated as heat. Low sounds travel in long waves that are less diminished by the same effects: the lower the sound, the less the loss. The strength of a low-frequency sound has a profound effect on its range. If you double the strength of a sound whose initial range is twenty meters, the range will increase to forty meters; if you double the strength of a sound whose initial range is two kilometers, the range will increase to four kilometers. So I saw that if we wanted to know the range of elephants' communication, we'd have to measure the strength as well as the frequencies of their calls in the field.

With this objective, I found myself, just two months after the zoo discovery, in Amboseli Park, Kenya, starting a study of elephant communication with Joyce Poole. All the groundwork had been laid before I came. Cynthia Moss had been following the Amboseli elephants for a decade and a half and knew all 650 members of the population as individuals. Joyce had completed a nine-year study of the male elephants in the population; Phyllis Lee had studied a cohort of calves in their early years, and David Western, Keith Lindsay, and others had studied the ecology of the park. Now I joined Joyce in the small research camp, five tents in a palm grove, where all this work had been centered. We worked together from January through March in 1985 and again in 1986.

Amboseli is dry in these months of the year. At noon the sky, blue in the middle and pale going toward yellow at the edges, broods hotly over sparse meadows of shimmering golden grasses. This is a good time to learn about the social structure of an elephant population because its members tend to travel between forests and water in discrete groups. The closest social unit is the "family," a group of a dozen or so related females and their offspring. Certain families have a strong preference for each other's company. The families so affiliated are a "bond group." Families and bond groups are often expanded by the visits of adult males, but on the whole males live rather separately from the families, in bachelor herds and independently. Large mixed aggregations of males and females form spontaneously now and then: when they break up, the animals return to their predictable social units. Guessing that vocal communication helps mediate all these movements and changes, and that powerful low-frequency calls underlie the coordination of movements over long distances, Joyce and I set out to record and measure as many elephant calls as we could while keeping track of the circumstances.

On some days, Mount Kilimanjaro appeared in the south.

Hovering, it did not seem to be attached to the earth, but it took up a large part of the sky. Gray-blue forest patches interspersed with tannish clearings floated above the plain. The tops of the irregular patches gave way to a tall and broad section denser in texture but weaker in hue, suggesting tundra. Very high above the tundra a broad white crest stood out in crisp contrast to the blue sky. "Nineteen thousand three hundred forty feet, and the white you see is snow and glaciers," said Joyce.

Snow and glaciers, on the equator.

Down on the plain, everything was trembling in heat. On the horizon, gray skyscrapers, tall ships, and long, square-ended tankers were lifting and running, becoming herds of buffalo or elephants or groves of trees and turning back into mirages, so that I wondered whether I was hallucinating. Some two dozen very large animals were drifting placidly toward us, swinging their trunks before them. Dwarfed by the mountain, they reminded me of domestic cows coming to be milked. "They've been in the swamp," said Joyce, and I saw that their legs and bellies were dark to a line halfway up their sides, and so was the bottom third of each trunk. Growing unevenly in height and density, they moved toward us along a trail that led to Joyce's small jeep. They surrounded and passed us, as little concerned as if we were a negligible bush. I looked out my left window at swaying bellies and thick knees draped in gray skin. A vast ear was waving rhythmically back and forth above my head: I felt a breeze. Other large bodies drifted behind, some ahead. I heard a very soft deep purr and looked up into an eye that was looking down into the jeep.

"Ulla," whispered Joyce.

Ulla raised her head and peered over the top of the jeep. In the direction of her gaze stood a broad old elephant with immense cabbage-leaf ears and a wizened expression that resulted from her having no tusks. "Big Tuskless," said Joyce. "Matriarch."

Ulla was looking down. Her front feet were kicking up grass clumps and raising dust, which was wafting in my window and landing on the spherical windscreen that protected the microphone. That instrument was recording the scuffing of feet and the thumps of earth on earth as the elephant, having lifted a clump in her trunk, flung it onto the ground; and the crumbling of dry soil on the salty crust, and the grinding of grass and dust between her molars, the growls and farts of her digestion, the scraping of her dry ears against her dry shoulders, many small hums, faint squeals, and faint rumbles. I had earphones on, listening to these sounds, which were all within my range of hearing. If there were sounds beyond my powers of perception, I would find out about them later, when I analyzed the tapes.

A little female calf was tagging along behind Ulla, tagged by the calf's slender-tusked older sister. "Ute!" said Joyce.

Ute's trunk was touching, stroking, sniffing, patting the calf's back as they moved along at the calf's pace. Ute's eyes widened as the infant, bumbling along, eyes and trunk on the ground, walked into the jeep—bump—grunted, growled, squealed, lifted her head and backed up suddenly, flinging out her trunk and ears, and did a little backward-moving dance. Alarmed by her sister's blunder, Ute ran trumpeting and bellowing to their mother. Immediately we heard large deep overlapping rumbles.

"Reassurance," said Joyce.

"From more than one adult?"

"Oh, yes, from several."

Ute shoved her infant sister toward their mother. Another calf, a four-year-old with two warts on her trunk, gave a loud rumble behind Ute, who again turned back. We heard a soft rumble from several voices, and the family completed its passage beyond the jeep.

"Ute is an incorrigible baby-sitter," said Joyce.

We started each morning by driving to an area where Joyce had often seen elephants. On some days, this led us into the middle of a grand happening; on others, we witnessed only an inkling of an event. Toward midday, the heat of the earth would begin to exceed the heat of the air and the change would create wind, making recording impossible. Then we would drive back to camp to pour water over our bodies, eat lunch, and rest under thatched roofs in the shade of palm trees. Most elephant families were also eating, bathing, and resting at that hour, having slowly moved out of the acacia groves, crossed a pan or plain, and sunk into one of the deep permanent swamps where their trunks served as showerheads and we could no longer accompany them. As we drove back, I would ply Joyce with questions about the elephants we'd seen and their groups and companionships and home ranges and history. Her impression of the variation of all these things over time provided a standard against which we measured our new encounters.

I kept extensive records on what we saw and heard, and our opinions about what it meant, and how these were supported by Joyce's past experience. I also kept records from which I could calculate the strength of each call and the distance it might travel. Overlaid on these systematic notes were musings and questions, arrows, stars, exclamation points, and guesses, guesses, guesses. There was much to be humble about. I was not surprised when Joyce and I, analyzing our tapes at the end of a month, found that the elephants had made at least three calls for every one that we had heard.

"... rrrrrrrrRRRRRRRRRRRRRRRRRRRRRRRRRRRRRRRR RRRRRRRRrrrrrrrrr ..."

A slow, deep rumble on a single tone, increasing in volume, fills the air for three seconds and then diminishes until we no longer hear it. The sound comes from ahead of the jeep, where, above a canopy of tall grasses and framed in the blue of the sky, the head and shoulders of a large elephant are coming into view, dipping and swaying as she slowly approaches on a well-used trail. Her trunk swings from side to side; her head dips with every step, and the dipping exaggerates the swing and the sway. The tip of the trunk is living a life of its own, opening and contracting and changing orientation, testing the smells near the ground on the right side, ahead, and on the left side of her advancing feet, to her sides and in the air ahead of and behind her. Her eyes look downward. Here's a heap of dry, decaying elephant dung (the smell is sweet): the great body hesitates, the trunk explores. The great body moves forward, displacing grasses on either side of the trail. She'll leave us to her left: the trunk sniffs left, the body hesitates; the trunk lifts, spelling **S** in front of and above the head, the tip swiveling, pausing; then the trunk swings heavily down to the ground again, and without turning her eyes to us she moves her great body forward.

It is hot inside a jeep in full sun on the equator. I am following Joyce's examination of the shapes and venations of ears, the length and angle and thickness and symmetry of tusks, the length of legs and breadth of heads and slopes of bellies, and occasionally the unique patterns of wrinkles. She whispers the animals' names, which according to Cynthia's system all begin with L. The elephant about thirty paces ahead of the jeep, who just gave the long rumbling call, is Leticia, the matriarch of the family.

"... rrrrrrrrRRRRRRRRRRRRRRRRRRRRRRRRRRRRRRR RRRrrrrr ..."

"Let's go," says Joyce, translating. The grasses behind the matriarch part and two younger adult females slowly emerge, with grass in their mouths, and their ears slowly fanning, each with a small calf at her heels. Grass tops are waving in other directions; soon five or six juvenile elephants are clustering with the first-comers.

In the shade beside the calling mother's body, the enormous fluted ears of a very small male calf are slowly fanning, together, apart, together, apart, like a huge gray butterfly opening and closing its wings. From time to time, his limber, stubby trunk stretches between his mother's front legs to touch one of her full breasts. After a time, his older sister ambles up beside him. He stills his ears and turns his head and lifts his trunk onto her head. The sister's trunk reaches to sniff his closer ear. The calf makes a faint growly sound and someone answers in a faint hum. The sister sniffs his farther ear, then lets her trunk fall loosely down, its weight resting on his neck.

For a minute, all is still. Then a larger, broader-headed young male emerges from the grasses and joins the two siblings. His trunk sniffs inside their mother's mouth, then down into his sister's and brother's mouths, and in one motion the smaller animals reach their trunks into his mouth. This seems kind of like ants, I think, which exchange drops of regurgitated liquid when they meet, and so learn about the composition and condition of their colony. A colony's responsiveness to its own condition is a beautiful thing to think about. I wonder whether trunk checking in elephants is a variation on that theme.

The three young elephants, their backs pale gray and smooth like the bark of beech trees, stand calmly side by side, parallel to their mother. Another long low rumble heralds two adult females who now join the family, trailed by their offspring. Ears flap and eyes are wide as they arrive; the old mother turns to greet them in the same posture of excitement, and a loud deep rumble spreads through the growing herd. More trunks reach to test mouths, ears, temporal glands (between the eyes and ears), and genital areas. This stimulates more group rumbling and further exchanges of sniffing.

Then all becomes quiet, patient, peaceful; the elephants stand together, waiting. We hear the "Let's go" rumble again.

Another mother arrives with two more calves. Another round of rumbling, ear flapping, touching, sniffing. Several calves nurse; others fan their ears at their mothers' sides or heels.

By the twelfth swell of contagious rumbles, all the gathered elephants have lined up behind the old mother singly and in pairs. She stands on a path made by the hoofs and pads of predators and prey alike and softened by elephant dung. After the fifteenth set of rumbles, six of the newly arrived elephants start moving down this path. "Lolita," Joyce whispers as a middle-sized adult female passes us. But the elephants closest to the old mother do not move and neither does she.

"What are they waiting for?"

"Laura. And Llewelyn, maybe, but I don't think so. He's eight years old."

The waiting elephants seem to be in agreement that the family is incomplete. Are they hearing Laura over the horizon? I hear nothing. Hot and confined in the jeep, I feel a twitch of impatience, in which I apparently differ from the waiting elephants. Not one is shoving, or wandering back to its previous companions, or falling asleep. As the group swells toward completion, every new arrival is the cause for a communal call. Laura arrives and is greeted. "We are together," I understand the call to mean, we, the members of Leticia's family—hello, hello, hello, we're together, all right.

All the females and calves are assembled. Still the family waits.

"Llewelyn," says Joyce. Over the tops of distant grasses I see a smooth gray head dipping and lurching as it comes toward us, the broad ears flopping asymmetrically. The width of the head, the rounded, muscular top of the forehead, and the long legs reveal an adolescent male. He approaches deliberately, in long bobbing strides. His legs, belly, and the back sides of his ears are coated with fresh, dark mud.

"Big brother, just going independent."

Covered with the evidence of a pleasure everyone might have liked to share, the large adolescent bull lumbers into view. His arrival is greeted with a last swell of overlapping rumbles. Joyce is surprised. I, too, am surprised, but without the benefit of elephant knowledge, I am viewing the situation as a human mother. No jealousy among the younger siblings? No swaggering by the mud bather? No reproaches from the waiting adults?

Llewelyn and the waiting elephants sniff and touch each other's mouths, temporal glands, ears, and under each other's bellies. Then the matriarch slaps both her ears and scrapes them forward against her neck—a sign that a change in activity is about to occur. She takes a step; all the other elephants start to move. It's twenty minutes since Leticia gave the first "let's go" call.

The family passes us in single and double file, their heads swaying, their trunks swinging, and stretching forward just above the surface of the ground. Without disturbing the stride each trunk explores the recent history of the path: elephants, with their eyes two meters above the ground, can collect this information as easily as does a mongoose loping along with his nose on the ground. At the rear of the herd, in the position often occupied by visiting adult males, a couple of lengths behind the last adult female but moving in synchrony with her, walks Llewelyn. The family moves steadily along until every elephant is out of sight.

What cohesion! What unanimity! What relishing of one another!

Cynthia Moss spent one week of each month in Amboseli, checking on the 650 individuals she knew. One day she invited me to join her in the census. "Oh, it's Qasmira," Cynthia said as we came into the proximity of a small family. "Look at her left side."

Behind the left shoulder of an adult female elephant was a vertical pocket about half a meter long, just under her skin. It contained somebody else's tusk—like an ivory sword in a perfectly fitting sheath. The broken end of the tusk projected a few inches out of the top, and the top edge was sharp and slanted. Long and slender, the tusk must have belonged to a mature female.

One of Qasmira's sisters had recently broken her right tusk. The raw upper edge of the sword in Qasmira's sheath matched the lower edge of Qatana's stub. Next to Qatana walked a very young calf. "Aha," we said, imagining that Qasmira had come between Qatana and her baby. Yet the sisters moved about casually, touching and testing one another like family members on good terms.

"Elephants will pull darts out of each other," Cynthia commented. I did not ask what kind of darts or who put them in—scientists wanting to prove something about the elephant's movements, or young Masai warriors wanting to prove their manhood?

One morning, we came upon the matriarch, Mary. With only a few members of her family, she was peeling bark from a branch of a large acacia tree. Mary's young bull calf stood between her front and rear knees waving his ears and swinging his trunk idly.

I felt idle myself, enjoying sweet fragrances and the light, fresh morning air, still but for bird calls. But suddenly a volley of roars, bellows, and trumpets scared me out of my reverie. Mary whirled around. In an instant, all the adult elephants were running toward us, their mouths open and their ears flapping. I looked over my shoulder to see four others converging on us from behind. "Freda, Fay, Fay's daughter, and Wedge," whispered Joyce breathlessly—"the missing relatives."

Rushing together, Mary and Freda pressed their heads together, then backed up and charged at one another. Their long slender tusks clicked and clashed close to my window. They grasped each other's trunks and pulled first in and then out, reminding me of a square-dance move in which partners hold hands, stretch apart, and draw together. Then they planted their feet firmly and shoved against one another. Loosening their grasp on one another's trunks, they roared and twirled in opposite directions until, completing the circle, they bumped rumps. Then they stood side by side, swaying. Each urinated and defecated urgently. Secretions from their temporal glands were streaming down their cheeks. Trunks low, they swung around again, raised their heads, and looked into each other's wide eyes, then lowered their heads, raised their trunks, and began sniffing— mouths, ears, temporal glands, vulvas—as they rumbled, and rumbled again. Meanwhile, the excitement had spread to the other family members, who were milling around in the dust. Even after the largest females had settled into sniffing, the air rang with bellows, rumbles, screams, and trumpeting from the rest, and the drumming of urine forcefully hitting dust. I noticed a stream of liquid spurting sideways from a young female's temporal gland, and rubbed my own temples, which itched as I watched. In a small clearing not far away, two pairs of young males started jousting. In the forest of moving adult legs a young calf called out a suckling demand; an abrupt growl signaled (I thought) a refusal; another young voice protested—the mothers were too excited to stand and nurse. Mary backed into her young calf and he squealed loudly—immediately a chorus of hums and rumbles responded. "Reassurance," said Joyce.

Had we parked, by chance, at a prearranged point of convergence, or had they chosen us as their meeting place? "Sometimes it does seem they choose us," said Joyce. Does such a greeting indicate a long and arduous separation? No, Joyce told me; elephants in the same family will greet like this even when they've only been apart for a few hours. Bond groups do the same thing.

Bond groups do the same thing: a diagram from an article on elephants' social system flashed before my mind. It represented, in a series of concentric circles, six levels of association of an adult female elephant. She stands, a little silhouette, in the central circle. The layer that wraps around her includes her calves. The layer that wraps around the family is the bond group. Of all the dimensions in an elephant society, this one intrigued me most.

"Are bond groups friendships, or extended families?"

"Maybe both," Joyce said. "We know for sure about one family, which enlarged and split apart. After the split, all the elephants continued to greet, whenever they met, in the manner of family, and if you happened upon one family, the other was likely to be near. But we also know of one case where they were *un*related!"

What did she mean by "unrelated"? Relatedness on the female side is easy to guess, since a female never leaves her natal family, but who could say which of the Amboseli elephants were related through their fathers? The terms weren't accurate or parallel. "Family" was being used to indicate a maternal relationship, "bond group" to indicate a behavioral relationship, and "clan" to indicate a geographical relationship. All at once I saw concentric circles around each of the greeting elephants, and concentric circles around Joyce, and around myself: I saw each of us in the world defined by our associations, which are defined by many different criteria. I thought of all the excited greeting I do, as often with friends as with family; I thought about cousins I hardly know, whom I hug when we meet for the first time. Feeling a little dizzy, I looked at Joyce.

"They sometimes greet me, too," said Joyce.

Then I remembered an experience I'd had with Bill, Liz, and Liz's son, Ramsay Thomas, shortly before coming to Africa. After we'd established that the elephants in the Washington Park Zoo were communicating infrasonically, we decided to visit another captive herd to make sure our discovery was not particular to one site or population. We drove down to Circus World in Florida, a brave little outfit that included a family of Brazilian acrobats, trained tigers, trained ponies, and five trained female Asian elephants, each with a yearling calf. You could see them all together under a red, yellow, and blue tent, bright in the southern sun and fluttering in the December breeze. Offstage, in a separate compound, lived Vance, the father of the calves, a dangerous male who did not perform.

The remarkable association between these elephants and their owners, Roman and Jean Schmidt, allowed us to confirm that during rumbling you can observe a fluttering, with an excursion of about one centimeter, of an area on the elephant's forehead where the nasal passage enters the skull. Jay Haight at the Portland zoo had called our attention to this occasional fluttering and suggested to us that it might coincide with infrasonic calls. He was right, and this provided the final proof that elephants were the source of the infrasonic sounds we had been recording.

But the elephants didn't vocalize very much during our week. On the last evening, Roman got to wishing we'd heard more sound. He decided to show us something he had learned from his father, who had been in his day a famous elephant keeper in the Barnum and Bailey Circus.

Five mother elephants and five small calves were quietly resting and eating hay in a very small stable. Stepping in among the elephants, Roman started to sing their names in a gentle, high voice, patting them and crooning to them. "Piccolo! Piccolo! O, yoiyoiyoiyoiyoi, yayayaya, ohhhhh, hummm." One of the elephants squealed in response, another gave a long string of squeaks (Asian elephants do that when excited), and then the rumbling began. At first it was made, I thought, by a single voice, but that voice was soon joined by others, making an unbroken deep rumble that continued for several minutes, waxing and waning in volume as voices joined and dropped out. Against that deep, throbbing bass line the descant began to include innovative long, modulated calls as well as squeaks. "Oyoiyoiyoiyoiyoi," crooned Roman, and an elephant's voice answered, "Oyoiyoiyoiyoi." "Sally," called Roman softly, "Sally." A long, drawn-out, wobbly descending high note answered, and Roman said, "Sally," and she did it again.

Holding a microphone and recording, I was amazed not only by the power and innovation in the sounds but by the tenderness and mutual trust among the animals and Roman. But suddenly the rumbling grew louder and harsher. Roman stopped singing. The elephants' voices died down.

"Whew! That puts me out!" he said, stepping out of the stable. Sweat was pouring down his face, his hands were shaking, and he needed to sit down. His bad leg—he'd been tusked by a bull elephant some years back—was hurting. He invited us home to his trailer, where Jean made tea for us all, and we looked at elephant pictures and circus pictures and calmed down. After a couple of hours, I referred to the experience we'd just had, but it was clear that Roman didn't want to talk about it. He said he didn't do that with the elephants more than once a year, and his father hadn't either. It wasn't a safe thing to do.

He'd been in the cage with them when it was going on. His own singing had released all that emotion. It was frightening enough for the rest of us, outside the cage: I agreed that it wasn't a safe thing to do. Now, in Amboseli, I found an interpretation for that event. Roman was greeting and being greeted as a member of an elephant family.

* * *

We started each day in the early morning, to take advantage of a short period of intense clarity for the eye and the ear. Just before sunrise it seemed as if nothing, no particle and no wave, stood between the perceiver and the thing perceived. But the sun at the horizon lit up millions of particles of dust, pollen, and insects; suddenly there were countless tiny specks in the foreground and an impression of general haze beyond. Within a few minutes, the changing temperature at the earth's surface produced a breeze, and the breeze softened and muffled sound.

One morning, in the earliest hour, we found ourselves resting at a crossing of two dirt roads as two mother elephants and their youngest calves approached. One calf was a male less than a week old, his limbs lanky and floppy, his wrinkly skin not yet filled out, the top of his large head covered with sparse red hairs, and the backs of his ears pink. The four were moving slowly through a sparsely grassy, dusty area. It was peaceful. Birds were spreading the news of their locations and territories—"huh huh," "huh huh," "huh huh," called the ground hornbill in a smooth mellow voice an octave below the doves and the plovers. Through headphones, the sounds were clear. I would hear distant elephants if they called.

Gradually, I did begin to hear them. They started as a pianissimo bass rumble, like a barely perceptible roll of drums under the chorus of bird voices. Looking into the distance, I saw the slowly moving silhouettes of two groups of elephants and predicted they would converge at the crossroads. They were stopping and starting, mixing and separating. Their front feet scuffed the dust, exposing the roots of grasses while their trunks twirled around the blades above, trying to get a grip. They were pulling up the grasses clod by clod; shaking and thwacking out some of the dust, lifting the clumps to their mouths. I was hearing quiet repeated rumbles of which, with even a whisper of a breeze, I would not have been aware. I was hearing faint sounds that might have been overtones of stronger sounds that the elephants, but not I, could hear.

The two groups mixed quietly with each other: now there were twenty-two. Then, with many low, soft rumbles, this larger group split again into two parts. One began to move away as a unit. All at once, we heard rumbles from several voices in the moving group. We looked to the source just in time to see a large female boot a very small male calf away from herself. Squealing and still propelled by the kick, the calf scrabbled through the forest of legs and into the open. As he arrived in a second forest of legs, we heard a volley of bellows and snorts, and low rumbles from a large, wide-eyed adult, to whom the calf ran and started to nurse. We concluded that he had wandered, and been returned to his mother by the departing family. The herds separated, heading for different feeding areas.

Wandering calves are treated differently in different circumstances, as I've learned by watching other people's documentary films. Cynthia's *Echo II* shows what happened to the little female calf Ebony when she strayed into a family more dominant than her own. She ended up under the belly of its matriarch, Vee, who pushed the calf into the rectangle made by her four legs. Ebony's mother, Echo, also a matriarch but in a subordinate family, called and ran excitedly to fetch her daughter. Vee's family chased Echo away while holding the calf prisoner in the forest of legs. Ebony and Echo both screamed, alerting other members of their family, who joined Echo in a raid on Vee's fortress and rescued Ebony.

Narrating the film, Cynthia described Vee's intention as "kidnapping." I wonder about her use of the term—in human kidnapping, a poor individual usually demands ransom of a rich one. Vee was not in this sense a kidnapper, for she already had higher status than Echo. I would describe her, rather, as a dominant matriarch using the tactics of a bully to reinforce her position in the clan.

Derek and Beverly Joubert filmed a matriarch taking over another cow's small calf in different circumstances, and felt that the calf's life was saved by the intervention. They were in Savuti, Botswana, a stressful environment where elephant calves are frequently separated from their herds and fall prey to lions and hyenas. Stuck in a mud hole, a very young elephant had been abandoned when a large aggregation that included its mother ran away from the spot in a state of high agitation. When another excited group of elephants arrived a few minutes later, the calf trumpeted and screamed. Some of the newcomers tried to release him from the mud but they, too, left abruptly, rejecting him with a kick. Once again the calf screamed piteously. Astonishingly, the second herd returned, dug and pulled the calf out, and led him away, stumbling, under the belly of the matriarch. The Jouberts reported that that relationship turned into a long-term adoption.

One day, I saw a very young male calf sally from under his mother to play-threaten his somewhat older but still nursing brother. The bigger calf gently nudged and herded his sibling back under their mother's belly to suckle. Then I asked myself: to care for a brother who competes with you for milk; or to care for a youngster from another family—why, and under what circumstances, and how often do social animals make sacrifices for each other? In a great moment for Darwinian evolutionists, William Hamilton, thinking about the same issue, predicted that the sacrifice will be proportional to the degree of relatedness. The more genes two animals share, the greater the likelihood that either will make a sacrifice for the other.

The Jouberts' story to the contrary, Hamilton's prediction has been borne out by many studies of social behavior in many species. Intellectually, I have come to expect it, yet the particular examples still touch me. I felt touched when I saw Qasmira and her sister moving peacefully together, one of them missing a tusk and the other carrying it in her side. Bless us all, I said to myself. However these social impulses are programmed, to be social is a complex assignment.

The wind never rose on the day when the wandering female and little brother were returned to their mothers—for the two events happened in the same herd within a few minutes of each other. We accompanied those elephants into the afternoon, and by midday they were loosely spread out in an acacia grove, variously resting and stripping bark from low branches. The bark was smooth and pink on the inside, and straight-grained so that it peeled off in strips eight, ten feet long. The resting and peeling elephants were engaged in their occupations separately, comfortable in the shade, and a large male had joined them without ceremony. Only one family group of nine remained united and moving: this was the family with the newborn male. We drove along parallel to them at a distance, watching through binoculars. They paused, as elephants often do when they arrive at a new kind of terrain. At the limit of a grassy meadow they faced a dusty grassless plain. A mile or two beyond the plain lay the swamp that was their destination.

The infant male reached his trunk to his mother's front leg, moved under her belly, lifted his trunk over his fuzzy head, tipped back his head, and nursed. Two other calves did the same under their mothers. Then, one after another, the calves sank down on their front knees. Kneeling in his mother's shade, the smallest one stayed in a half upright position for a few seconds before he flopped over sideways, his upper ear lying like a huge leaf over his head and shoulder. His eyes closed; his fat belly rose and fell as breaths filled and emptied him; his mouth fell open, showing a circular entrance to the throat—a mouth prepared for a nipple. Under another mother three other calves were heaped one upon the other.

They lay in pools of shade formed by the generations of their female elders. Their mothers, aunts, great-aunts, and grandmothers stood side by side in a half circle protecting the young of the herd from two dangers—the sun, and us. Two of the adult females lifted their trunks and coiled them on their up-curved tusks and closed their eyes. The other trunks drooped symmetrically around the half circle; as the muscles relaxed the trunks grew longer until they touched the ground. One grew so long that it made a circle on the ground like a thick rubber hose. The elephants closed their eyes, and their bodies swayed. Every now and then one of them slowly filled her trunk with dust, lifted the reservoir above the heads of all, and showered the family with a slowly settling coat of reddish dust. They became a terra-cotta sculpture, everything still except the breathing and the slow filtering down of dust. Sleepy myself, I stopped taking notes. A timeless interlude passed.

Suddenly, the smallest calf staggered to his feet, violently rattling his ears so that they threw off a shower of dust, then ran to his dusted cousins and clambered over one after another in a burst of playfulness. They leaped up wide-eyed, trumpeting and blowing out dust. Naptime was over.

I laughed to myself. Who says the matriarch makes a herd's internal decisions? This herd had changed leaders from hour to hour, the youngest calves had made most of the decisions, and all that had been required was for the rest of the herd to agree. How, then, shall we generalize about an elephant family's social hierarchy?

This much was clear: at each level the hierarchy acts in the service of the young. It's easy to see how this has evolved, since the young are so few and so costly to replace if lost. The investment goes on and on. The female gives birth only once every four or five years, for first there are two years of gestation, then two of lactation, which inhibits ovulation. Then come the years of protection and training. A female elephant starts to breed only after about eleven years; for a male the figure is almost tripled before he's a significant breeder. Everything depends on the care that sustains the young animals to adulthood, as with people; and that, I suppose, explains the evolutionary rise of the community in long-lived social mammals.

The more closely you watch elephants, the more complexity you see in their communities. Studying them with evolution in mind becomes a stimulating challenge, approaching the challenge faced by those who ask evolutionary questions about humans. I have seen, for instance, adult elephants protecting the experiences and experiments as well as the bodies of their calves, and have wondered what is accomplished. Adults stand in a protective phalanx while their youngsters assert dominance over animals that hardly compete with them—zebras, or monkeys, or wildebeests, or our vehicle—shooing and threatening, ears wide and trunks forward, trumpeting. The adults stand by as reinforcement: are they taking pleasure from the feistiness of their young? Once I saw an elephant mother do a subtle trunk-and-foot dance as she, without advancing, watched her son chase a fleeing wildebeest. I have danced like that myself while watching my children's performances—and one of my children, I can't resist telling you, is a circus acrobat. Does our dancing improve the performance, and (an evolutionary question) does the enthusiasm of the audience contribute to the reproductive viability of the performer?

However it is all accomplished, there is this concert, this pageant, of communal behaviors, collectively drawing the members of elephant families to one another. Only rarely do you hear of a predator attacking an elephant calf, and I assume the rarity reflects the predators' awareness that, should they attack, they might find themselves in a sorry fix.

Peter Ngande, the cook and general assistant in the Amboseli elephant camp, once saw that promise realized, in an encounter between a solitary lion and a herd of elephants. While working in a fossil-digging project in another part of Kenya, Peter noticed the lion crouching and glancing from side to side as if frightened. A herd of elephants was approaching, and the landscape somehow trapped the lion so that he couldn't get out of the elephants' way. At the last moment the lion leaped forward, dug his claws into the shoulder of the lead elephant, a large female, and hung there. In a single motion the elephant reached her trunk over the lion's body, grabbed him by the tail, ripped him off, and, using the tail as a handle, slammed him onto the ground repeatedly until he was dead. The elephants then broke branches from some nearby bushes, and covered the dead lion with them—a sort of burial—before they walked off.

One day during a later study of elephants, my research partners and I were watching an elephant herd at a man-made watering trough. A very young calf fell into the deep end of the slanted trough and gave a wild bellowing scream. Instantly an aunt and two siblings ran to the calf's aid. They had just filled their mouths with water but had not yet swallowed it; as they ran, water gushed out of their mouths as if they were fire hydrants. Falling on their knees beside the frightened calf (who stood upright with her head, trunk, and shoulders exposed), they reached their trunks under her belly to try to lift her out. As they struggled, their screams, bellows, and rumbles were added to hers. Instantly more help came out of the forest. From an observation tower that we had erected near the trough, we'd been surveying the local wildlife all morning and had not noticed the thirteen mature female elephants who now ran forward and drew the infant with their trunks to the shallow end of the trough. Safe and pampered, she clambered out amid a pandemonium of reassuring rumbles.

It was in this same place—where we spent every day observing the same terrain and often the same individuals—that I realized how much the quality of female leadership in free-ranging elephants varies with personality. Our site was often visited by a family of twenty-three that had a shared leadership. Apparently equal-aged, the largest individuals, whom we called Nervous Tuskless and Eleanor, were as different in character as Mutt and Jeff. Eleanor was easygoing and even-tempered: she spent as much time as the younger elephants drinking, bathing, dusting, and resting, and, secure in her surroundings, led the herd at a leisurely pace from either end of the line or from its middle. Nervous Tuskless, on the other hand, was beset with apprehensions. She would stand extremely tall at the edge of the group, spending the smallest possible time drinking and the rest of her time in a stiff alert position, guarding, freezing, and giving alarm signals, always anxious to lead the family away.

We saw Eleanor and Nervous Tuskless and their herd only at the artificial water point where we spent all our time. This was the sole source of water in a vast dry area. Our project introduced the pervasive smell and noise and activities of humans into the place, which had previously been relatively free of people, and it's my guess that this accounts for Nervous Tuskless's nervousness. With only her behavior as evidence, I suspect she had survived some human maneuver that destroyed the rest of her family,* and had joined Eleanor's group, where something—perhaps age and relatedness—led her to claim a quotient of responsibility for the group.

Frequent disagreements between Nervous Tuskless and

---

*The elephants in this area had been culled repeatedly.

Eleanor suggested that, as among people, elephants' perceptions of reality can differ. It was interesting to watch the family in relation to its two authorities. Perhaps in response to Nervous Tuskless's frame of mind, the herd was more high-strung than most. Drinking or resting was often interrupted by her contact calls to distant elephants, and by unusually frequent bouts of intense listening, and by sudden panicked departures when we could spot nothing wrong. Eleanor remained, in spite of these interruptions, relatively relaxed: she'd respond to her comatriarch's bursts of concern, would stop drinking to listen, but only briefly. Nervous Tuskless's fears undermined the herd's self-confidence enough to alter its patterns of feeding and drinking, but it did not appear to aggravate them. It is possible that in the future, this old elephant's weather ear might save the herd. But in the meantime, I imagined, she was depriving them of a certain kind of well-being that would have been theirs had Eleanor been their only leader.

Before I knew this family I wondered whether a misguided elephant matriarch could doom her family, so unanimous did each family seem to be in its compliance with the decisions of its leaders. Now I think of the situation as more complex. To a certain extent all the members of a herd participate in leadership, as I learned one day when a leaderless elephant family came under our tower. After drinking they spent close to an hour unable to reach agreement about where to go next. Two or three subgroups formed, setting off in different directions. Each group, soon discovering that the whole herd was not following it, stopped, vacillated, and returned to the center, soon starting again in a new formation and direction, from which it soon returned again, and so forth. We had an array of microphones set up that would have captured a "let's go" call in the area, but none occurred, nor did I see the stereotyped behavior that is the usual response to that call. The herd seemed disoriented. In the end, they reached a decision that seemed to result from agreement without vocal communication. With a medium-young adult female in front, the whole group moved together along a previously abandoned path. For as far as I could see—about a kilometer—they all stuck together, and they did not return to the water hole.

I guessed that this family had lost its matriarch. In her absence, each of several potential leaders had gained a following, but all the leaders and followers seemed to sense that the group should not split. As soon as the whole group began to move as one, the vacillation was over.

I have no idea how conscious all of this was, but it has its parallels in conscious human behavior. One of my friends at home is the clerk of the local Quaker meeting. Quakers go to great extremes to avoid a hierarchical power structure. My friend participated in a gathering of clerks from many meetings—leaders of the leaderless—"to develop a query that would help us move toward unity with the process even if some may not agree with a given conclusion." The clerks wrote in their query, "In trying to arrive at unity of spirit do Friends realize that unity is different from unanimity or consensus?" The cautious, compassionate effort reflected in these words reminds me of elephants even if agreement to agree in elephants is not conscious. The disoriented elephants seemed more obedient to process than concerned about where to go. Faced with various impulses about how to spend the day, the unity they had reached was simply to stick together.

Still, it was a shocking moment when I first understood the strength of elephants' attachment to one another. Driving into camp one evening after a long day of censusing in Amboseli, Cynthia called to Joyce out of the window of her Land Rover, "Sarah isn't with her family. I wonder where the carcass is."

"Do you mean . . ." I asked, interrupting.

"Oh yes, a matriarch is always with her family," Cynthia answered.

We found Sarah's carcass the next day. I asked myself, who was this animal that had never been alone until the last day of her life? At what level was I seeing the whole organism? At the level of the individual, or the family, or the bond group? I couldn't reach a satisfactory answer; there was so much interdependence at each level and among and between levels.

When the wind came up in the early afternoon, Joyce and I would leave our adventure regretfully and return to camp. There we found much to be done. I had tapes to label and prepare and writing to do; Joyce had countless tasks and preoccupations with the camp and other people. Sometimes I joined her in a visit to Masai friends or to other European researchers in the park. But usually we parted company for the afternoon and Joyce drove away, leaving me with urgent instructions not to go far on foot, for there were lions around.

This restriction might have been frustrating had I been in good health, but I didn't feel well during most afternoons in Amboseli. I lay around dizzy and hallucinating under the spell of the heat, the antimalarial drugs I was taking, and eventually (in the second year) a case of malaria that I contracted in spite my efforts to avoid it. Gradually, my symptoms came to include the shimmering sound of cymbals in both ears and a wobbling, burning sun before my eyes—for such a visual experience I recommend to you the opening scene in the film *Lawrence of Arabia*. I later learned that these symptoms were caused by an overdose of antimalarial drugs. My difficulties were compounded at night, when I became delirious and had many troublesome dreams. Fortunately, these troubles subsided by morning. Some afternoons were all right as well. Then, in camp alone, I took the opportunity to see how others had interpreted the things I was encountering for the first time.

On one such afternoon, I looked up "matriarchs" in a book called *Elephants,* by Keith Eltringham, a Cambridge University professor who had participated in an elephant management program in Uganda. He noticed that elephants' attachments are particularly clear when they are terrified, injured, or dying, and quantified his observations. His chapter called "The Social Life of Elephants" contains the following summary:

> Sometimes one female, the matriarch, is very much older than the rest. She is probably the mother, or grandmother, of the others and she is very much the leader. In times of trouble she will defend the group and the rest look to her for guidance. If she runs away they will follow her, but if she turns around and attacks they will charge with her. This was often brought home very forcibly to me during immobilization programmes. If one darts a young female in the group, it is extremely difficult to chase off the matriarch. She will stand guard over the stricken animal, trumpeting loudly and attempting to lift it to its feet. The others follow her example and one is then faced with a milling mass of furious beasts. One tries to avoid this debacle by waiting for a female to wander off a little way before darting her and hopes that the matriarch will not have noticed. An alternative is to dart the matriarch herself. The difference in the reaction of the elephants is striking. In this situation, they seem to have no idea of what to do and rarely make any show of resistance as they are shooed away to stand in a forlorn group, anxiously watching the proceedings. Their first reaction when the matriarch falls is to run to her, and this is put to use in culling operations in which whole family groups are usually taken out. . . .

> It is not clear how leadership is exercised in family

groups lacking a clear matriarch or in those with more than one matriarch. . . . It was found, during cropping, that, if one matriarch was shot in a group consisting of two or more family units, her followers would abandon her and run off with a new leader. . . .

"Cropping" means treating elephants like a crop, and killing them in large numbers. Cropping procedures are also sometimes called "harvesting." These days people prefer the word "culling," which shunts the emphasis toward the reduction of population size and away from the collection of valuable ivory. Under the new name, the practice continues in several African countries.

It was terrible to read Eltringham's chapter, not only because of what the elephants had suffered but also because of the decisions the author had made. How terrible it seemed that he'd stood taking notes on elephants' behaviors during death as manifestations of their social life. What is this distance, this vow of objectivity, that science permits in or exacts of the scientist? I should not be in science, I told myself as I struggled into sleep.

Sleep came while it was still light. Perhaps the camp around me went about its business: I knew nothing. But in the middle of the night, I awoke. The moon had risen full and was flooding the meadow, leaving dark shadows under the palm trees on its border. A wave of sound was passing through those trees, a soft low purring. Slowly it became two waves moving down the trees on either side of the clearing, waxing and waning. Close to my tent, a third wave was beginning. Elephants were all around me, calling and answering.

4

RIVALS AND MENTORS

In contrast to the family stands the independent bull. Golden afternoon sun is glowing on his chest as he rips out a tall bush by its roots and swings it in a great circle, an arc of red-brown dust flying over his head. It flames outward against the central blue of the sky, doubling the illusion of the bull's size. This is the individual, M10; no group subsumes him.

"M10"? Do the Amboseli researchers refer to male elephants as numbers and to females by name? Yes, for historical reasons, and yet the naming seems to indicate ambivalence—toward science, perhaps, toward the animals, toward gender. When Cynthia started the project, she gave the females personal names. Soon, Harvey Croze joined her, to study the males: he gave them numbers for the sake of objectivity. In her doctoral dissertation in Cambridge, Joyce used Harvey's nomenclature, but back in camp she and Cynthia assigned the males names as well. The few that stuck are disparate; there's Dionysus (from Mount Olympus), Thor (from Norway), Iain (from Scotland), Bad Bull (from Hell), Pablo (from Spain), Oloitipitip and Saibulu (from Kenya), and Beachball (from Coney Island). I found that I preferred numbers to this medley. But the females' names, with their family relationships encoded in them, pleased me. The Amboseli team was aware of the naming confusion, of course, but it is hard to change a name once everybody is using it.

M10 is swinging an uprooted bush that flings dust into the air and enlarges his image. He is in his prime, which is to say that he has been alive for forty or more years and is growing steadily in dominance, with the top in sight. His status gives him increased access to fine grasses and barks and sometimes precedence for water. He moves slowly between and within his favored drinking and feeding places, at his leisure joining and leaving families, and joining and leaving temporary aggregations of males, displaying his enormous strength but hurting nothing—he adjusts the placement of his feet to allow a tortoise to follow its course uninterrupted. His behavior suggests that he is enjoying several kinds of experience. In the afternoon, the presence of another male stirs him to pull up bushes and push down a tree; but when the two of them meet in the evening, they raise their trunks to test each other's open mouths, and having tested there they slide the trunks across each other's foreheads to sense each other's temporal glands, and then to test each other's ears. Or if the two are up to their knees in water with trunks submerged, each allows just the tip to emerge from the water under the other's belly, and after clearing the hose in a slow, quiet, bubbly exhalation, he uses it to test the scent of the other's genitalia.

This is the same kind of inquiry that females make, but from infancy onward the responses of bulls to what they perceive have been different from their sisters'. Young females love to baby-sit, but young bulls love to chase things, they relish the exhilarated, chin-up, feet-splayed rush and the sight of other animals in flight, and they magnify the impact of their assaults by chasing in pairs or small gangs. Once I saw a rush of which the object was a butterfly. Eyes wide, a gang of young male elephants collectively weighing some twenty or maybe forty tons thundered to a stop as the small fairy, white and weightless, rose up out of their midst. Then each turned on his heels and fled.

To be an adult male is to have experienced about eighteen years of bullying, chasing, and feeding in the best places, and to have passed through the massive change that is adolescence. During adolescence he is one day with his birth family, tagging, like Llewelyn, ten elephants' lengths or so behind a close formation of females as the family moves between drinking places. The next day, he's wandering alone but not so far as to be out of hearing of the sounds of the family. For half a day, he joins a casual assemblage of adult bulls; they casually trunk check with him as he arrives but do not greet him with calls. They graze and drink beside him; they pay no attention when he drifts away toward the end of the day to find his family, who may, in his early wanderings, greet him with calls. The third day, he's with the family. The fourth, he's tagging behind a different family, inciting other young bulls to pushing and pulling matches. Then he's back with his birth family, but he shoves somebody at a water hole and the adult females turn on him with loud admonishments and chase him a hundred meters away. He goes farther or he returns. He tries asserting dominance among animals who know him, and sometimes the acquaintances are tolerant, sometimes intolerant. He walks away as an independent bull, but finds himself the smallest and most subordinate in any group of bulls he joins. For three or four years he vacillates between these different social worlds and different experiences of himself, learning new rules all the time.

Adolescent bulls are sometimes treated tenderly by older bulls. One day, Joyce and I watched Ed, a mature bull, sparring with young Conrad, who was about two-thirds his size. The match was unequal and careful. They clashed tusks and then locked them together, pushing. As they pushed, Conrad wound his trunk around the combined configuration of their tusks, holding the two heads together. Both bulls then pulled but nothing happened. Conrad slumped and wriggled, looking confused, and unwrapped his trunk. The bulls backed apart and ran together, tusks clashing–Ed held his trunk down while Conrad curled his high over his head, out of the way of Ed's tusks as the faces bashed together. They locked tusks. Conrad lowered his trunk onto Ed's forehead while both shoved, their legs forcing them forward, shoulder and hip muscles bulging. Ed forced Conrad back; Conrad broke away, raised his tail, and fled; Ed gave chase. As Conrad ran there was an unfamiliar sound– pop-pop-pop in between footfalls. "Poor little Conrad," said Joyce, "he didn't manage to pull his penis in before Ed started chasing him"–and he was kicking it as he ran. Both males stopped running and rested, while Conrad retracted his penis, not a quick process, for it was five feet long. The bulls sparred again, this time with Conrad prepared for flight. But Ed was easy on him, the contest ended quietly, and they separated. It reminded me of a practice session between a master and an apprentice, or of the humorous jousting matches my adolescent sons used to incite when a favorite male mentor would come by our house for a visit.

I once saw in Etosha another interesting example–as I interpreted it–of an older male showing consideration for a younger. It was October, locally known as "suicide month" because of the heat, and this was an unbearably hot day. Two elephant bulls, one very large and the other very small, were standing together in the open sun at midday about a kilometer from a water hole. The older bull had closed his eyes and was swaying when the younger moved in very close and touched his left front shoulder. The older lifted his huge left ear and the younger moved under it. It became a sun umbrella, whose outer edge slowly settled onto the far side of the younger's head. In that intimate position the pair stood for a long time without moving. As the older bull dozed off, his shading ear relaxed and started to slip into the crack between the animals. This woke him. He opened his eyes suddenly and restored his ear to its former posture. I wondered whether it heated him up even as it cooled down his young companion. Or, since the underside of the ear, where the veins are exposed, was now in the shade, were both elephants being cooled?

One day during the same expedition three of my associates came upon a group consisting only of bulls, one of whom was lying down, apparently injured or ill. The other bulls were trying all sorts of maneuvers to get him onto his feet, and the assisting behavior continued throughout the half hour that my friends spent with the group.

I offer these stories as suggestive news about males. Male bonding in elephants is presumed to be temporary, but I reserve judgment on this issue. The same males are found in bull areas year after year, and particular males have strong affiliations—nor are temporary associations necessarily unimportant. There is still much to learn about males as communal animals.

It's true, though, that after adolescence such social activity as males engage in includes far more chasing and bullying than you see from females. Bulls more often use bushes and trees as props—Zimbabwean researchers report that a single bull may push down fifteen hundred trees in a year. Much of this is showing off; the presence of a serious adversary brings on bouts of furious pulling up, throwing, and digging. This branch could be your trunk stretching as thin as a noodle, this dust your body flying over my head, these recalcitrant roots your tusks locked against mine. On the surface there is play, mock indifference, mock rivalry; underneath, there is growing individuality, grow-ing difference, real rivalry.

"I love ya, ya know, but you're in my space," I heard one of my growing sons say to the other after a scuffle, and before a hug. Watching elephants during the analogous passage in their lives, I wondered whether they heard anything like that from each other when, occasionally, one would lay his trunk on the head·or the neck of the other and then relax it. A mixture of friendliness and pressure—a hug, I said to myself.

Unlike most mammals, bull elephants become sexually mature a full decade or more before they're socially mature, by which I mean welcome as mates. A bull can father a calf in his twenties, but other elephants in his population won't be keen on his doing so—fertile females will reject him, and dom-inant males will chase him away. Nonetheless he tries, grab-bing chances to mount estrous females in spite of their protestations during moments when there's no powerful bull around to drive him away. It's when a bull reaches his thirties that the hormonal condition called musth begins to endow him with the social status that qualifies him as what wildlife managers call a "prime breeder."

Elephants are distantly related to antelope, and musth is probably a kind of rut. It increases the testosterone in a bull's body fluids and makes him aggressive in the presence of an-other bull. A bull in musth spends a good deal of time alone if he is not defending a mate: everyone knows it and gives him lat-eral room. He acquires vertical room by holding his head a foot higher than normal. His legs lengthen, neck stiffens—everything about him rises up. You can recognize a bull's musth from any distance if you can see his silhouette.

You can also recognize the condition by his smell. Like an ant, he lays a trail of odoriferous urine to mark his passage; the faster he walks, the faster he dribbles. When female elephants encounter a musth bull's urine, they announce it to the universe with an uproar of vocal and behavioral excitement.

The bull's own sound also announces his musth. He makes deep, slow, guttural pulsations that the Amboseli researchers call "musth rumbles." He paces alone across plain or pan, pausing frequently to musth rumble and then freeze, listening with spread ears for distant responses. He listens more when he's in than out of musth, and responds, with calls or movement, to the calls of an adversary or of a female in estrus. A circumference surrounds him within which other elephants know about his presence and his condition, and know what he is looking for. As night comes on, his calls travel farther, for a temperature inversion in the atmosphere forms and creates a sound layer of increased transmission.

Musth occurs at different times of the year for different bulls in Amboseli, but the calendar timing for each bull is roughly the same each year. Joyce tells me that as many as fifteen bulls may be in musth at the same time. During the days of musth, the bull's posture changes; the urine dribbles; the musth-specific temporin (a pheromone that announces his condition to others) trickles slowly and stickily down the cheeks from each temporal gland, leaving a dark streak that passes under the chin behind the mouth. The glands swell, a source of discomfort, I suspect,* contributing to the bull's irritability and to another aspect of his posture, his tendency even as he walks to lift and coil and rest his trunk on his tusks or hang it over one tusk, relieving the pressure on that side of his swollen face. Everything he did playfully as a four-year-old he now does irritably: what were play tussles are now serious fights, and favored wrestling partners are adversaries. Other males not in musth, even males much bigger than he, hear his musth rumbling and give him wide berth. But to

---

*There are mahouts in Asia who also endorse this notion, Joyce says, but she disagrees.

another bull in musth, the rumble is a challenge and an announcement of status–probably of identity as well.

The other bull behaves accordingly. When a bull experiences his first musth, he is still small in relation to the other musth bulls. He spends his energy fleeing, and it soon runs out. After a few days you see him again with clear cheeks; no more trickling, dribbling, or musth rumbling, just a peaceful fellow feeding and drinking among his peaceful peers. But every year thereafter will include at least one musth period, which will transform his relationships with all the elephants that surround him. The periods will last progressively longer, until musth occupies a quarter or more of the year. Coincidentally he will be increasingly preferred by females and feared by males, with the result–we speculate–that he fathers an increasing proportion of the young elephants in the population. Gradually, his periods of musth will come to encompass the time of year when most females come into breeding condition. Toward the end of his life, some of these processes might reverse, but so far in Amboseli no bulls have lived to experience the reversal.

It turns out, as other populations are studied, that the way the Amboseli bulls stagger the timing of musth may be unusual. It probably has to do with the extraordinary circumstance that there is always abundant water in Amboseli. All possible stages and conditions of elephant males and females are simultaneously present in the population: is this not quite a piece of choreography? You could never stay long enough to understand all the ever-changing relationships. Almost every day, I heard Joyce exclaiming in amazement over some unexpected new happening. One day, we watched a small calf suckling from the teat of a bull in musth. "Babies get away with *anything*!" said Joyce, squealing with delight.

*   *   *

M10, a huge bull elephant with thick symmetrical tusks who walks with a swagger, is moving slowly through the middle of an expanded elephant family. He swings his trunk in a stiff, strange way and lifts it to rest on one or the other of his broad, symmetrical, slightly splayed tusks. His urine, which contains a much-exaggerated concentration of testosterone, is dripping steadily from his penis, darkening the fronts of his back legs and marking the path he walks on. The combined smell from his musth urine and temporal gland secretions is sweet, lemony, and pervasive. In fact, he stinks.*

He reaches out his trunk to test a pool of urine left by one of the females in the bond group that surrounds him. After him, several other large males extend their trunks in the same gesture. Each one sniffs, wrinkles his trunk, blinks his eyes, and lifts his trunk to the roof of his opened mouth where he shunts the inhaled smell of female urine to the vomero-nasal organ, which enables him to evaluate females' reproductive condition. One after another, the bulls do this—it's called "flehmening"; they lift their trunks again and again. Someone is in breeding condition.

M10 knows who it is and so do we. He probably knows it from her urine. We know it from the behavior of fifteen-year-old Flavia, and the odd fact that she is separated from her family and surrounded by males. Hugely larger than Flavia, M10 approaches her. She walks fast, holding her head tall and her eyes wide, turning left and right among elephants and bushes, apparently trying to wipe off her suitor. M10 follows, and suddenly seeing a break, runs at her. Flavia gives a rough, blood-

---

*Dr. Betsy Rasmussen has analyzed the urine, temporal-gland secretions, and breath of captive male Asian elephants. When an elephant is in musth, all three substances are rich in a set of volatile compounds called ketones. These virtually disappear when he goes out of musth.

curdling scream and flees. Her scream draws a crowd of females and four adult males. She makes a beeline toward our vehicle, running. We can't get out of the way. The following elephants turn to threaten us, lifting their heads, flaring their ears, and rumbling loudly, and Joyce says, "They're blaming us. They do that." I feel a burst of anger—my four children, bigger than they realized, used to shout "Mum's base!" as they chased each other, meaning that it was unfair to knock down whoever clung to me, with the result that I was sometimes knocked down instead. Flavia is using our jeep as base, and not in jest: she's circling around it as M10 pursues her. Each time M10 gets close she screams, and the whole herd closes in on us.

The excitement spreads and becomes general. Not far from Flavia two musth bulls smaller than M10 are challenging one another. One of them, Saibulu, shakes his head, his huge ears flapping to the left and to the right. He runs at the other, who twirls round, lifts his tail, and flees silently. From a hundred meters away, we can't hear his footfalls.

A large old bull with both his thick tusks broken and chipped to half length now moves quickly toward Saibulu. The newcomer is Thor. Thor towers over Saibulu, whirls, cracks his ears with the abrupt motion and sharp sound you can get by snapping a wet towel, walks sideways toward Saibulu, and that is enough. The gesture strips Saibulu of his status: Saibulu turns, lowers his head, and moves quickly away alone, leaving no urine trail. Thor follows to complete the encounter.

My sympathy goes offstage with routed Saibulu, but the drama of the dominant hero continues in front of us. The drama has gone internal, and now resides in remembered and imagined power, and in strategy, as in a chess game. The player M10 stands within a few body lengths of Flavia, guarding her. Eight other players, all males, surround them. Six are small males standing in a circle around the pair. Beyond that circle stand two males more powerful than the six small males, but not as powerful as M10. All nine players are standing motionless and concentrated, as if participating in an incredibly important game. We stay and watch the frozen scene for several hours, and I'm riveted to my seat, waiting for an old balance of power to give way to a new one, but nothing happens. Had Joyce not known the game, had I stumbled onto the chessboard unenlightened, I might have thought myself among inactive bulls, so still are they holding. Gradually the wind comes up. We look at each other and Joyce starts up the jeep and drives us away. The pieces are laid out on the board. Who know how long it will be before one of them makes a false move?

When we find M10 and Flavia again, quite early the next morning, they are surrounded by at least two hundred elephants, spread about and grazing on a plain close to the edge of a grassless pan. Quickly assessing the situation, Joyce explains succinctly, "They have gone into consort." M10 walks close behind Flavia, who glances coyly over her right shoulder, and then over her left, at M10 as she walks, as if measuring her distance from him; he, following, seems to be measuring it as well. A careful, graceful dance between two dancers, each with attention only for the other, has replaced the static game of yesterday.

Surrounding and closely observing the pair are nine small males. Beyond them and protected from M10 by their presence is Thor of the broken tusks, who routed Saibulu but ranks lower than M10. The relative status and positions of the males are the same as in last night's formation, but some of the individuals are different. Flavia and her consort are the sun; the other elephants are planets held by gravitational forces—desire, jealousy, and fear—at a certain static distance from them and from each other. M10's only real competitor, Thor, protects himself from M10 by standing behind the layer of young males. A favorable moment (if M10 falls asleep, for instance) might enable them to rush his prize in a cohort, but it's highly unlikely that even one of them would succeed in mating under the circumstances. They are flanked outwardly as well as inwardly by males of greater status who watch the situation jealously, nor would Flavia relish the approach of a young male. Nonetheless, being young and male, they take the chance.

Around the planetary system, a great many other elephants are going about their lives more or less as usual. More than a dozen members of Flavia's family are moving toward the swamp. After a time, we do likewise, predicting that the bulls and Flavia will come this way. They do. M10 waves and flaps his ears as he slowly approaches. Then he stops and opens his mouth and makes a dry, oscillating musth rumble in his throat. He flaps his ears and waits. After fifteen minutes he rattles again. He walks a little, waving both ears in an elegant asymmetrical but circular motion, so that one is forward while the other is behind, like the blades of a fan, wafting the smell of his temporal secretion toward the elephants at the swamp. He calls again, and I note his forehead vibrating. He stops walking and calls a fourth time while ear-flapping. He rumbles a fifth time and ear-waves. He folds his ears in a threat, walks to the water and slaps his trunk down on it, blows out through his trunk, and rumbles again. *Take that.* We hear a dry, pulsating rattle, the audible overtones of a powerful call with fundamental energy outside our range of hearing.

The families that have been bathing and drinking are leaving the swamp; to my surprise, they are calling in contagious, overlapping calls. "Bond group greeting," announces Joyce. For once I feel a reservation about her translation, for this did not strike me as a greeting. Several of the elephants are turning on the jeep. Blaming us again? Suddenly Joyce, whose eyes have not left the dominant male, grasps my arm. "He's lost her! M10 is following the wrong female! Everybody knows he's lost her!" The rumbles are rising and we begin to hear trumpeting. M10's trunk is snorkeling above his head, searching for a whiff of his lost mate. Now others are doing likewise.

Joyce's voice is tense and loud. "This is dangerous, because they don't know what to do!"

Suddenly about twenty females and calves close in on the jeep, their rumbles escalating. A small adult female emerges in front of a small calf and blocks its path. The calf roars in surprise and consternation, calling our attention to the oddly behaving female—oh, she's Flavia! Again our vehicle is base—she's using us to ward off her unwanted suitors. M10 now approaches from behind, but not before several young bulls reach their trunks under Flavia to smell her vulva.

Flavia crosses in front of the jeep. Now M10 passes just behind her, dribbling urine profusely. Joyce heaves a sigh of relief: "He's found her." His enormous trunk, draped over his right tusk, swings above our heads as he passes. Flavia circles the vehicle with M10 on her heels and an adult bull not in musth following closely in M10's tracks. There is a rumble. Within a few seconds that bull yields silently to a larger bull also not in musth. Both of them are insignificant in this hour of courtship. The jeep is insignificant, too, but now that M10 has found Flavia, there is nothing to blame us for. Joyce has lost her fear.

M10 waves his ears and gives a final musth call, then, rising up onto his rear feet, embracing Flavia's hips with his front legs, laying his trunk the length of her back and up over the top of her head, he mounts her. Underneath her his penis, fully engorged and six feet long, curls into a sideways **S** and seeks the entrance. Flavia holds still and permits forty-five seconds of success. M10 slides backward, dismounts, and stands aside quietly.

Standing alone—truly alone—Flavia now begins to sing her song, a series of deep, loud, arched notes repeated over and over again. Each shuddering rumble rises up out of silence and expands in volume as it reaches its peak pitch and then descends as it subsides into nothingness. By the third call, other excited voices are joining in, overlapping with Flavia's: all are rumbling at once, neither in synchrony nor in sequence. Only Flavia's rhythm is repetitive, and her voice, slower and lower and more extremely inflected than the others, is recognizable again and again. Suddenly, she breaks out of the sequence and starts trumpeting, in a series of unorganized, brilliant, high-pitched, wheezy, excited sounds. The surrounding elephants blow their trumpets in response. Flavia ear-flaps, and several females urinate thunderously together. Flavia's estrous calls resume, but each one is successively flatter and softer than the one before. Her companions huddle around the spot where the mating occurred, reaching out crisscrossing trunks to smell the semen that has leaked onto the ground. The singing stops, the rumbling subsides over here, resumes over there, breaks up into fragments of sound, and stops.

"The FB family is acting as if she's a family member," says Joyce. "They're the only ones who got excited."

"*As if?*"

"Yes. Flavia's an elephant without a family. Even her baby died. She *is* the family."

What is the evolutionary explanation of this ceremony, then? My mind fumbles to take in what I have just learned. We're surrounded by more than a hundred elephants from seven families—Joyce names them all—but only one family is vocalizing and excitedly investigating the site. We don't know whether their relationship to Flavia is a matter of shared genes, friendship, or adoption.

As we drive home in the early afternoon, Joyce comments on the moment when M10 lost Flavia. "I've seen a male lose his female for two or three hours. She's mounted by lots of small males, she panics. The subordinate male is in such a hurry he doesn't set up his position as a high-ranking guard, he just chases her, she runs, everyone chases her; either there are many mounts or many chases." I think about the estrous female. Once she is guarded, she can eat and drink and rest without being pursued.

But estrus is brief, and the period of protection is even briefer. Back in camp on the following evening, Cynthia reports that late in the afternoon she saw Flavia mounted by a smallish bull. "M10 wasn't far away: he was angry, and stomped over, shaking his head."

"Now all the young males will mount her," Joyce predicts. "She's no longer in her peak. And M10 will stop guarding, and start looking for another estrous female." The following morning confirms this prediction. We have trouble finding Flavia, for she has melted back into her adoptive family. M10 is not far away, but Flavia's attractive powers are gone. Of everyone present, it seems that only Joyce and I remember the events of the preceding days. M10 moves gradually away from Flavia and us, pacing here and there, his trunk to the ground in a bushy grassland as if searching for something.

The quarter year that M10 spends in musth will constitute most of his time among females. As musth subsides, he will resume his peaceful association with other nonmusth bulls in bull areas, and wander about nonchalantly by himself, browsing and grazing. He won't seem fazed by the demotion from highest to the eighth-ranking male in the population. He will still be fertile, and in the unlikely chance that he finds an estrous female unaccompanied by a male in musth, he will attempt to copulate with her. But the "sultan in his brain" was put there by the extra testosterone that comes with musth, and will be withdrawn as the testosterone diminishes.

As one male goes out of musth and descends on the dominance ladder, another ascends. Joyce has noticed that M22, the second-ranking male in the whole population, huge, with enormous, symmetrical, splayed tusks, has begun standing alone, and feeding alone—not near other males—and holding his head tall; she wouldn't be surprised . . .

So all of this is going to happen again.

But not yet. In mature bulls like M10 and M22, musth is slow and steady in its growth and decline. For the time being, we continue to find M10 rumbling; listening; searching; joining, testing, and forsaking families, his urine dribble waxing and waning with circumstances; and within the week he is courting a new estrous female, Zita.

This time the situation is more complex. Not only M10 but Thor, his slight subordinate, has found Zita. A closer rival of M10, M7 has also arrived, trailing fourteen younger males. M7 has only one tusk. He must have lost the other decades ago, for his trunk is enormously thick: I imagine its extra muscular power more than compensates for the loss of a piercing weapon. Like the constellation that twice formed around M10 and Flavia, a new circle of young males now forms around M10 and Zita, buffering them from M7. Zita, however, is declining M10's advances. What does she know? M10 keeps giving musth rumbles. What does he know? Is it M7 who is disrupting the relationship, or is M22 on an olfactory or acoustic horizon that I can't perceive? Zita, far from entering into the slow dance of consortship, is maneuvering to keep a young male between herself and M10. Because of the presence of older males, the young male who serves her in this way doesn't dare mount her.

Now a new bull arrives, but he is not the one I expected. He is Saibulu!—the young male we saw trounced by Thor only two days back. Joyce laughs quietly and whispers that yesterday she noticed him without signs of musth, but here he is again dribbling urine, draining temporin, holding his head high, and musth rumbling.

Suddenly Joyce stiffens, for from another direction yet another musth bull of Saibulu's size, but older than Saibulu, is arriving. This is Pablo. The female elephants rumble excitedly as the several bulls converge. Our heads dodge from side to side, for things are beginning to happen all around us.

But the site of the action is directly behind us. CRAAAAAACK!! Saibulu has leaned with all his weight on a huge dead tree. It is splitting at the ground and tilting over as on a hinge, cracking again and again at its stump and slowly descending. The tips of the bottom limbs strike the ground and are crushed; the limbs themselves sever from the trunk. The hinge opens wider, the earth rises up to slam against cluster after cluster of higher branches, and one set of limbs, branches, and twigs after another is shattered against the ground. Meanwhile, a shock wave passes through the branches on the upper side, swaying them wildly and erratically, like branches of standing trees when they are lashed by storm winds. But here it happens so abruptly—and the branches, being dead, are so dry—that they also break at the trunk, fly into the air, and fall onto the ground, splintering beside the crushed branches.

The whole process takes longer than I would believe possible, and is shattering not only to the tree but also to the composure of the human observer. Before it is half completed, I am close to tears. But Pablo is not impressed. He swings around and charges. His tusks clash against Saibulu's, he gives a brutal shove, and Saibulu turns and flees, a cloud of dust enveloping his disappearing form.

Without a moment's pause Pablo now marches forward to lock tusks with Thor. Thor holds his own, announcing the start of a contest quite different in character from the last. Silently, slowly, the bulls fold their ears into front-facing **V**s, and push. Their cheeks are streaming with temporin, and urine is streaming down their back legs—urine mixed with testosterone and pheromones. The air stinks.

Many other elephants are coming too close around the jeep and around the fighting bulls. Some are backing up, others are moving forward, and the air is loud with rumbling, bellowing, and trumpeting. In relation to this mob, Pablo and Thor now do something very interesting. They pull apart from each other and from the crowd and walk away parallel to one another, separated by about two elephant's lengths. And the crowd does something equally interesting. It does not follow. But Joyce cranks the starter of the jeep. We will follow—at a respectful distance, for neither of us wants to be in a vehicle that's being used as a surrogate tree or bush.

Moving crablike and looking into each other's eyes, Pablo and Thor mirror each other's movements on the two sides of a dirt road that they keep exactly halfway between them. Their unnatural posture makes me shudder. It's clear that their cooperative behavior is the preparation for a duel.

I am glad to have left the crowd. I dislike crowds just as I dislike being base, and the spirit of this crowd has reminded me, suddenly, of something I wanted to forget—the day when my brother, sixteen years old, challenged my father, forty, and they came to blows in our dining room. My memory of the event is not softened by its rapid outcome, in which my father reinstated his dominance. For me, my sister, my mother, and a friend visiting me from school—for all the women in the house—the physical fight was an event we would never forget or understand.

How many of the female elephants are closely related to the bulls who have been challenging one another and fighting all week? How can the females turn their back on the battle, given their communal imperative? Hearing all the vocal activity, I am reminded of women. I think they're maneuvering in the interest of peace, each female concerned about the group she considers—whether by an old or a new definition—her family. But they're also interested in who will win!

I feel a surge of relief as we move away from them. We drive along parallel to Pablo and Thor, placing our bets. It seems an even match. Thor's stubby, broken tusks will put him at a disadvantage, but he is older and more experienced than Pablo. He is significantly dominant to Pablo when both are out of musth. But he has been in musth for several months already. Pablo is full of the energy that musth imparts during the first weeks.

All at once, Pablo crosses the dirt road they have been using as a center line. With folded ears and draining glands, he and Thor clash tusks, lock together, and shove.

The contest is strangely formal, divided into more or less quarter-hour bouts separated by ten-minute breaks, and lasting in all three and three-quarter hours. During the breaks the contestants graze and browse as if unoffended by the company they are keeping, as in a college contest, where men give their all to beat each other and then sit down side by side eating oranges. We ourselves rest during the breaks, grateful for the routine until a bush suddenly flying through the air, showering red dust down on the hurler, calls our attention back to the match. From too great a distance I make a faint recording, picking up only twelve musth rumbles during the whole fight.

Well into the fourth hour, Thor sidles away from Pablo during a break, and puts a bush between them as if in quest of better fodder. Then he moves a little farther and there are two bushes between them. Glancing behind himself, he moves farther still, wheels around, turns his back, and flees in a cloud of dust, over a kilometer back to the crowd of elephants he and Pablo had left behind at the start of the duel.

Pablo takes stock of the situation, saunters down to a nearby water hole, and has a long, thorough, luxurious mud bath. He does not wallow, but uses his trunk to slowly spray himself all over; in the end he is dark and slick. Then he stretches out his trunk and touches it to the ground, and starts walking steadily along on Thor's trail. His eyes are half closed: he reminds me of a blind man with a cane. The smell of Thor's tracks seems to be leading back into the crowd. "Strange," says Joyce, "usually the loser does not join the crowd but makes a clean getaway." We parallel Pablo, wondering when he will have had enough.

As he enters the crowd, Pablo's eyes suddenly open wide— he has encountered a startling odor. He spins around in a sudden challenge to another male. *"M7!"* exclaims Joyce. "Who does this Pablo think he *is*?"

Once again, she has made a valid prediction. Within a minute Pablo is fleeing with an enormous one-tusked elephant on his heels. Pablo's tail is in the air, and M7's trunk extruded. They thunder away and disappear over a small hill.

A deafening, chaotic uproar—screaming, bellowing, and trumpeting—now breaks out on all sides of us. The structure of the crowd disintegrates. Elephants small and large stampede past us, their stiff legs swinging out sideways, their bellies at eye level, screaming. I screw up my window, cover our equipment, and buffer my head. *This is it.*

I don't know how many minutes pass before I realize that I was wrong. I am sitting inside of Joyce's vehicle, she is in the front seat, and we are surrounded by silence.

I bang my window with a fist to shake off the dust. A circle of blue is beginning to appear in the top center of the sky, above a thick, slowly settling curtain of brown. Slowly, the blue expands. Slowly, the curtain lowers, revealing crowns of still standing trees. We begin to see the battered earth in the foreground. The field is empty.

Although the jeep's windows are closed, it has filled with dust. Joyce turns to look at me. She is a figure made of dust except for the whites of her eyes and her teeth. She is smiling, but obviously not about the thing we have just witnessed. Her mind is engaged again with the saga she's been following for these last nine years. The little guy pushes over the tree as a challenge to the big guy, who routs the little guy and challenges a guy his own size, and routs him and challenges a bigger guy, and so on until it ends in mating or blood or a full-scale stampede. "I adore Saibulu," said Joyce. "He's bad, but I adore him."

5

DANGERS

THE PEOPLE AT HOME WANT TO KNOW ABOUT THE DANGERS. I start by telling them stories about the breathtaking moments—the stampede, for instance. Then I say that most of the time I felt pretty safe, because the elephants were habituated to our presence and we to theirs. Habituation—familiarity—makes it possible to explore many dimensions of social behavior that you would never otherwise know about. But there is a danger in it, in that you may take it for granted. Habituation is a continually developing relationship, which, like other relationships, depends on mutual trustworthiness. Sooner or later, one of the participants is likely to take the other too casually, and disregard the rules.

It's my opinion that Joyce and I violated the proper boundaries of habituation toward the end of our work together. "I pushed you into it," Joyce said afterward; yes, and I gave in. I agreed to help her test her notion that the depth of an elephant male's musth rumble announces his seniority. We would drive perilously close to all the musth bulls, one at a time, and make them growl into our microphone repeatedly, threatening us while we recorded. There was no chance of collecting such a sample passively, but if we irritated the bulls we might get it before my research permit expired.

A few days into the venture, we approached a large bull named M51. His face and legs streaming with evidence of musth, he walked up to the jeep that had driven offensively close to his drinking pool, put his right tusk slightly inside the window over Joyce's lap where she sat at the wheel, and made a fine musth rumble right in her face. Then he withdrew and stepped to the front of the vehicle, tapped the tusk on the hood of the vehicle three times, turned, and went back to splash in his pool.

"That's it for me," I said when the blood had come back into Joyce's face. "If you want to keep on collecting calls this way you'll have to find another partner." But we were in agreement and called a halt to this aspect of our research.

That evening, we told the others in camp about what had happened. It reminded me of an experience I'd had in 1971, on the northeastern coast of the Peninsula Valdés in Argentina. I was a member of a pilot trip led by my husband, Roger Payne, to find a site for a long-term study of the behavior of southern right whales. Roger, our friend Ollie Brazier, and I had run into a difficulty: there were no boats for hire. So an Argentine diver took us to a spot where the ocean currents carried whales very close to shore, and loaned us his eight-foot pram for a day. As it turned out, Ollie and I had the adventure while Roger struggled far inland with a truck, stuck on a beach made of stones so round that he could not move forward. Hearing by walkie-talkie that a whale was moving down the current toward us, Roger told us to go ahead and launch the boat without him. By the time he arrived, we were back on the beach in the aftermath of an experience to which we ourselves had been the only witnesses.

We lifted the pram into the water and, just as the current drew the whale past us, we entered the current and cut the engine. The whale turned around and swam back upcurrent toward us. Suddenly he disappeared and a round-topped, shiny, blue-black wall considerably wider than our boat rose up beside us. If we'd understood the anatomy we'd have looked down rather than up, for the wall was the underside of the whale's flat chin, and his eyes were just below the surface, surveying the bottom of the boat: he was "spy-hopping." Two minutes later he was horizontal again and facing downstream but moving backward toward us, which created strange tight ripples on the surface of the waves. Slowly and powerfully he moved his tail from side to side—a threatening gesture, as we later learned, from a tail twice as wide as the pram was long. He backed the tail under the bow of the pram and lifted us up. He held us steady for a full minute, two people on a tray six inches above the water's surface. Then he gently set us down. Amazed, Ollie and I sat in the boat and did nothing. The whale drifted ahead for a minute or two, backed up, made the sideways motions with his tail, and lifted us again, the same as before. And again—three times, like the three taps of M51's tusk. After the third lowering Ollie pulled the starter rope and turned the pram northward against the current. For a few minutes the whale accompanied us, spy-hopping first to one side of us and then the other. Then he turned downstream and disappeared. After a short time, a series of distant blows down-current and glimpses of dark bodies and tails told us that he was joining some other whales.

"He," I say. Actually we did not know the sex of the whale.

Why had the whale taken such care not to hurt us? It would have been easier to demolish the pram with a moderate slap of that huge tail. Why, in Amboseli, did the elephant M51 warn but not injure us? Haven't I twice been given the benefit of the doubt during a moment of high-handed intrusion?

Well, maybe. But the question is a projection of my human experience. Humans intrude high-handedly and give the benefit of the doubt, but whales and elephants may not think in such ways at all. What can I say about the mental experience of the elephant, and of the whale, if I just stick to what I saw?

That there was forbearance. That it was deliberate. And that it was communicated in a manner that was both subtle and clear.

The challenge of describing animal experiences becomes obvious when you try to make a lexicon or dictionary, translating the calls of other animals into a human language. How can you study communication without translation?

Joyce and I thought that we knew enough about some of the calls we'd recorded that we could start making an elephant-English dictionary. We would make spectrograms and match them up with meanings. From the Rosetta Stone it has been possible to work backward into revelations about the society that created it: wouldn't the same thing be possible from a lexicon of elephant calls, and what would we learn?

Dictionaries assume that sounds fall into discrete structural categories—vowels, consonants, syllables, pitches, inflections, timbres, duration—which match categories of meaning. Dictionaries assume that every "word" has a certain referent with a given breadth and depth and content. Joyce and Cynthia claimed they could translate more than two dozen elephant calls in Amboseli, could even recognize them with their eyes closed. Joyce was my dictionary in Amboseli: I faithfully recorded her translations along with every call she translated. Often she had a sense of who had made it but I didn't, for calling elephants seldom open their mouths. For every call, we announced her level of certainty about the caller's identity, the call type, the circumstances, and the distance of all potential callers from the microphone. By "call type" we meant our guess at the call's function. To name functions for another animal's vocalizations is to take a leap of the imagination, but we had to start somewhere.

In family groups, we heard calves calling for help in a variety of ways. Joyce's call types included suckle rumbles, suckle cries, suckle distress screams, lost calls, and distress calls. We heard groups of adult females and single mothers respond to these calls with reassuring rumbles (two call types). In times of social excitement we distinguished between greeting rumbles, roars, bellows, screams, and various kinds of trumpeting, including a long half-muffled, half-shrieking sound that was always associated with play. One day we watched two calves running away from their mothers through a field of grass much taller than themselves with their trunks stuck out straight ahead of them, their tails straight up in the air and their ears flapping, play-trumpeting at top volume as they escaped!

A number of calls were obviously important to group dynamics and coordination. There were attack rumbles, "let's go" rumbles, contact calls and answers, coalition rumbles, and "discussion rumbles" (usually, I thought, about where to go next). Sometimes elephants seemed frightened or surprised by something strange, and we heard trumpet blasts and snorts. We suspected but never successfully recorded a purely infrasonic alarm call.

When females competed for dominance, they made rumbles. Different rumbles, including the musth rumble, occurred during dominance disputes between males. Last, but not least, there were loud, important calls associated with reproduction. Zita's estrous call, her family's excited chorus when she was mounted, and the females' calls when males sniffed their genitals were three call types of this sort.

Joyce considered each of these a distinctive category. In her book, she wrote, "Of the twenty-six documented vocalizations made by adult elephants, nineteen are made only by females, three are made by adults of both sexes, and only four are made exclusively by males. (An additional six calls are made only by subadults.) Of the twenty-two calls exclusive to females, nine are calls typically given in chorus with other family members, while thirteen are usually made by an elephant calling on its own."[*]

The project that had brought me to Amboseli was much narrower than the dictionary. I wanted to know whether the calls that seemed to function over long distances were well designed for that purpose. The answer seemed to be yes. Zita's estrous calls, for instance, were powerful—117 decibels at one meter from her throat—and most of their energy lay below 40 Hertz. Musth rumbles were as low as 14 Hertz.[†] At such intensities and frequencies, these calls would carry several kilometers.

Some years after my 1986 visit to Amboseli, a Cornell student named Greg Gerst and I approached the dictionary question by trying to put some of Joyce's translations to the test in an orderly way. We selected the hundred calls she had been surest of from nine call types. We measured a few aspects of their shape, duration, pitch, and amplitude, and asked a computer program to sort them into categories. Then we compared the structural categories to Joyce's meaning categories. If we'd found a good match we'd have said, "a call that looks and sounds like this probably means that."

But what we found was a terrible match. The calls made in

---

[*]Joyce Poole, *Coming of Age with Elephants* (New York: Hyperion, 1996), pp. 131–32.
[†]A bass singer's low G is 98 Hz, about three octaves higher than a musth male elephant's call, and more than two octaves above 20 Hz, the point below which we label sound as infrasound. (When a frequency is doubled, the pitch goes up an octave: thus, 40 Hz is one octave above 20, and 20 is one octave above 10.)

similar behavioral contexts fell into several of our structural categories. The calls in the same structural categories fell into several of our behavioral categories.

Were Joyce and Cynthia wrong in their classifications? I doubt it. More likely, the problem lay in the analysis. Probably elephants rely on more and other features besides the ones Greg and I measured. Probably they emphasize the importance of certain features differently. Probably there are more call types and more structural types than we recognized (there must be, for elephants recognize each other's voices, and a population contains hundreds of individuals: a distant contact call elicits a response only from members of the caller's family). A more radical idea also offers itself: perhaps we were guessing wrong when we expected elephant calls to be representative, like human words, with the same sounds always interpreted in more or less the same way. Dictionaries work for people, but who is to say that the minds of elephants work like human minds? It would not surprise me to learn that elephant calls are richer in emotional content and poorer in symbolism than human words.

The project loomed huge ahead of us, requiring a larger sample of recordings than we had and a more sophisticated analysis than we had time for. Greg graduated and took a job in California. But for me, still surrounded by elephants, the lexicon question lingered. One fine morning I woke up realizing that we had overlooked two obvious structural categories into which all calls fall. A call is the work either of a single voice or of a set of overlapping voices. Since overlaps would obscure the features we were measuring, Greg and I had excluded all overlapping calls from our sample. In so doing we'd bypassed a question I could easily answer: were overlapping calls made in some kinds of groups and not in others?

Mya Thompson from Oberlin College helped me take a fresh look into the Amboseli data and within three days we had confirmed my hunch. Overlapping calls had occurred only when females were present. The presence of females was thus encoded in these calls even if one knew nothing else about their context.

This observation is enriched by details from Joyce's ongoing studies of elephants' sexual behavior. On days when no estrous female is calling, adult males take their chances by visiting families and sniffing the genital areas of all the adult females they meet. The males are rather quiet as they do this. Males not in musth tend to visit families for several days at a time, but musth males rove between families urgently, leaving at once if their search establishes that none of the females is in estrus. If a male finds one who is, or is close to it, he flehmens—lifts his trunk to the top of his mouth where there is an entrance to an organ with special diagnostic tissue, and inhales. A certain facial expression reveals a positive diagnosis: he communicates it without making a sound.

Females, on the other hand, make an outburst of communal calls if they encounter a male in musth or even a pool of his urine. They call collectively when a male sniffs a family member—loud vocalizations follow each test, and some of them run away screaming. They call collectively when they greet relatives, and when they reassure offspring, and when any one of them is mounted, and after mating. Families band together when one of their members is in estrus, and the larger the group, the noisier. Adult males listen more when they're in musth than when they're not, and they preferentially visit large families—identified as such, we imagine, by the amount of noise they make.

In short, even without a dictionary we can say that the vocal behavior of the different genders illustrates their experiences of life. Here are the males visiting and revisiting the experiences of competition, with only occasional sallies into cooperation.

Their rather quiet, solo, individual announcements serve as warnings to competitors and invaders, but silence predominates among males. A male does not announce his discovery of an estrous female, for instance. His silence suggests a competitive motivation, for why should he attract rivals?

The females, by contrast, spend most of their time visiting and revisiting the experiences of communalism, and only occasionally express their individual imperatives. Given that most of their announcements are buried and immersed in each others' announcements, it seems that the point of them must be largely communal. What information do the females' group calls transmit, to distant elephants and to the calling animals themselves? Would it be wrong in the crudest analysis to start our translations of them all with the pronoun "we"?

If I were trying to offer evidence that elephants are self-conscious, I'd mention these observations. I'd suggest that male elephants have a sense of themselves as individuals, and females have a sense of themselves as members of communities. I'd point out that male elephants, abiding by the simple rules of competition among individuals, are easier to predict than are females, whose decisions depend on what they are learning hour by hour from a large, ever-changing community. I'd say (probably getting myself into hot water) that this reflects a difference in consciousness.

A male's evolutionary agenda is straightforward: he must look after his own well-being, and he must beget offspring. To beget offspring he must master the art of the dominance hierarchy and be selected by robust females to father their offspring. In or out of musth, he competes with a few other bulls of roughly equal status, in compliance with a set of formal rules. In between challenges, he eats, gets strong, and mates. He is responsible only for himself.

A female's agenda is far more complex. She, too, must look

after her own well-being, she must choose the best of males and beget offspring, but also this: she must rear her calves to adulthood. Her success in this task demands a complex and communicative association with the members of an extended family. Keeping track of the conditions of all these individuals in their changing locations is not easy (take it from me), and relying on others is dangerous! I think about all this as I remember that it was not aggressive males, but confused females, who endangered us during the day that we spent with fighting bulls.

But the greatest danger that most field biologists have to contend with has less to do with aggressive and confused wild animals than with keeping balance among people.

While Joyce and I were recording elephants in Amboseli, Iain Douglas-Hamilton was flying all over Africa making aerial surveys of elephant populations. His intent was to count living elephants, but he ended up counting a great many corpses, the work of poachers. While I was at home preparing our conclusions from the first round of data on elephant communication, he was in Nairobi publishing his conclusion that over half the elephants in Africa had been killed for their ivory in the preceding ten years. Of all the countries he could reasonably survey, Kenya, Uganda, and Tanzania were the hardest hit. Poachers had killed more than three-quarters of Kenya's elephants, most of them in national parks.

With this information burning in her mind, Joyce put her research aside one year after she and I had completed our work together. She moved to Nairobi to devote her energies to the politics of conservation. Cynthia before her, and Iain before them both, had made similar decisions. None of the East African elephant researchers had lost interest in research, but there was a higher priority. As our paths diverged, I recognized their sacrifice. They would be engulfed in human arguments that had very little to do with elephants as animals and a great deal to do with elephants as currency. Their work would be disheartening and infuriating.

As for me, I was thinking on a smaller scale, just trying to straighten out my notions about elephants. I was acknowledging the error of my impression that what we'd been recording in Amboseli was "natural" behavior, like what we would have recorded if the elephants had been altogether wild. As I studied our spectrograms, I saw that the elephants' calls were small shapes superimposed on a bed of braided horizontal spaghetti, and the spaghetti was the prints of the low-pitched voices of tourist vehicles stopping and starting. As visitors gorged themselves on wildlife spectacles, their average stop was less than one minute. And in between our recordings, our own vehicle had added its voice to the uproar that must be a significant experience for animals sensitive to low-frequency sound.

I was thinking about what is lost when wildness is lost, and realizing that habituation is not just a slight modification of a wild nature. It's a huge step toward tameness, in which all kinds of odd circumstances are accepted as normal. What's the final stage in tameness, if not domestication? Elephants as farm animals? I asked the question bitterly, and then I examined my bitterness.

The replacement of a pleasant illusion with bitterness is a serious danger for anyone whose work involves the documentation of mounting losses for which the human community is responsible. A pessimistic frame of mind can lead you to reject your connection to the human community.

I admire Howard Nelson's poem about this dimension in the experience of Dian Fossey:

She sat among dark lives on mountains,
among those who do not change.
To choose another species over one's own

isn't natural, or admirable, exactly—
but who doesn't have some flaw?
Hers was the size of the gap between human and gorilla.

When she was on the TV show
with the famous, well-dressed comedian,
she was relaxed only when she spoke gorilla.

... *"Naoom, m-nwowm, manouum—naomm, naoumm."*
The gaze of the mountain gorilla simply rips your soul open.
She's buried among gorillas.

It was a rage she was in.
It was a love she was in.
To give one's life to sit down among the animals
    is a strange, great thing.

In her cabin high in the mountains of Rwanda, Dian Fossey committed herself to the welfare of a population of gorillas at the expense of her relations with local African people, and one day she was murdered. Then many of us spoke quietly about our own experiences of alienation.

The spirit in the Amboseli camp was as enlightened as the researchers knew how to make it, yet there was a touch of alienation. It reminded me of the Argentine whale camp where my husband, four children, and I, with a shifting array of associates, had spent the best part of a decade studying southern right whales. On the unpopulated shore of an enormous pristine bay, we were bitten by the desire to protect a population of whales that would migrate every year across the cruel and ignorant South Atlantic Ocean.

We hadn't been there long before our uncommon ambition made us the focus of local curiosity. Unannounced guests arrived, making it difficult for us to do our work. One day, with official sanction, we bolted a padlock on the gate to camp, and started behaving exclusively "on behalf of whales" in a land that was not our own.

Soon afterward I noticed our four young children furiously digging pits on a beach miles from our camp, and I went to join them. I learned that they meant to make a cover for each pit, and to disguise each cover with beach sands, sticks, and stones. Anyone not forewarned would crash through the covers and be trapped in the pits, which the children called "tourist traps." So we were raising a brood of semiconscious dragons, and they were helping in the defense of a treasure we thought of as ours.

Attachment to anything you privately and intensely appreciate can make you as intolerant, irrational, and possessive as a demented lover. You don't have to know the object of your attachment; to be the only one who meets its gaze is sufficient: sitting among animals has this danger along with the rest. For so few sit there, and so little is known by those few, and what is known is so vital and so callously disregarded by outsiders. If outsiders would make the same commitment you've made, everything would change, but should they look and not make it, the violation would be unbearable . . . so this place is private. *And sacred.* Go away.

Is this sense of a sacred trust an illusion? I remember one day when such a sense rose up in me from nothing in the course of two hours. What had evoked it was the sight of a natural formation and a great many piles of sun-dried elephant dung.

I was one of twelve campers who had awoken that morning—August 19, 1987—on a drab rubbly clay roadless stretch of desert in a desolate part of Namibia called Damaraland. We were searching for evidence of the "desert elephants" who live in the region. An aura of mystery surrounds these endangered creatures, who, though continuous in genus and species with the savannah elephants, are culturally different. They walk as much as seventy kilometers a day between water and browse, and drink only once every three or four days. It is not their way of life, however, that is diminishing their numbers, but their vulnerability to poachers.

As we drove across Damaraland in a pair of Land Rovers, with wet towels on our heads to keep the heat from concussing us, the landscape became increasingly lifeless and rugged. From horizon to horizon we saw a brown rock-strewn plain flanked by utterly barren hills, buttes and mountains that rose in layers and tiers, each receding layer fuller of haze and blueness and paler than the one in front of it, till the last five or six layers were only pale clear blue. Our eyes burned from scanning the horizon for life. I felt that a journey to the farthest, bluest hills would take several days, with no water the whole way, and when we got there we'd still be seeing brown gravel plains strewn with rocks. Perhaps I'd see one or two little golden springbok on the way, perhaps a cluster of frightened gemsbok, perhaps a sprig of dry golden hay here or there—nothing else . . .

We came to a tree and the tour leader said, "We'd better stop for lunch here; it'll be tomorrow before we see another tree"; and we stopped for lunch, although it was ten in the morning.

The trip had been organized for a group of important and sophisticated conservationists, including Russ Train, president of the board of the World Wildlife Fund (the organization that had sponsored our project), on the basis of a casual suggestion of mine. I myself had wanted a glimpse of the desert elephants, but I now felt worried and let down. Where was the wildlife in this remote and so-called priceless place? I couldn't talk or listen comfortably at supper, and in the morning I went off for a solo walk to get control of myself. I was quite far from the group when their trek started, which is how I came to do it mostly by myself, following their route over a trail of old, soft elephant dung, straw-filled and odorless.

The dung led between a pair of rocky hills and onto a little-used animal trail that ascended gently in a rock-strewn crevice ten or fifteen feet wide. After a few minutes, the trail increased in steepness, its walls becoming nearly vertical. After two hours, it had became a jumble of fallen rocks; it would be alarming to meet a herd of elephants coming the other way here. Still the dung led upward. At last I rounded a corner and drew an astonished breath. There, in a sun-struck passage between dark walls, a natural staircase strewn with elephant dung led infinitely up into the center of the mountain.

I began to feel I was having a spiritual experience. Vertical striations in the rock walls drew my eyes up as if I were in a cathedral. At the top of the staircase I saw a cul-de-sac, framed by vertically streaked blue-gray rock walls on three sides. "Organ pipes," I said involuntarily. I climbed to the top and saw a small sandy area with a hole about six feet in diameter in its middle. Rather deep below the surrounding sand lay the surface of the only water in a vast area, a pool dug by elephants. That was the treasure in the mountain. And what a treasure—we ourselves had traveled more than a day since our last sight of water.

The rest of our party had already enjoyed the spectacle for half an hour and were ready to descend, with the exception of my friend Blythe Loutit and her little dog. Blythe was a Namibian resident who knew and loved this place. Very quietly we rested in it together. Then I noticed a big flat rock projecting from one of the walls ten meters above the pool. I climbed up hand over hand, thinking it would be fine to look down and imagine a herd of elephants mounting the stairs to the secret pool their ancestors had created. I reached the rock and saw its top surface. Again I caught my breath, for it, too, was covered with dried elephant dung. I imagined a noble matriarch with a desire for overview, clambering up the cliff as I had done.

Blythe waited for me in the shade partway down the staircase, giving me time alone. In camp we found the rest of the party as harmonious as ourselves. Something about the experience seemed to have rested everyone's soul. We *live* in our imaginations. *La vida es sueno,* as Don Quixote said: Life is dream.

Never mind whether our dream was sacred, mystical, imaginary—we needed it. During the ten days of our trip we saw only two elephants—a pair of bulls traveling together along the base of a gravel ridge—and it was not the experience we wanted. They were so far away as to be hardly visible, but at the sound of our two Land Rovers they panicked and started to run. Regretting our presence, we got out and watched them through binoculars. We saw one and then the other loop his trunk into his mouth; then we saw sudden splotches of dark appear on their backs and sides. Drawing water out of their throats, they had splashed it on their bodies, cooling themselves as they fled. I would not have chosen to be the cause of this behavior. The sight and sound of us had deprived the very animals we wanted to see of all the water in the landscape—water from their own throats.

Was the elephants' fear of vehicles my fault? Was my existence partly responsible for the disappearance of the wild world? There's a profound pessimism in that question, which I often ask myself. It comes to my lips when I receive newsletters from the African Wildlife Foundation, my channel for information about the elephants I knew in Amboseli. Recently, a "fax from Cynthia Moss" was reprinted as follows:

I HAVE TERRIBLE NEWS! ANOTHER OF
AMBOSELI'S OLDEST BULL ELEPHANTS HAS
BEEN FOUND SLAUGHTERED IN NORTHERN
TANZANIA.
     THIS TIME IT WAS "M10," A 50-YEAR-OLD BULL
WHO WAS SHOT SEVERAL TIMES AND HIS TUSKS
WERE REMOVED WITH A CHAIN SAW. . . .

M10 WAS LAST SEEN ON 20 JANUARY 1996
HEADING TOWARD THE TANZANIAN BORDER.
ONE OF OUR COLLEAGUES TALKED TO SOME
MASAI LEADERS JUST THIS SIDE OF THE
BORDER IN KENYA. THEY THINK M10 WAS
KILLED ABOUT ONE MONTH AGO WHEN THEY
HEARD THREE GUNSHOTS. THEY SAID THERE
ARE ALSO TWO OTHER CARCASSES NEAR
WHERE M10 WAS KILLED. . . . WE THINK THESE
TWO BULLS ARE "THOR" AND "ANDREW."

WITH THESE THREE BULLS GONE, WE HAVE
LOST ALL OF THE BIG . . . BULLS FROM THE
WESTERN AREA OF AMBOSELI EXCEPT M51. . . .
THE MASAI LEADERS SAY CATEGORICALLY THAT
ILLEGAL HUNTERS KILLED THE ELEPHANTS.
THEY CLAIM TO BE ABLE TO TELL THE
DIFFERENCE BY THE WAY THE CARCASS IS
HANDLED. . . .

"Believe it," I said bitterly. "M10, Thor. No. No."

M10 is dead. Thor is presumed dead. I already knew that
Pablo and Saibulu had been killed. Only three of the big bulls I
had known are still alive. One of them is M22, whom I last saw
displacing M10 and becoming Zita's consort. One is M7, who
routed Pablo and precipitated the stampede. The third is M51,
who spared Joyce and me in our day of foolishness.

I got to my desk and wrote a miserably small check considering the size of the problem. I shared what I had in the spirit of
a sacrificial prayer. "In remembrance of you," I said to M10 and
Thor, Pablo, and Saibulu. To M51 I said, "In remembrance of
your genius for communication. Three taps on a resonant surface. Watch out."

6

DOUBLE BLIND

Since science is without morals, it offers itself as a sanctuary from the dangers of emotional commitment. Happy fishermen, we biologists stand together on the pier casting and reeling, mesmerized by a certain shimmer visible from this or that angle, enchanted by the concentric rings here and there, imagining things just below the dimpled surface. If something leaps into the air, we all lift eyebrows together as if we were one great being with one eyebrow—*that*? Is it alone, or part of a school? What else lies below?

I'd come home from Amboseli thinking that I understood the elephants' grand scheme of communication. Meanwhile, Bill Langbauer had moved to Ithaca. He made spectrograms of the tapes I'd collected with Joyce Poole. We studied them together, and agreed that they seemed to confirm our hunches about long-distance communication. But the fish was still in the water, for we hadn't *proved* that distant elephants responded to these calls. Estrous calls *seemed* to have brought males from all over the countryside, but how far had they actually walked? And had not there also been attractive *smells* of fertility? And might not a *chain* of communication have occurred, with each call functioning over just a short distance?

Bill designed an experiment to narrow down the possibilities. Over what distances do elephants respond to one another's low-frequency calls? he asked. An enormous loudspeaker mounted on top of a van would be the source of the calls; it would sound but not smell like an elephant. We would build an observation tower over a water hole and surround the pool with an array of transmitting microphones. A pair of video cameras on the tower would record the visible behavior of all elephants who came to the pool, while the mikes would record their acoustic behavior. Every now and then, the van would broadcast a prerecorded elephant call from one of several faraway spots at measured distances from the tower. We would examine our tapes for evidence of perception: ear raising, holding still, turning to face a new direction, walking in that direction, rumbling.* We'd repeat the experiment using different calls, different locations, and different subject elephants.

Many repetitions would be necessary, because the elephants' responses to our broadcasts would be added to their responses to all the natural events of the day, and we couldn't control the timing of those. Sixty trials, testing female and male responses at two different distances, might be enough. Back at home we would analyze the tapes to compare elephants' behaviors during periods when there had been broadcasts with periods when there were no broadcasts. We would analyze the results statistically.

Neither the people who made the videotapes nor the people

* We had established these as normal responses to other African elephants' calls in a preliminary experiment in the Toronto Zoo.

who analyzed them would know the exact timing, location, or contents of the broadcasts. The signs of perception we'd measure wouldn't depend on our knowing anything about the meanings of the calls. In both respects Bill's design was simple and elegant–words of high praise in the scientific world. "It'll be double blind," Bill said, "to keep our personal opinions and expectations from biasing our observations."

"Ugh," I said, playing dumb. "My favorite occupation is forming opinions and expectations."

"Be my guest," said Bill. "You can still form them." We laughed. There was a little rivalry between us. We often played roles, each exaggerating a personal quality of which the other was mistrustful–I the dumb female who couldn't tell her brain from her heart; he the smart scientist who couldn't see the world beyond his blinders.

We did the experiment in Etosha, a vast, wide open Namibian park where we could occupy a large area free from tourists. Three park rangers built us an observation platform five meters high, fifty meters to the south of an artificial pool, or "fountain," a trough with a little overflow beside it. The place, called Dungaries, was scruffy and remote, and off bounds to tourists. It wasn't unusual for a ranger to drop by Dungaries on a free day. He'd sit on a log polished by elephants' tusks and hides and smoke a pipe. He might chew on a strip of *biltong*–the salted meat of giraffe, gemsbok, springbok, or other game animal he'd shot for baiting lions or wild dogs or hyenas. Or he'd gaze into the distance, and think about things. Or maybe he wouldn't think, but he might hum a sentimental tune from his Dutch ancestors, the Voortreckers. He'd check the pump and the rain gauge, and before he left he'd stroll around the edge of the fountain picking up ivory chips that had split off from elephants' tusks while they were dueling, the way my son John used to pick up Tehuelche Indian arrowheads near our whale research camp on the bay in Argentina. Arrowheads, ivory chips–souvenirs of male rituals–totems.

The observation tower's legs were made of telephone poles, of which the park had a surplus, although other wood was scarce. Its supporting structure consisted of two tall vertical **X**s, held together and stretched apart with wires, the entire system requiring not a nail. My father, who had held a barn together with block and tackle, would have admired it. As the truck pulled the tower onto its feet, four unperturbable bull elephants watched from the side of the fountain.

The fountain was filled from a shallow subterranean well by a solar-powered pump. It was the only source of water for many miles around and very popular with elephants and other animals. Several kilometers to the west we set up a tent camp inside a fence that had formerly surrounded a ranger's horse camp. It was amazing to me that they used horses in the Namibian parks. There were places enough where a vehicle couldn't go, but the park was overrun with lions. I thought about the horses, smelling lions, and about the danger of their nervousness to their riders. Inside the horse camp we ate, talked, slept, and ran a generator all night to recharge the exhausted batteries that ran the microphone transmitters by day. As we cooked, I thought about the delicious smell of a horse in the nostrils of a lion. Outside the fence, over the rumble of the generator, we often heard lions and hyenas calling in the night. Sometimes, a set of tracks in the morning told us that a lion had walked around the camp fence in the night.

"Let's go, campers," Bill would say in the morning. "Let's move it, team."

In the first year, the team was Bill, Liz, my daughter Holly, and I. We set up an array of microphones and made video recordings of elephants that came near them. Our microphone system didn't work as it should have–the first year of a project is ever so–but Holly was talented with a camera and Liz with a pen, so we brought home quantities of descriptive material. In the second year, ready for the experiment, we brought a bigger team: Bill, Liz, Russ Charif, Loki Osborn, Lisa Rapaport, and myself. Like Bill and me, Russ and I had known each other some twenty years, having met through research on whales. Loki and I also had an old connection through studies of whales, but Etosha turned his head, and he was soon a student at Cambridge University, studying elephants. Lisa had spent many months studying the Asian elephants in the Washington Park Zoo; we'd met there and discovered common interest.

"Let's move it, team." We'd drive over to the tower. It was four kilometers away, a distance we'd have liked to walk, to overcome the claustrophobia of life inside fences, but there were lions around. Some days some of us ran beside the van–good for everyone except the driver. Approaching the trough area, we'd pile in and drive slowly so as not to disturb animals that were drinking or waiting to drink. Then if we saw a kudu, or zebra, or giraffe, or warthog, or springbok, or gemsbok, hyena, jackal, or lion near the trough one of us would say, "Let's wait till they've drunk before we put out our batteries."

Not all those animals were drinkers–the huge, powerful antelope called kudu, for instance, were said to be independent of surface water. But kudu were strangely shy, and if they seemed to want to drink I hated to disturb them. We'd wait ten minutes; three might move one step toward the water. A subtle panic would break out among the nine behind them; all twelve would withdraw eight steps. Fifteen minutes later, everything would be quiet, and seven, after craning their necks anxiously in all directions, would take two tenuous steps forward. "Dammit," Bill would say after an hour of this, "we've gotta get started."

Sometimes I quarreled, baring my teeth on behalf of the Thirsty Animal–*No!* Bill bared his on behalf of the Experiment–

We've gotta. After a few minutes we'd drive into the array, scattering animals as we attached a huge truck battery to each of the little transmitting microphones.

It soured me to upset the animals. I complained to Bill that to the extent we disturbed the natural situation, our results would be distorted. "That doesn't matter," Bill explained. "It will just be noise in our data." We hadn't promised that the animals, even elephants, would feel comfortable with us around. We had only promised to film them sixty times while playing sounds to them. We were sampling their perceptual abilities, not their natural behavior.

Two people, usually Russ and Loki, would disappear in the van with the speaker on top, to be the broadcasting team for the day, taking a walkie-talkie for contact with the tower. The rest of us would climb the ladder and get ready to record and film whatever elephants came into our area. Once ready, we often waited all day, for elephants tend to take their mornings easy, and strike out for water only toward day's end.

The fountain lay in the center of a dust bowl that encompassed most of the square kilometer visible from the tower. Before the bore hole was dug, the area had been a sparse mopane forest, its floor covered with grasses interspersed with sharp-edged white calcareous rocks. Now the grasses had been trampled, thinned, dug up, and buried in dung by a multitude of animals. The trees had been pushed back and knocked down by elephants, and stripped of their bark. But for all of this, mopane is hard to discourage: the small, gnarled trees coppice when laid on their sides, turning branches that touch the earth into new sets of roots. Logs laid down by competing bull elephants were soon likely to have trees growing up at both ends. These logs were smooth, hard, and shaded on either end by leafy umbrellas. They were nice to sit on.

Coppiced mopane trees ringed the edges of the clearing.

Looking out from the tower, we used them as reference points to identify the heads of the eight most-used elephant trails that converged on the Dungaries fountain. In the clearing stood the branchless stumps of a dozen dead mopane trees whose roots had refused to let go when their tops were killed. The feet of these vertical stumps were scarred and burned. Much of Etosha burns during the dry season, sometimes by design–for burning enhances the growth of grasses–sometimes as the result of lightning, and sometimes as the result of careless camping. A major fire spread from our own camp one day, when a dust devil uncovered a buried but not quite extinguished cooking fire, lifting sparks that ignited a pile of tinder.

The earth was all light here–light silver, light gold, light tan, light olive, light gray. The lightness burned our eyes. In early afternoons a small breeze fluttered the dry mopane leaves and their silvery bottoms reminded me of the leaves on my aspen trees at home. The afternoons also brought dust devils and small tornadoes, raising cylinders of earth and natural debris hundreds of feet into the sky, swirling them as if they were in the force field of a huge eggbeater, and flinging them into the distance.

Dungaries was overgrazed, overbrowsed, hoofbeaten, and burned. Such a place can't regenerate the vegetation that the animals attracted to it eat; the desolation spreads outward, and yet it has its charms. It was nice for all kinds of thirsty animals to find the soft elephant dung carpets covering the sharp rocks and converging on the fountain like the spokes of a wheel. The vertical mopane stumps in the clearing became beautiful to my eye once I got used to them. Mopane wood is as hard as ebony, and these, varying from one to four meters tall, each one unique in shape, made prime rubbing and scratching posts for many visitors. Elephants, rhinos, and warthogs would move from one to the next, relieving the itching inside their hides, until the burgundy heartwood shone in the sunlight. One tall stump, broken off at about three meters and free of bark at the top, was specialized for tusk sharpening.

Mopane trees were on my mind a lot. Small, gnarled, deciduous though they were and with only a few dry winter leaves clinging to the tips of their branches, they provided the elephants' primary nutrition in the dry season.

"How can such a scrawny forest support such huge families? I don't see how elephants can afford to be social. They'd be better off solitary, like rhinos." On the tower, I was trying to start a conversation with Bill, Lisa, and Liz, to help us survive the heat until the elephants might start arriving.

"Mmmm." End of conversation. Already, by ten o'clock, it was too hot to think. Even under the shade cloth we'd spread over the tower, we needed wet towels on our heads. I probably wasn't the only one fantasizing about jumping into the amber-colored water in the trough.

We took turns climbing down the ladder, to stretch out under the tower or seek a little shade under the solar panel. But to descend was to leave the theater in the middle of the play, or while new actors were gathering in the wings. The communal faintheartedness of the kudu was about to show, or the awkward, ambivalent sociality of the long-faced hartebeest, or the graceful acrobatics of the springbok, or the loftiness of giraffes who guided their fawns from the top of stilts without the benefit of sound, so that I wondered whether giraffes, like elephants or bats, make sounds outside the range of human hearing.

Warthogs came, dutiful in motherhood, jaunty and fearless. Much larger beasts made way at the fountain for a line of trotting piglets that held their tails straight up in the air. One afternoon a solitary honey badger zigzagged toward us, guided by its nose through rocks and bushes. Having heard the legend that if a honey badger gets a man's scent it will run at him and bite his testicles, we put on quite a show as we scrambled up the ladder. But neither our presence nor our performance was noted. The honey badger scurried from one bush to the next, urgently sniffing roots, stems, and holes in the ground. Liz knew this to be normal, for she had encountered a number of honey badgers during her years in Bushmanland and never seen signs of aggression toward human beings.

Ostriches came, four to six at a time, fluffing out their great body feathers and swinging them above long shapely legs and below a long shapely neck: I thought of Toulouse-Lautrec. Jackals came, and bat-eared foxes, and a hyena, and mongoose, but we waited for elephants.

One noon when I was the tower lookout, and it was too hot for man or beast, and not an animal was in sight, I kept myself awake by pondering the costs and benefits of being a social rather than a solitary animal. How can elephants "afford" to be social, when one elephant alone may eat three to five hundred pounds a day of grass, bark, and leaves? Costs and benefits: the economic language reminded me that evolution is indifferent, devoid of sentiment, like the world of money. If adult elephants practice love and compassion, the chances are that these attitudes promote the survival of their young. The same is true of any trait—it's a genetic accident which will persist as long as it doesn't cost too much. The costs of a trait may increase if the environment changes; when they outweigh the benefits the trait dies out, sometimes taking the population or even the species with it. The devastated landscape of Dungaries was a good backdrop for such a thought.

The social system that has evolved in elephants is oddly like that of sperm whales. Linda Weilgart and Hal Whitehead pointed this out to me, and included me in an expedition to the Galapagos Islands where I saw it for myself. Twenty-one whales surrounded the sailboat, moving in synchrony—they were all females with calves. "Is this like elephants?" asked Lindy. Yes, it was. We had listened to them through hydrophones as they started surfacing together, and we'd heard many overlapping calls (clicks). They'd come up swimming in formation, parallel to one another, and I was reminded of the way elephants sometimes walk in single file when nothing about the geography makes this necessary. Sperm whale family groups are permanent associations, Lindy told me. They're closely related, and they share in the care of their calves. For a feeding mother to dive to the depths where she will catch her prey she must hold her breath longer than her newborn calf can do; one or more of her sisters will stay with the calf on the surface.

Elephants are the largest land animals, and sperm whales the largest toothed whales, in the animal kingdom. Of all animals they have the largest brains, which are also, in both species, large relative to their body size. Brain size gives a rough measure of mental flexibility—some say intelligence—and large mammalian brains are associated with complex sociality. Sperm whales and elephants have both evolved a lifestyle that resonates of ours as well—long lives, few offspring, a high investment in each offspring. Communal family care offers insurance against losing the slowly developing offspring: it's easy to imagine that these traits evolved together. The lives of the bulls are also similar. They spend enormous amounts of energy competing for dominance and they grow to be three times as massive as adult females. Because size is an important factor in dominance, and dominance is a key element in breeding, the bulls may be sexually mature a decade or more before they are big enough to be important breeders.

This suite of characteristics, separately evolved on land and in the sea, has produced a pair of particularly well-adapted species. Sperm whales populate all the oceans; and the ancestors of elephants, in their peak abundance, populated every continent except New Zealand, Australia, and Antarctica. But with the advent of modern human technology, the story is turning on itself. The advantages that sperm whales and elephants gained through the evolution of their complex sociality are maladaptive in the face of mass killing—whether hunting, poaching, or culling. The physical separation of males and females, supported in elephants by their long-distance communication, is so great that wantonly reduced populations may never recover. When they do, reproduction is so slow that it takes decades free of exploitation to restore a population. To compound the difficulties, the individuals of greatest commercial value are old males and old females—the prime breeders and reservoir of traditional memory, whose survival is most crucial to the survival of herds.

I sighed and turned away from the empty landscape. "Somebody else take over," I said as I climbed down the ladder to spend a few minutes in the shade.

In the van, Russ and Loki were passing the day on an empty stretch of pinkish earth exactly one kilometer to the north of the observation tower. Russ had connected the speaker's wires to a loose truck battery. Loki had stretched an awning over the side door of the van. He sat under the awning to make up a tune on his guitar—in the absence of water, there were no animals to watch or to bother. Russ settled into a shady spot with a book on the practice of Buddhism. Loki's song was about the breathtaking excitement of life in the bush. In that mode they passed four hours.

"Tower to van." Russ jumped to the radio on the dashboard.

"Van to tower."

"We've got Mohammed and Hannibal."

Russ leaned over the seat and selected a recording that he hadn't played to these bulls before. Sometime in the next ten minutes he would broadcast it for forty seconds, and Loki would measure the output of the speaker to make sure its strength was 104 decibels (dB), plus or minus two.

Back on the tower we wouldn't hear the broadcast. The upper frequencies to which our ears were sensitive would have dropped out within a few hundred meters of the speaker. The lowest frequencies, which the bulls might hear, would be below our range of hearing.

Our video cameras were recording. At the trough, the very large bull Mohammed and his smaller companion Hannibal were drinking, splashing, dabbling, dangling their trunks in the muddy overflow. Through my viewfinder I watched them, and watched the passing seconds, which showed as white digits against the blue sky on the screen, 4:44:53. 4:44:54. 4:44:55. At 4:45:02 both elephants lifted their heads as if in one motion. Out went four ears, spread, lifted, and stiffened. Two bodies froze, all motion stopped. Very slowly Mohammed swung his head around to the left, and slowly back to center, and around to the right, as if scanning half of the world for sound. Very slowly Hannibal did the same. 4:45:50—the white digits in the camera's sky. If the elephants' behavior was a response to a broadcast it would be over by now, for a broadcast never lasted more than 40 seconds, and was not repeated. Everything after that would be a response to a remembered experience.

Both bulls turned, two slow parallel rotations from south to west to north. Mohammed swayed forward and took his first step. North. Hannibal moved behind him. They passed the overflow from the pool; neither stopped to test it—an unusual absence of interest. They walked into a grove of winter mopane trees, not on a game trail. They stopped after three minutes, and froze for half a minute. They stopped again after six, holding perfectly still for another half minute. They resumed each time on the previous orientation. At 4:56:00 they disappeared into trees heading north. We looked at each other. Because of the double-blind protocol, we didn't know where Loki and Russ were and whether a broadcast had been played, but we grinned as the big bulls disappeared. It occurred to Bill that in case our guess was right, Russ and Loki should know what was coming their way. He picked up the walkie-talkie. "Tower to van."

"Van to tower."

"Just wondering if you have any last words for your loved ones," said Bill.

In the evening we learned that Russ had broadcast a series of five elephant calls at 4:45:00. They were Zita's estrous calls, my recording from Amboseli. The broadcast was over by 4:45:40. At 5:15:00, Mohammed and Hannibal strode past the van, continuing north without a pause. They were searching for something, but not for two young men in a Volkswagen Combi.

The results from all the trials in our experiment indicated that elephants hear and respond to each other's loud calls from distances as great as four kilometers.* An area of at least fifty square kilometers would be filled by such a call at a level that a listening elephant could hear. This didn't tell us about the limits of perception: they undoubtedly heard more than they responded to, and their responses to close sounds were probably more pronounced than to distant ones. But what we had found was a long distance for overland communication–long enough to explain most of the coordinated events that had been reported.

By now the story has been expanded by two meteorologists, David Larom and Michael Garstang, who recognized the

---

* We had to make an extrapolation in order to reach this conclusion. Because our loudspeaker was not capable of reproducing elephant calls at their original volume without distortion, we played back all the recordings at half volume. When the power of a very low-frequency sound is halved, so is the distance it will travel. We calculated the distances over which elephants would have responded to full-volume calls by doubling the distances over which they responded to our half-volume playbacks.

importance of a relationship between atmospheric conditions and the transmission of low-frequency sound. They measured air temperatures at various heights above the earth throughout a dry season in Etosha. They found a dramatic temperature inversion within three hundred meters of the ground on most evenings, which usually persisted through the night until dawn. They made a model predicting that the layer so formed would deflect low-frequency sound back down to the earth instead of allowing it to dissipate in the sky, and greatly increase the distances the sound would travel. At dusk, a loud elephant's call might be heard by another elephant 9.8 kilometers away; it would be heard by the listening elephants within three hundred square kilometers. At midday, the calling area might shrink to one-tenth that size.

The enormous daily expansions and contractions of their acoustic world must have important consequences for land animals with low-frequency, long-distance communication—consequences for them as predators, as members of social groups, and as prey; as listeners and as callers. Do they call more during the hours when the calls will go farthest? The answer, at least for elephants and lions, is yes. It's an answer qualified by subtleties that reflect the interplay between several evolutionary pressures. For female elephants, there are advantages to being able to communicate over long distances, but come nightfall these are offset by the likelihood that their calls will attract the attention of lions. Lions, the master predators, are the master callers of the night. It seems not coincidental that female elephants do most of their calling in the late afternoon, when sound transmission is good but not perfect and the lions are still asleep.

At one hour before sunset the heat and glare were almost unbearable. At ten minutes before sunset the sun had sunk to three degrees above the horizon. The intensity was beginning to drain out of it, and it was growing in size. As it paled and grew, it sank faster. Huge but almost colorless, it slid behind the low forest and was gone. Then everything began to relax—the earth, the air, the brow, the pupils, the scalp, the throat, the ears, the cheeks, the mouth, the tongue.

Whirrrrr-r-r-r-r. Whirrrrr-r-r-r-r. Whirrrrr-r-r-r. Wings near the water as hundreds of sand grouse landed to drink and were quiet. Darkness settled. The space expanded. It became huge and empty. The smallest sound would be audible.

Then I said to myself, shall I go to the horse camp and eat and rest, now that the day's work is done, and be ready to face the heat and brilliance again when tomorrow dawns? Or shall I stay, now that it is cool, now that everything that was oppressive has been drawn off into the sky, and the players in the drama of the night are getting ready for their performance? I looked around to see who else was thinking the same, but just then a chill ran up my spine. A low groan was coming from the eastern corner of the tower. It rose in pitch and volume, swelled to a full-throated peak, and slowly descended, losing volume. *rrrrRUh . . . rRRUHh . . . rrRRUhh . . . rRRuh . . . Ruhh, uhh, uh, uh, uhh, huh, ruh, ruh.*

Had a lionness lay here unnoticed in the grass all day? Indeed. Now we heard a faint response, almost an echo, from beyond Kudu Hill in the west, followed by silence. Several more voices called from the southwest, overlaying, alternating, overlaying. *Huh huh, huh, huh, huh.* A single voice called from the east.

We took turns at night on the tower and there was never an uneventful night. Here's a recollection from Russ: "A large group [of elephants] approached under moonlight from the west. A hundred meters away we could clearly hear the crunch of every footfall on gravelly ground. Then at fifty to seventy-five meters they froze for a minute. When they resumed walking, they passed under us in utter silence."

One night, Holly used the light of the moon to film twenty elephants departing from the tower area after they had drunk. As they started to leave the fountain, a subgroup containing two adults, two juveniles, and a newborn calf turned back abruptly to face it. With ears stiffened and lifted, they froze in their tracks while the rest of the group continued walking. Those who had frozen soon followed the others, but ten steps later the entire group froze, facing forward. This freeze lasted a full minute—a very long time for twenty wide-awake animals, infants as well as adults, to hold perfectly still. Eventually an old female broke the stillness and the entire herd walked into the forest, unanimous.

You can't look at that bit of film without sensing things that you might ignore at midday. Reminded of what it is to be a prey animal, and of what it is to be a social animal with responsibilities to distant others, you ask yourself whether your own listening skills are sufficiently honed. Watching animals who achieve silence when it is called for—never mind that there are dozens or even hundreds together, and that some weigh ten tons, which makes silence of the feet difficult, while others are but a day or two old, which makes silence of the voice unlikely—you remember that in humans, as in elephants, communication is only as good as what is received.

To use silence so well: if I could choose for people one attribute of elephants, I'd choose this.

At the end of the first field season, Holly and I stayed on in Etosha, searching for private adventure. On the first day of our independence, we encountered a group of elephants in a large natural pool called Ajab involved in behaviors I'd never seen before. Out of the pool, which lay glistening before us, heaved an immense, dark, shiny bulk—an elephant head so coated in mud that the whites of the eyes didn't show. It lunged into the air, flopping its long and indecently relaxed trunk upward and then flipping it backwards, releasing a great sling of mud—dark droplets flew out and made an arch against the clear sky— *whoosh!*—the head flopped over onto its side and sank, leaving a seething crater on the surface. Displaced water rushed to the center of the crater just as another huge, dark, asymmetrical shape rose up beside it. We strained to understand the anatomy—that ridge could only be a backbone, making this lump a fat haunch. It swelled and lumped but failed to produce a head: an animal must be rolling under the surface. Now a close circle of mud began to seethe, revealing what appendages?—something that squirmed like large thick snakes, or, I thought to myself, like the penises of right whales when a cohort of males competes simultaneously for a female who lies belly-up avoiding them and they reach over her, groping at the surface: I had watched scenes of this sort with mixed emotions from the cliffs in Argentina. But these elephant parts were not penises. They were trunks wound together and slithering apart, all covered with "slip," to use a potter's terminology.

A rounded back now rose up with two trunks slithering along its upper surface, but the heads beyond the back and trunks remained submerged. We tried to count the animals: joked about counting the visible body parts and dividing by some integer—four? But now a fifth surged out of the depths, breaching like a whale, with its ears flung out sideways. This creature landed on its back, wallowed, and disappeared in a new crater surrounded by thick in-curling waves. Suddenly out of the crater's center rose the heads of two large bull elephants with broken tusks. Their identical texture and degree of emergence and facing positions gave them the appearance of mirror images carved out of clay and set on a platter for display. But the faces rushed at each other and locked together—I gasped, realizing that a jousting match had gotten started underwater. Immediately, a third large, black head surged out of the mud, slapped its trunk across the back of one contestant, reached into the mouth of the other, and the three of them fell over as a unit into the turbulent pool.

I was beginning to see the elephants as monsters and the pool as a prehistoric sucking tar pit. Beside it, four yearling calves were enjoying a game of pig pile. They were sliding one over the other into a shallow pool of mud, landing on the sides of their rumps with their legs beside them or splayed in the air. They achieved a pile four deep, facing the deeper water. Then the top animal swooped down into the lake, and in a mighty splash disappeared as someone trumpeted.

Holly and I trumpeted, too—we laughed until we hooted. We hooted in resonance with the wild slippery fun, and admired the grace of circumstances that gave us this experience on the day we forsook our commitment to blindness.

7

BE REASONABLE

THE LIONS IN ETOSHA WERE NUMEROUS AND BRASH. THERE was a large bearded lion who lay against one of the legs of the first observation tower we used, a tower over a natural water hole called Gobaub: his was a daunting presence, because we were up on top. One evening, after he left, we descended to drive to our camp, but on the way we encountered a heap of four adolescent lions just waking in the shade of a large tree. They were energized by our vehicle and chased it the way dogs chase cars, snarling and racing, and one pounced on the back bumper as we hurried to get out of range.

Flip Stander, one of the parks people who had built the Dungaries tower for us, was studying the nocturnal hunting behaviors of the Etosha lions. He took us out one night, predicting that we'd see a piece of remarkable teamwork if the seven lionesses in the pride he called Okondeka were in a communal hunting mood. He predicted they'd take up positions in the shape of a horseshoe, with the oldest female, Number 27, in the center and the younger ones on the edges. In this formation, the group would creep slowly toward a herd of springbok, partially surrounding them. The open mouth of the horseshoe would close when young Bravo, having slipped away from her position as the team's left wing, would charge from center rear, driving a central springbok into the jaws of Old 27.

"It's a compelling image," I said to myself. "Now let's see what really happens." In the dark of the night, we sat in Flip's truck and watched with him; a searchlight covered with a red filter allowed us to see without disturbing the action. Scanning the light back and forth, Flip whispered a running commentary. "Here they come—that long body, that's 27." A long-bodied lioness slunk into crouching position behind a bush a hundred meters in front of us as three shorter animals moved away to her right and three to her left. "That's Collar 4, she'll go to 27's right," and we watched Collar 4 hide beyond behind a clump of grass some fifty meters to 27's right. "There goes Bravo," and the searchlight caught the flank of another slinking animal far to the left just as she disappeared over the horizon in a sparse mopane grove. "Here come the springbok." Many eyes glinted as the light struck them. The glints were dispersed and at different levels, telling us that the little antelope were innocently grazing as they came. One passed close to a hidden lioness: the predator did not stir.

"Watch the second springbok from the right. Here comes Bravo." Suddenly there was a rush from the forest beyond the herd of springbok. Hooves thundered as the herd fled in all directions, but the second springbok from the left leaped forward with a scream, into the jaws of the long lioness. Immediately the horseshoe closed in on itself. Six lionesses rushed to the center, growling and snarling at each other, tearing apart the warm body, which gave way with sounds as of ripping canvas. Fifteen minutes later there wasn't a scrap of flesh or bone left to tell the tale, which explains why Flip was the first to recognize the springbok as the principal prey of the Namibian lion.

The lionesses did not rest. We drove along behind them, and watched, within the hour, the same players repeat the performance on another playing field. Over the years of his study, Flip had seen it, with variations, 486 times. When key members of the pride were away hunting elsewhere, others substituted for them, and the order of the substitution was predictable, revealing a functional hierarchy in which each player had learned and practiced more than one specialty. When fewer than seven lionesses were present, only the most important positions were filled.

This, too, I said to myself, is communal behavior.

At dawn, the seven lionesses, full of meat and bones, lay down and fell asleep, pressing their warm breathing and digesting bodies against one another.

I had chosen Etosha as the site of our research in 1986 and 1987, for reasons that were partly personal. My son John and his friend (now wife) Ann Edwards were also to be in Namibia in the seasons when we would be there, working for a foundation dedicated to the survival of the Namibian Bushman people and culture. Eliazbeth Marshall Thomas's brother, John Marshall, was running the foundation, and Liz would be with us in the field, as would my daughter Holly. It was a delightful prospect, that our two families would be close together and able to help each other.

But the time I spent in Bushmanland turned out to be a short, heartbreaking experience. The Bushmen about whom Liz, as a young woman, had written so eloquently in *The Harmless People* were now no longer hunters and gatherers. The South African government had granted them waterless land when it took their own away, leaving them dependent on outsiders and for the first time impoverished. To supplement what they could do for themselves the government had instituted a dole, from a bush station where alcohol was sold along with basic goods, producing some of the same troubles it produces in our sorrowful American Indian reservations. In the face of these realities, the Bushman Foundation was involved in a bitter and frustrating struggle. As if that was not enough, there was bad blood between the foundation and the Department of Nature Conservation and Tourism. Caught between well-meaning institutions, how could we feel anything but disillusioned, and, more important, what could we do?

We who were working with elephants wondered whether our project, with its foreign money, foreign personnel, and foreign objectives, was contributing to the sort of social imbalance the Bushman Foundation was struggling to redress. This was on Bill's mind when he planned our second Etosha expedition. He suggested we could offer a course in animal behavior for Namibians who otherwise seldom entered the domain of the national parks. We had become aware of a small institution called TUCSIN, the University Center for Studies in Namibia, which offered a few motivated indigenous students the opportunity to improve their education, for the standard school system mandated segregation, and the black schools lacked the resources and advantages that were given to the white schools. The TUCSIN students were from other cultures, not Bushmen, but the opportunity to interact with them appealed to us.

In the service of this idea, I walked one day in early June 1987 under the tin roof of the central offices of the Department of Nature Conservation and Tourism in Windhoek, the capital city of Namibia.

The officials in that department called their building "the rabbit warren." It would have been too small for their business even if there had not been so many of them, and each so large and deep-voiced and opinionated. It was funny to hear a pair of them booming their greetings as one squeezed respectfully past the other in a cul-de-sac at the end of a narrow hall: "Good afternoon, Dr. —." "Good afternoon, Dr. —, I hope you remain as fit as you claimed to be when we did this a few minutes ago."

"Good afternoon, and what brings you here today?" boomed the official I had come to see, when I caught him in a corner. He waved his hand to suggest that we should squeeze our way eastward along the central hall until we spotted an unoccupied nook or cranny. As I followed him into the dark warren I glanced over my shoulder at the street. Our truck was parked far enough up the hill so as to be inconspicuous, and Bill and Loki were in it. They had insisted on my being the one to make the inquiry because I was "good at schmoozing."

"It's an idea about a service we'd like to offer the department, if you'd like," I said. "Our team includes four teachers of animal behavior. We've all wanted to give something back to Namibia in thanks for our time here, and it occurred to them that they could teach an observation-based course in Etosha for Namibian students. They'd do it during the week when I'll be off in the desert with World Wildlife Fund people."

"But this is quite appropriate. I'll have to ask my colleagues, of course—which week did you had in mind?"

"First week in August."

"Pity. Unfortunate. It's the middle of a term. But I assume you've talked this over with the Academy?"

"Actually, we were thinking of TUCSIN students," I said. "The dates are all right for them."

Everything in the room suddenly shifted and scuffled; a scowl appeared on my host's face. He drew a deep breath as if to fill a bagpipe and stiffened and stepped so close to me that, had the day outside not suddenly grown quite dark, I would have been standing in his shadow.

"Dr. Payne," said my host, honoring me with a title I have never earned, "this is a *great disappointment*. Until now we have

had an ideal relationship, last year you did an excellent piece of science without meddling in the affairs of others, you were model visitors; but now it seems you're becoming *political*." His voice rose in pitch and did not lower in volume. I do not remember the particulars of what he said, apart from the word, many times repeated, "bl-l-lecks."

When he had subsided at last, I said, "Isn't it you who are being political, and in the face of a reality you can't afford to deny? You are a manager of wildlife in a country that is soon to be run by black people. Unless they know the parks there won't be a wild animal left in ten years for you to manage—"

BOOM!

A bolt of lightning had struck so close to us that it felt as if it might have hit the building itself. The room and early afternoon sky darkened. Although no rain was expected for five months, a volley of rain and hail began to pelt the tin roof over our heads so violently that any continuation of our discussion was out of the question. We had to wait.

After several minutes the storm had passed and with it, astonishingly, my host's resistance. He asked me quietly, "Where would you like to teach it?"

I asked my host where he would teach it if it were his course. "In Okaukuejo," he replied quickly, "where the staff can show the students the ecological institute. The students could stay in the visitors' campground, and . . ."

It was my loss that I was away in the desert during the week that the course was taught. In a series of methodical observations, nine enthusiastic adult TUCSIN students documented, among other things, the vigilance of kudu in relation to the circumstances around them. They documented the rate of elephant ear waving in relation to changes in air temperature. "But the only thing we couldn't do," Loki recounted, "was to persuade them not to talk politics. They couldn't contain themselves—at night they'd be outside the tents, waving their arms and shouting."

A few years later, Namibia declared its independence following a peaceful revolution. I'd like to think that our small intervention had something to do with the continuing vigor of Namibia's wildlife after the transition, but in truth I have no idea whether this is the case. The only thing I can report for sure is my own satisfaction on the day when the right words came to my lips and Jove confirmed them with a thunderbolt.

Although there were exceptional days, I often felt troubled in Namibia, and thought of it, somehow, as a place that divided body from soul. I was uncomfortable acknowledging the thriving wildlife program when I knew so much about the unhappy indigenous population. Our research procedures, favoring after-the-fact assessments over spontaneous observation, went against my inclinations even though I understood their value. More to the point, though, there was a contradiction in my own behavior. At home my parents were unwell. Namibia wasn't where I should have been.

At the end of a day's work, I'd sometimes leave the others and drive away, to try to find my balance. That's what I was doing one afternoon at the end of August 1986, while my partners, back in camp, were disassembling a piece of equipment for the umpteenth time and joking about new ways of combining rice and beans for supper.

We had a two-way radio in our vehicle, a universal exchange and gossip channel, to which the parks headquarters had instructed us to listen continuously in case anyone wanted to reach us. I had objected to this requirement, for I didn't want human voices to disturb the natural situation and sap our attention. Understanding my objection, headquarters had reduced our listening assignment to one early and one late hour of the day. But when the evening hour came on this day I defaulted on this responsibility along with the rest.

By the time I returned to camp, the sun had set and the land gone dark, for the moon was waning and would not rise for several hours. The coals in our small campfire glowed, offering a little light. We ate a quiet supper, anticipating the coolness that would soon arrive, and listening to a pair of little Scops owls calling back and forth in the mopane trees over our tents. Then Bill sighed and said it was time to start the generator, to get the batteries charged for the morrow. But just as he was about to pull the starting rope we noticed a low rumbling sound, the rumble of a vehicle moving rather fast.

Tourist vehicles are not permitted to move at night, and our camp was far from the parks people's usual trajectories. The sound of an engine meant something serious. We stood up and waited.

The driver was Malan Lindeque, our closest Namibian colleague. He had been trying to reach us by radio for several hours. "It's a message for you, Katy," he said kindly. "A phone call to the station. One of your parents is not doing well. The transmission was bad, I couldn't tell which one—"

"Damon!" I said.

I dived into my tent and stuffed my knapsack. Without discussion, everyone joined me, and within five minutes we were heading for the Windhoek airport, six hours to the south. Bill drove; in the backseat I closed my eyes and leaned against Holly, who held her arm around me. A striking vision appeared to me, the figure of a strapping young man in the form of a Matisse cutout. Huger than a mountain, he strode across a mountain range with seven-league boots on. "Damon," I said. "He is coming free."

I arrived home in time for his last three days. Sam, the youngest of my four children, had come from Oberlin, Ohio, and we waited together in the hospital, glad to be together. In the course of those days Damon gave us three pieces of advice.

The first was, *Let's be peaceful.*

There was a pause that lasted I don't know how many hours, and then the second piece of advice, in an intense, husky voice. *Katy, be reasonable.*

This was advice from one who had given equal time to reason and unreason. I should have seen it as a revelation and paid attention. But I was in a mood for love, not reason.

I squeezed his hand, and answered, with humor in my voice, "Okay, I promise. Just as reasonable as you."

My father frowned and turned toward the window, where Sam was sitting. "Who are you?"

"I'm Sam," said Sam, in a deep strong voice.

"Sam," said Damon, *"pursue!"*

In the middle of that night, he died. Sam and I went home to Mary. She greeted us in her schlafrock, the embroidered green woolen bathrobe she'd worn all my life. Seeing the news in our faces, she said, calmly, "Oh, good." There was a bowl of perfect, ripe peaches on the table under the north window: with steady hands my mother cut them up, and we ate them in honor of Damon's passage.

Sam and I both followed the advice intended for Sam, and neither of us followed the advice intended for me. Sam became an acrobat in a circus. I continued to follow my nose, careless of the consequences, and to recall Damon's advice only when I found myself in trouble.

I recalled it intensely on the last night of our second Namibian field season, a year after Damon's death. I'd stayed on in Etosha after the others departed, because I wanted to record lions roaring. I was aware that lions, like elephants, call back and forth to one another over large distances, and that their voices are impressively low and powerful. By making a few measurements I thought I might link these two observations.

In the afternoon, I had recorded a large lioness near the main tourist camp and found her voice stronger than the most powerful calls we'd recorded from elephants. I decided to spend that night waiting for her or another lion, my sleeping bag spread inside a fenced-in area in the main tourist camp, my recorder at the ready. At sunset, I threw down my bag two or three meters from the fence and crawled in.

By the time I noticed that there was a large hole in the fence, patched with chicken wire, Yellow Mane had arrived. Not a lioness but a lion, who sat down, pressed up against the hole, and looked into my eyes. On my belly and elbows, I stretched my back and craned my neck to return his gaze.

I lay as still as I could, for I remembered an instruction from my childhood: In the presence of a threatening animal, you must hold perfectly still so he will think you are dead. I looked into his eyes, since that's what I was doing when he arrived, as unblinkingly as possible (as if dead). After a while, the moon began to rise behind the lion, back-lighting the hairs on his shoulders, his whiskers, and the long hairs of the mane around his face. They stood out gold against the darkening sky, lifting and wavering slightly with his breathing. Without shifting the direction of my gaze, I was aware that he was surrounded by a halo. Neither of us blinked. My eyes smarted. It grew darker.

All at once the top of the moon began to show above his head. In a minute it would shine into my face. I held perfectly still. Yellow Mane held perfectly still, looking into my eyes.

The moon climbed higher and higher: it was perfectly full. Silently I spoke to Yellow Mane, acknowledging my stupidity. He did not move; he was relaxed and alert, his mane blowing sideways in a sudden breeze. I did not move but I thought I might collapse, for my arms were all pins and needles. I had been lying in this position for three hours.

The moon rose higher. Yellow Mane's mouth slowly opened: he was panting gently. A long drool ran down his tongue, stretched out toward the ground until it was half a meter long. It rolled and dropped off his tongue and hit the ground, making a wet sound.

He drooled but he did not lift his paw to reach through the hole. I thought, He has acknowledged that I am food and has not reached for me. He has decided not to do it.

Not to do it, or to spare me? Which did he decide? The difference is great. Was the decision pragmatic or merciful? Or was it not a decision, but a waiting?

My arms were numb. The moon reached the zenith and slowly rolled back behind my head. Now it was I who saw every detail in the lion's face. His eyes were exquisite, brown and gold. Neither of us blinked.

Hours passed, and everything very slowly changed. The sky behind the lion's head slowly became a blanket of gray. His eyes darkened and lost their glint, and then my shadow came between us, then that and all shadows disappeared. The moon has set behind me, I said to myself. Twelve hours have passed since the start of our vigil.

Yellow Mane stood up, looked away from me, turned sideways, stretched his huge, muscular body from neck to tail, gave a long, loud yawn, turned his back on me, and walked away. A few minutes later there was a scream a short distance up the fence. I walked up and saw Yellow Mane standing over a freshly killed kudu.

That night ended my work in Namibia. I returned to Ithaca and stayed for three years.

I spent much time, then, with Mary. I joined her for tea at her house on most afternoons, and we often read aloud. Chapter by chapter and volume by volume, we read Mary Moorman's delicate, slow, beautifully detailed biography of Wordsworth.

It occurred to me to ask Mary one day whether she thought of Wordsworth as a romantic.

"I'm not sure. He wrote about what he saw."

"How about Damon?"

"He was a romantic."

"And you?"

"No. I'm a realist."

In her last week Mary had two dreams. In one, Death said to her, "This is how you'll know. If there's a light fall of snow and it falls over your whole face and body and doesn't flutter or move, you're dead."

"That's smart," Mary told me when she woke up. "This is a new way to be sure when somebody's dead. Watch the snow."

But in a second dream, which came immediately after the first, Death said to her, "If it were not so, I would have told you." These are words from John 14, that Jesus said to his disciples when he was about to die. His next line is, "I go to prepare a place for you."

"Then I said to Death, 'In that case we'd better tidy up,'" said Mary to me. "Then I in my long green schlafrock and you in a long white nightie, floated around the house. We found that everything was ready.

"I have such a clear view of the long green schlafrock," she mused. "I was above the situation and saw myself below. You— often in a dream you have a perfectly solid sense of a person without seeing 'em. I mean, there wasn't any question that you were there although I didn't really visualize you exactly."

Then she said to the visiting doctor, "Everyone's hopes are up. They think I may make it over the border."

"Your hopes included?" he asked.

"Yes."

But she lived on, a few days more.

On the last day, I asked her whether she wanted reading, but she said, "No. Silence—and presence." Inside her head she was hearing the last chorus of the Mass in B Minor. "Only Bach could have ended it so simply."

After a time she asked, "What are the words?"

"Dona nobis pacem."

"No—to the Agnus Dei."

"Qui tollis peccata mundi, miserere nobis . . ."

"*Miserere,* that's the word I wanted."

Have mercy on us.

My parents' ashes are scattered in a small country graveyard on a hill where they used to walk during their last summers together. Black raspberries grow wild around the edges, bordering a row of unkempt old maples that slowly drop their branches onto the gravesites, and are favorite drumming sites for woodpeckers. In May a patch of gone-wild lilies-of-the-valley fills the ditch by the road. When Mary first thought of this graveyard, she sent me to find out whether you can hear the wood thrushes and veeries that sing in the gorge across the road. I found them singing so lustily, you could hear them from any grave.

In winter, when it gets so cold in these parts that the snow sublimes—rises up and becomes air without melting—it occurs to me that my parents, too, may have sublimed, and become spirit. But in spring, when everything has substance, I encounter them in the veeries and wood thrushes and lilies-of-the-valley. Occasionally I have a new experience that reminds me of an unfinished conversation with one of them. The night when the gaze of a lion cemented in me a passionate desire to be reasonable—that was such an experience.

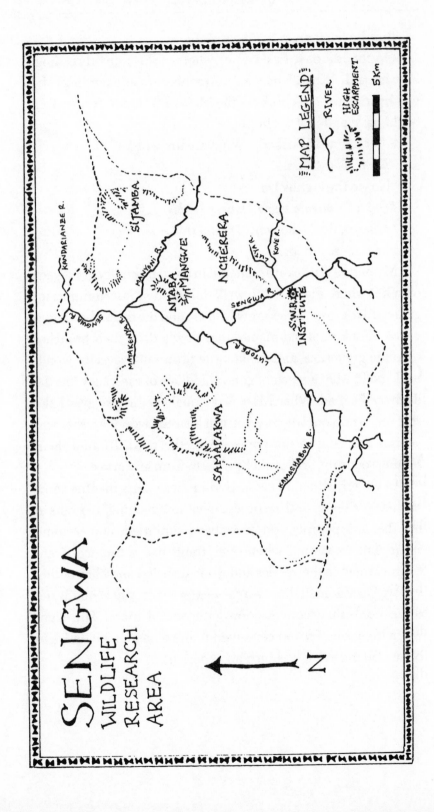

SENGWA
WILDLIFE
RESEARCH
AREA

N

MAP LEGEND
RIVER
HIGH ESCARPMENT
5 Km

KANDARIANZEE R.
SITAMBA
MANYONI R.
SENGWA R.
MATAKENYA R.
NTABA
MANGWE
NCHERERA
KOVE R.
SENGWA R.
S.W.R.O. INSTITUTE
LUTOPE R.
SAMAPAKWA
KAMASHABOYA R.

8

THE CALABASH
THAT IS HEAVY

CHITENDE CHINOREMA NDECHINE MHODZI. THAT'S A SHONA proverb, from Zimbabwe. The calabash that is heavy is the one containing seeds. And the heavy calabash, for me, was Sengwa.

The landlocked country of Zimbabwe lies north of South Africa, east of Botswana, south of Zambia, and west of Mozambique. Toward the end of its years as the British colony Rhodesia, Rowan Martin, a Rhodesian of Scottish descent, pursued a graduate program in tropical ecology at the University of Rhodesia, studying the movement patterns of elephants. He radio-collared several dozen elephants from a single population and tracked them over several years to find out where they went and on what schedule. While analyzing the movements of adult females from different families, he noticed that certain pairs of families appeared to coordinate their movements for weeks at a time, over distances of several kilometers. This struck him as remarkable and he asked himself how they were managing to do it.

Cynthia Moss heard about Rowan Martin's observation,

and told me. The work was unpublished, so in 1986 I went to Zimbabwe to meet Rowan—now assistant director of research in Zimbabwe's Department of National Parks and Wildlife Management—and see for myself. I returned with Bill Langbauer in 1987 and the three of us, intrigued by the way our discoveries seemed to fit together, designed a collaborative project to examine the connection between elephants' use of infrasound and their coordinated movements. It would take us three years in preparation, for this was a complicated project to plan and fund.

Rowan and Bill would design a new sort of radio collar that could transmit not only the elephants' movements but also their loud, low-frequency calls back to a receiving station where they could be labeled and stored in computers. We would collar female elephants from different family groups, and simultaneously follow their movements and record their calls. We expected to find that coordinated movements between separated families were organized by their calls. We would analyze blood samples for genetic relatedness. We expected to find that the relationships reflected by vocal behaviors and movement patterns were genetic as well as social.

We would work in Rowan's former research site in central Zimbabwe, the Sengwa Wildlife Research Area, an area of about four hundred square kilometers centered on the convergence of the Sengwa, Manyoni, and Lutope Rivers. This area had been a reserve since 1965, when the Sengwa Wildlife Research Institute was constructed near its southern border. In those days, the area was remote and the local human population sparse, due to the presence of the tsetse fly, which carried a disease fatal to people and livestock. The institute's initial mission was to figure out a way to get rid of the tsetse fly. Once that was accomplished, the area became no longer so sparsely populated or so remote, but it has remained a place independent of tourists, a place whose life is rooted in its own soil.

Even now, Sengwa is a long day's drive from the capital city—a long day for both body and soul. You speed westward out of Harare on a double-lane highway between irrigated fields of maize, pumpkins, beans, and cabbages, enchanted by the slowly revolving and crisscrossing arches of water in the air. Five or six hours later you have left these signs of prosperity far behind. The tarmac road has reached its end in the squalid, teeming center called Gokwe, whose main square is a parking lot for dozens of dilapidated buses, with hundreds of people camped between them waiting for other buses. The people are variously immersed in and defending themselves from all sorts of dealing, debauchery, and thievery. You must do your business in Gokwe quickly, and your business is to fill all possible tanks with petrol. You feel a bite of fear in Gokwe—you who are irrigated and mobile, passing through a center where so many are dry and waiting for buses, and selling their meager bundles of roofing grass. A hundred years ago the land you passed earlier, that now produces the cabbages and displays the arches of water, belonged to the ancestors of these people. It is upsetting to think about the displacement of the ancestors and the consequences for the descendants.

After Gokwe the dirt road slows you down; you are no longer above it. You join sand and dust, and its ruts throw you rattling and zigzagging among donkey carts and oxcarts and barefoot pedestrians, everyone waving to everyone else.

You begin to pay attention to small clusters of round clay huts with thatched roofs at the sides of the road. Each cluster is a "village," a communal farm inhabited by a single extended family. The clay floors of the huts are continuous with the earth that surrounds them, and the area encompassing all the huts and the storage shed—an open-topped platform on stilts, piled with produce and fodder—has the multiple functions of a courtyard, and is swept clean several times a day with brooms made of twigs. If the courtyard contains a shade tree, there will likely be chickens, dogs, women, and children under it. If there are goats, donkeys, and oxen, they live in separate corrals.

The villages were here before the road, and a village near a road means many more villages inland, with paths running between them. Hand-painted signs mark the intersections of paths with the road: "Bus stop." It seems strange to see the words in English, given that Shona is all you hear in this area, but English is Zimbabwe's designated national language, in which most school lessons beyond second grade are taught.

At intervals of a few dozen kilometers, the road broadens beside a community store, a rectangular concrete building with a corrugated tin roof and a large sign over the brow of its single, central door. The Manyoni School Bottle Store and Butchery is such a one. It offers tinned goods, candles, matches, soap, enameled metal plates and cups, cast-iron stewpots, a little clothing, soda, and beer—basic requirements for survival, but the prices are much higher than in Gokwe.

People gather outside the store, hoping that a bus will come. Some chat cheerfully, oblivious of heavy grain sacks balanced on their heads. Others rest under shade trees, having thrown down the maize, cotton, and thatch they hope to sell in Gokwe. The women, wearing long, colorful printed skirts and kerchiefs, have babies strapped to their backs and babies at the breast and children at their knees. Some of the women are plump, but the men are lean to the point that every muscle and sinew shows. They wear straw hats and carry sticks for prodding livestock. Some cluster together, tired, intense, and talkative—drinking.

Not far from the store stands a dusty diesel-powered mill where homegrown maize is ground into the staple of life, mealie-meal. Mixed with grain dust, the earth here is a lighter color than elsewhere. The people who wait are not animated;

some of them sit in their donkey carts, tired, perhaps weak from malnourishment.

The afternoon gets hotter. You have been long on this Mafungabusi Plateau. It is dull, scrubby, dusty, depleted—to your Western eyes, neither wild nor agricultural. You have not seen a single wild animal. Perhaps things will change at Charama; everyone has said that you must get to Charama by sunset. You drive on and on.

Suddenly you reach a place where the earth has been cut in half, and one half has sunk several hundred feet below the other. You are on the top half, looking over the cliff you must now descend. On its face, you see rugged ledges and vertical red earth and the wreckage of vehicles that failed to get here by sunset—mostly buses. You must now turn and back-turn, narrow and blind, all the way down this face, recalling that it is the only passage for donkey carts and oxcarts, power vehicles, livestock, and pedestrians. If you have a passenger, send him or her ahead to signal from each outer curve what is coming from below, and at what speed, and occupying how much of the track. Waiting, you can get out and stretch, and look along the wall to the west. The sun, which sank a quarter hour ago below Charama's upper horizon, is still a few degrees above the horizon that lies below. But onward: the sun is sinking and the rider is waving—the road is yours.

By halfway down, you've descended into night. You travel the last hour in darkness. In the morning you wake up in Sengwa, and you don't know how you got there.

July 16, 1990. A large elephant lay on her left side on the sandy bank of a dry floodplain, her left ear spread out under her cheek on the ground, her right side swelling and falling with slow, deep breaths. Tranquilized, she had been lying in that unlikely relationship to nature for half an hour. Long drafty inhalations and sonorous exhalations emanated from her trunk, which was casually slung on the ground in an upward curve in front of her open but glazed eyes. About two dozen men surrounded her, some the color of ebony and others the color of cherry wood, most of them wearing the army-green uniforms of Zimbabwe's Department of National Parks and Wildlife Management. Eleven light-skinned people, including three women (of whom I was one) were also present, wearing shorts and T-shirts. I was concentrating on the elephant's rising and sinking side as it blotted out and then revealed the forested horizon beyond. I felt a burden of responsibility because, as the senior member of a visiting research team, I'd just been given the privilege of naming the elephant. Her light gray skin was textured by deep wrinkles, varying in geometric pattern and hairiness over different sections of her body. A pair of enormous soft breasts lay sumptuously between her front legs in the position of human breasts. My mind groped in the domain of goddesses and heroines. Athena? Demeter? Casseopeia?

Around me the Shona language flowed, gentle and fluid, its vowels like Latin vowels, its consonants soft, its words many-syllabled, its sentences punctuated with explosive exclamations—"!Ah!!" "!O!" "!Eeee!"—in pitches above and below the current. The sound of the men's voices, animated but not heated, entered my ears pleasantly, like a brook tumbling down a stony gully. I stopped to listen, recognizing a word, "computer." Then it was on several tongues: "computer, computer." Like a three-part bubble it floated, bobbed, duplicated, flowed on the stream of words.

Rowan Martin glanced at me with a quizzical smile. "Her name is Computer," he said.

"Wait," I said.

"Too late," said Rowan. "A name can't be changed once it's given."

Around Computer's neck ran a wide strip of machine belting, its ends bolted together under her chin, where a massive lead weight would hang when she stood up. It would counterbalance a bright-red homemade fiberglass case the size and shape of a large loaf of bread that was attached to the belting and would ride between her shoulders. The case enclosed two radio transmitters with their antennae and fourteen lithium batteries wired together. The total weight of the package that Computer would now carry continuously was nearly sixteen kilograms (about thirty-five pounds).

Rob Ramey was crouching beside Computer's extended left ear. "Got it," he said, holding up a test tube full of blood. "Okay," said Mike Kock, the vet. "Get to safety. I'm going to inject the antidote and she'll be on her feet in a minute."

We moved quickly into the woods and climbed onto the flatbed of an ancient battered truck. In a few minutes I heard, through the chatter of human voices, a long, loud elephant rumble, and Mike's feet scrambling through the bush. "She's up," he said. But my heart was down. The first elephant we had collared had been named for an electronic instrument.

"I think Computer is a fine name," said Bill.

"Oh, Bill," I said.

Computer's collaring completed our day's work. People crowded into the field station's dusty old Land Rover and our old Land Cruiser. On the back of the flatbed truck, I moved to where I could hang on to a wooden wall behind the cab. Next to me a short, upright, elderly man, Christmas Vurawa, and two young men, Didimus Hapaori and Timothy Chifamba, clung for their security to a huge spare tire. I smiled at Christmas. "I like your name," I said, when we reached a level stretch of road.

Christmas smiled back, his central upper tooth, very white, dangling loose and swinging with the motion of the truck. "I was born on December twenty-fifth, a long time ago," he said in a deep, growly voice. "In 1939."

"And I in 1937." I responded instantly, appreciating his confession: everyone knows that age has its drawbacks. But Christmas turned to face me, pressed his hands together, thumbs against his chest, and bowed, looking down respectfully. Didimus and Timothy let go the tire, turned to face me, pressed their hands together, and bowed. I bowed in return and smiled but they did not smile as they greeted me, an elder.

As the forest opened, the driver shouted, "Hold on!"—for there is only one way to get across a sand river without four-wheel drive. The flatbed plunged over a drop-off, accelerated across fifty meters of sand, lurched up a clay wall, and, roaring, climbed a steep hill. There we stopped at a junction of three dirt roads, broke into different languages, and dispersed on foot. Most of the men walked down a dusty trail toward the compound a couple of kilometers below, where they lived in humble circumstances, without electricity or private water and most of them without their families. The rest of us walked up the main drive to the institute, whence we would disperse to spacious cottages with verandas, peeling linoleum, and bathtubs six feet long. Passing the workshed, we greeted the mechanic; passing the flagpole beside the elevated water tanks, we greeted the office orderly, who was striking the national flag. Each greeting had three parts: *"Maswerasei?" "Ndaswera, maswerawo."* *"Ndaswera, taswera."* How did you pass the day? I passed it well, if you did, too. I passed it well, so we all passed it well.

On the previous day, Rowan and Bill had explained to some thirty people—most of the staff—how the project was going to work. The fourteen "scouts" (mature, experienced field assistants) would soon be doing most of the radio tracking. Young and middle aged, these men were Shona, Ndebele, and Tonga, and their surnames were beautiful to tongue and ear. Maramba

Gubunja, Hapaori, Chingoma, Mutunha, Shumba, Gava, Nya-makusa, Mbanga, Masarirevhu–these were Shona names, pronounced with clear consonants and Latin vowels. Ndebele was closer to the throat with occasional clicks and wetter consonants: Mahlangu was pronounced "Machshangu," where the *ch* of the *-ach-* is like the German *ich*, and the *ng* is soft as in *ing* and the wetness between the *-ach-* and the *-sha-* is a gush, a luxury in a dry country.

Of the eight American biologists and engineers, half of us (Bill, Russ, Loki, and I) were companions from Etosha and before. Bill's wife, Lillie Wilson, had joined us, and the Cornell engineer Steve Powell, and a young couple, Rob Ramey and Laura Brown, Cornell graduate students in population genetics and conservation biology. From Harare, Debbie St. Claire Gibson and Mike Kock were well known to the Sengwa staff. Debbie was not only a pilot but also an ecologist and a recent director of the institute; Mike was Zimbabwe's leading wildlife veterinarian. Debbie and Rowan planned to help us whenever their other responsibilities permitted. Sengwa's officer-in-charge, Ian Coulson, and Aaron Bhiza, the field station manager, would keep things going from day to day.

We would collar sixteen adult female elephants from thirteen different family groups. Every three hours around the clock for three months, we'd get a compass bearing to each of the elephants from two tall antennae, one on the high mesa, Ntaba Mangwe, and the other seven kilometers to the south at the field station. We'd locate the elephants by crossing the bearings. Scouts would manage the Ntaba Mangwe tracking and the nighttime tracking at the institute. Bill would oversee the data acquisition at the computer station in our office, where we were now all gathered. He showed how we would feed the tracking data into our computer, while it was simultaneously receiving all the powerful calls all the collared elephants were making and storing each sound in its own file, labeled by time and the name of the calling individual.

The scouts burst into such animated conversation that the next day I supposed they'd named the first elephant out of admiration for our computer. But as I now know, circumstantial naming is frequent. River is a common name for a child born by a river. Death is a common name for a child born in a time of death. Nor is it a bad omen to have a name that doesn't reflect your parents' hopes for you. In this respect I was more superstitious than my indigenous companions.

Back at the station after the collaring, Rowan kindly promised me another chance. That evening, gentle Steve Powell suggested the name Babe. We'd known a captive Asian elephant named Babe a few months earlier, when we were testing our pilot collars in the Burnett Park Zoo in Syracuse, New York. She had died in childbirth, and we'd felt bereaved.

With Babe's name secured in my mind, I felt fine the next morning as we—our team, a dozen scouts, and Rowan, Mike, and Norman, the darting team, piled into vehicles and headed for the center of the research area. Overhead, Debbie's plane was already circling; we were hearing her voice on the radio as she searched for an elephant to collar. She would direct the vehicles to a stopping place. Carrying a radio, the darting team would stalk the chosen elephant on foot and dart her. The rest of us, some two dozen people, also carrying a radio, would move in on foot to help with the collaring, the collection of blood for genetic analysis, and to make some standard measurements that would reveal the animal's age, status, and health.

Our work started with the mistaken darting of a small elephant. We left her sleeping, since it would be dangerous when she woke up, and waited for Debbie to guide us to another. Debbie soon radioed down that a large female was guarding the darted animal. "She's charging me," Debbie called as the plane swooped in wild low dives over the place of the elephants' vigil. "Not a problem," radioed Rowan (Rhodesian humor: he meant, it's not a problem because you're in an airplane.)

"She won't go," Debbie again. "She must be the matriarch."

Rowan said, "I've got another dart if she's not interested in leaving."

The plane made six more swooping circles.

"There are a hell of a lot of elephants around."

Another circle.

"She's loath to leave her."

"Confirm, the big one's loath to leave the down one."

"Roger."

We turned back through the forest and the men darted the big one. She was Babe, but the naming occurred without ceremony, in the midst of confusion. Several younger elephants were on their knees attempting to lift the young female Babe had been loath to leave. They got her onto her knees but she fell over. Then, in a confused, stressful reaction, they jabbed her with their tusks, and ran away.

"There are thirty elephant around you," Debbie called down from the circling plane.

Babe fell a little way off in the woods. Debbie dived over her, trying to frighten her family members away, but her half-grown son sat down on her uppermost teat and stayed there. After a while he stood up but immediately sat down again on her shoulder.

"Look here, Rob," said Rowan, "this is your chance to get a skin biopsy." Rob needed tissue samples from elephant mothers and their calves as an indication of the proportion of genetic material shared by close relatives in the Sengwa population. Either blood or skin would serve the purpose; we would soon draw blood from Babe, and here was her calf, sitting on her. So the rest of us moved into the woods to let the darting team approach Babe's son with a dart gun. We heard two shots and men shouting as they tried to drive more elephants away from the fallen matriarch.

In time they were successful, and we all moved in.

To crouch beside a tranquilized animal that might kill you if it weren't unconscious is a strange experience. I crouched by Babe's head to have this experience, although I only half wanted it. For some reason I made a recording of her snores–I suppose to justify my presence.

But it didn't feel like something I should do. I felt as I had felt one evening in Etosha, when Flip Stander had used our observation tower to dart a lion that he wanted to relocate to another place. We helped him lift the enormous, powerful, paralyzed body into his pickup truck, and so loaded, he drove away. But before he left there was a half hour when the lion lay unconscious before us, and Flip, while writing numbers in his notebook, invited us to touch him. We did so for the sensation. We snuggled into his coarse mane and lay against his neck. We pulled his lips apart and slid our fingers over the canines and examined, with Flip, the molars. We smelled his breath. We pulled back the lid of his right eye and looked into it–alive, clear, frighteningly beautiful. We pressed our fingers into the enormous muscle in his right foreleg. Holding the paw in my two hands, I kneaded my knuckles into the hot gray pad, and the claws shot out.

As we indulged in these violations I felt less than comfortable. To investigate another human being without his or her permission is rarely all right: people everywhere know that, and have taboos against it. For some people, and I am one, this taboo extends to other animals. A sudden shudder ran up my spine as I thought that when the lion came to, hundreds of miles from his former terrain, he would smell my scent and know that I had explored his body.

Crouching beside Babe, I felt a similar sense of transgression. It was a relief when Mike's needle had restored her and the small elephant (perhaps Babe's daughter) to their senses, and we watched them disappear into the winter-leafed forest. We people from our five human cultures then stood quietly together for a few minutes, recovering our sense of normalcy.

By two weeks later, we had learned enough about the performance of Babe's and Computer's collars to proceed with the rest of the operation. With help from a Mobil Oil helicopter, the same team collared the last fourteen elephants in three days. We worked in three layers. On top, Debbie directed the operation from the plane. Under her, the chopper maneuvered Mike into position for darting. On the ground a large crew moved about on foot and in vehicles as before, entertained by Rowan's and Debbie's wry radio exchanges. D: "The bloody vultures think there's a cull on." R: "Don't hit one." D: "Is anybody out there? They're right next to you, lads!"

We all enjoyed the adventure, with its plane, helicopter, trucks, guns, and camaraderie. "It's fun," said Andrew Masarirevhu, the scout who had been assigned as our special assistant for the season. "Fun, like war." This was a subtle remark from a sensitive young man who had fought in the war for independence, and noticed his own contradictory feelings.

On the second day I rode in the chopper. Rowan, the vet, and the pilot shouted over the noise of the motor, and occasional words reached me in the backseat. After a few minutes I heard "extra freight." The chopper sank to the ground and Rowan told me to get out. "We'll be back once we've got one."

I jumped out near a steep knoll under the escarpment called Sijamba. As the chopper whopped off into the sky, I climbed the knoll. Almost immediately, there was another sound, a deep, soft thundering. It was the pounding of feet in sand as seven elephants fled below me, their ears pressed against their necks, their eyes wide in terror, so closely packed together it was as if they were one organism with twenty-eight feet. In their wake, a cloud of dust rose up and choked me.

Within a few minutes the chopper was back. I pointed at the tracks. "Did you see them?" The men looked at the freshly beaten path, and then at one another. "You'd have been pulverized," said the pilot. "Get in."

Heavy again with extra freight, the helicopter rose up awkwardly, lunged over the edge of an outcropping, and dropped beside a large "recumbent Jumbo" (Rowan's term). Her two calves stood above her on both sides. The air throbbed, condensed and battered by the helicopter's still revolving rotor. Thus accompanied, the scene reminded me of a wartime movie. At the same time the thought of a medieval Pietà entered my mind, two angels beside their fallen mother, with a barren sand-colored escarpment looming above them. I shouted, "I think this one is Sijamba."

"A very good name," shouted Rowan.

On the third day I flew in the plane to help Debbie search for Runyanga, or Crooked Tusk, a female elephant reputed to be as large as a large male, with a following of as many as forty other elephants but no small calf of her own. She was notorious for ambushing and chasing scouts during the ten days of each month when they were assigned to "transect duty." This duty took them on foot along fixed paths, each one about six kilometers (three and three-fourths miles) long, where they recorded the occurrence and abundance of mammals. The twelve transect paths in Sengwa had been surveyed in the same way during ten days of every month for more than a decade. The central paths crossed the Sengwa River and ran up into a thicket that Crooked Tusk seemed to consider her property. It was commonly referred to as

Fuck-up Thicket, perhaps because of the many routines that Crooked Tusk had upset.

The reputation of this elephant interested me: I wanted to collar her to find out what her life was like. An old matriarch would seem likely to make loud coordinating calls. But most important, a collar would enable us to warn the scouts of her whereabouts. Rowan said he had unsuccessfully tried to collar her more than once in the past. He would search in an airplane, she would suddenly disappear: he believed she knew what was going on. He thought she had a secondary home range centering on a set of springs north of the Sengwa boundary, and urged us to look there if Fuck-up Thicket was empty. If we could find her, she would receive our last collar. In fact we had, in a sense, reserved it for her. With every collaring we had spoken again of our hope to collar Crooked Tusk.

We found no elephants in either of the reputed home ranges, but as we returned to the Sengwa-Lutope confluence I spotted a very large elephant with heavy tusks, the right one strangely splayed out. The ground team moved in, tranquilized and collared her. We felt happy and successful.

Two weeks later an elephant twice the size of the elephant we had collared was sighted in the Manyoni, with a family the size of a bond group. Her left tusk was twice the length of the right, and so skewed that it pointed straight up into the sky. When the news came in I was with a group of scouts: they hooted with laughter and burst into animated chatter. I saw right hands, and then left hands, thrust upward and stretched high, amid an outburst of laughter. A long monologue by Christmas followed, to which everyone listened with rapt attention—his gestures indicated a moment of terror, a panicked flight, a narrow escape, and an endless wait in a tree. Everyone doubled over in hilarity. I wasn't sure whether the scouts were sorry or glad that we had failed to subdue the elephant with whom they had this relationship. But there were now two Crooked Tusks in our repertoire, the more illustrious one as untraceable in the forest as Moby Dick in the sea.

On the evening of the last collaring, the visiting experts from Harare treated us and the Coulsons to a sunset feast on a great rock overlooking the Sengwa. Near us stood a thatched hut called Colin's Bar, and below that an empty concrete swimming pool that no longer held water. The site reminded our laughing hosts of their fine old colonial days when Zimbabwe was Rhodesia, and Colin Craig was director of the institute. They said the elegant but deteriorating state of the institute mirrored the state of the country, which had gone downhill since independence. Nevertheless we feasted on steaks, red wine, fruit, salads, bread, and fine cheeses they'd brought from the city, and on their rambling reminiscences. The Coulsons, Martins, Debbie, and Colin had spent years together in Sengwa with each other and with the institute's First Family, Dave and Meg Cumming. Rowan, a bagpiper trained by the queen's own piper during his college years in England, used to attract elephants by playing his bagpipe. The Cummings had adopted a family of orphaned warthog piglets; then, realizing that the infants needed their mother for body heat, had taken them into their own bed to warm against their bodies—oh, sweet life in the bush! The red went out of the sky and the stars came out, sharp points in the clear black air. Across the river we heard lions roaring. Up the river by the Coulsons' house, a hyena answered in a series of rising whoops. We weren't the only ones who were well fed and well content.

Early next morning the team from Harare departed to urgent duties in other parts of the country. The helicopter tilted and twirled away into the distance amid a huge cloud of roiling dust. After checking a sandy runway for warthog holes, Debbie, too, took off. Dipping her wings, she sent us a last sunbeam; and then a lovely silence settled on those of us who had stayed.

"Well, campers," said Bill, "let's get to work."

In our spacious, airy office, our computer was already filling with data. Bill and Russ sat down to see how everything was proceeding. Rob took his samples of skin and blood and disappeared into the room we called the chemistry lab. Lillie started the three o'clock tracking session. Sibanda Mafohla Mbelekelwa found us at our various occupations and told us it was time for tea. The routine had begun.

Tea was served at ten in the morning and at three in the afternoon. Institute officers and visiting researchers were welcome, but lower-ranking employees were not, except for the friendly old Sibanda, who carried in a tray with tea, sugar, milk, and mugs, and set it on the table, saying, "Tea?" and silently left after everyone had greeted him.

The mugs were blue pottery. They had elephant heads on them—the trunks were the handles. The task of serving tea started when Sibanda walked down to the workshop to crank the mighty generator, for the kettle was electric. We Americans would learn to schedule our use of electricity around the necessity for tea.

Tea was served in the library, the most beautiful room in the main institute building, which—designed by Dave Cumming—was in all respects beautiful. The building had the form of an **H**, in which the horizontal limb was the backing for two courtyards, one facing north and the other south, each framed by a row of large, quiet offices. The offices opened onto raised concrete walkways surrounding the grassy center of each courtyard: the walkways were broad and roofed, and had the cool, restful feeling of porches or verandas, and the roofs were supported by arches that rested on pillars. Each patio and the design of the whole had the aspect of a monastery. The library was the largest room, in the center of the west wall. It was cool and welcoming even on the hottest day. Its outer wall was a pair of large glass doors that opened onto a porch and, the whole building being built on a high bluff, looked northward out over the estate of the Sengwa Wildlife Research Area.

Not far below the porch but invisible through the forest lay the Sengwa River. In the center of the view, the flat-topped, square-edged mesa called Ntaba Mangwe, or Mountain of the Vultures, rose suddenly more than a hundred meters straight up out of the valley, seven kilometers away. Beyond Ntaba Mangwe and on both sides of it rose other mesas and escarpments, framing the valley with odd-shaped blue walls. In the evening you could stand on the porch watching the red sun descend over all of this. This is peace, you would say to yourself. But each day there were two opportunities to take tea with the officers, and realize with a shock that the political and physical life of a small remote reserve is as complex as that of the cultures that support it.

On that particular afternoon, only the station officers took tea. After three years and two months of preparation, the rest of us campers were getting to work.

9

ON NTABA MANGWE

THE FIELD OBSERVATIONS WERE MY RESPONSIBILITY. WE needed to know what the collared elephants were doing so we could interpret the calls we were recording from their collars, and understand some of their movements. We needed to know the locations of elephants and herds that were not collared: otherwise how could we say whether elephants were communicating over long distances? Intermediate animals might be passing messages along the line.

Rowan had warned us that close or continuous observations would be out of the question in Sengwa, for the elephants, having been culled repeatedly, were notoriously shy. Accepting that the task would be difficult, I wrote an extra vehicle and assistant into our budget. But when the time came these resources were needed twice over. Rob had belatedly recognized his need for biopsy samples from local elephant mothers and their calves. He couldn't safely collect these samples without two nimble assistants and an escape vehicle.

Rob's need worried me in more than one way. To have someone stalking elephants and shooting at them with a dart gun would introduce disturbance while we were trying to study undisturbed behavior. I called for a group meeting—the first of many that Bill dubbed "sourdough meetings," since anything we pushed down soon rose again. I was persuaded to turn the observation vehicle and assistants (Laura and Andrew) over to Rob. Rob, for his part, promised to finish his darting as soon as possible, and to keep it to mothers and calves in families other than the ones carrying collars. As for the observation protocol, there was a comprehensive view of the research area from the high mesa Ntaba Mangwe. An observer could be stationed there indefinitely without a vehicle, and in between tracking sessions, the tracking scouts could lend a hand.

This decision was necessary, but Ntaba Mangwe was close to only about a quarter of the range of the elephants we had collared. Without a vehicle, observers couldn't quickly get to areas where interesting things were happening, as indicated by the incoming acoustic and tracking data. So I complained, but not very loudly, because on a personal level I liked the new plan very well. For it now seemed that I was going to spend a lot of time on a single great height and get to know it.

This prospect called up many happy memories. Just north of the back field in the farm of my childhood, a broad, energetic creek called Taughannock tumbled over a cliff in the highest straight-falling cataract east of the Rocky Mountains. Many were the midsummer days that I spent lying on the smooth gray slate ledge with my nose hanging over the brink of the falls. Beside my elbow a sheet of water sped out into space and fragmented into a thousand sparkling droplets that danced downward to a green boiling pool, so far below that I could hardly see it. They flew at different rates and in different trajectories, forming layers of descending **V**s, each of whose unique

paths and shapes and speeds reflected the local winds and vac-
uums in the space between the waterfall and the empty half
cylinder that backed it. Black and wet and fragrant, that space
was a miniature of a vast amphitheater formed by the canyon
walls. Inside the canyon I liked the knowledge that I was only a
tiny and inconsequential person.

The farm experience was sixteen years behind me on the
day when my husband and I chose a beach at the base of high
cliffs as the site for our whale research camp in Argentina–a
camp where we and our four children would spend the best part
of our lives together. I would make it my business to be a cliff-
watcher, leaving the boat work to others. The view from those
cliffs changed by the minute. The tides, like those in the Bay of
Fundy, varied with the phase of the moon by as much as thirty
feet. At fullest tide I would peer down at whales swimming
against the cliff wall; in the lowest tide, the sea met the land half
a mile out. Even on a rare calm day, whale spouts were barely
visible out at the glistening interface, and what lay under the cliffs
was a collage of tide pools, and our children exploring them.

Memories of Taughannock Falls and the Valdés cliffs always
elate me. And by whatever means old experiences activate new
ones, my heart was lifted on the day Rob, Andrew, Laura, and
I drove up the sandy, rocky, tilted track on the south side of
Ntaba Mangwe–the old Land Cruiser growling–rounded the
last ridge, and saw sky everywhere. A peregrine falcon and a
pair of black eagles were circling on the updrafts made by rising
heat striking the vertical wall of the mesa. We walked to the
nearest edge and looked four hundred feet straight down to the
valley floor, out to a horizon that disappeared into haze and the
curvature of the earth, pale blue at its farthest edges, with distant
hills and ridges. Sixteen elephants were crossing the sand river
beneath us in single file. They looked like a string of ants on an
odor trail.

Laura, Rob, and Andrew stayed with me all morning. We four had been working together continuously during the previous eight weeks, Andrew teaching the rest of us the lay of the land; now we related our recent experiences to what we could see from the top, and to my topographic map. Each of us was a lover of heights. Laura had hiked in the Rockies and the Himalayas; Rob, a rock climber, had mastered Half Dome and El Capitan in Yosemite; Andrew, inspired by the distant silhouette of the Nyanga Mountains from his village in the eastern highlands, had named his second son Hillary, after the climber who had reached the top of Mount Everest.

I spent the rest of the day exploring the top of the mesa. In area it was at least a square kilometer, maybe two or three if you included the whole top surface, for it was fissured into three main masses with numerous buttressed wings and outcroppings. With a mild amount of clambering I got extraordinary views of elephant terrain in every direction, each one a different study in earth history. This mesa must be the hard core of an ancient high plain; other relics of it were apparent in neighboring escarpments and ridges that projected into and shaped the three deep river valleys. In ancient times the whole area may have been as uniform as the Mafungabusi Plateau, but water had broken through. Centuries of rainy seasons had washed soft earth away from hard rock and left behind skeleton without flesh. When the evening sun struck it, the skeleton turned all the colors of the canyon country in the American southwest, from a blazing orange too painful to look at to the softest old rose; and the colors and vertical formations struck chords in my heart, as if an organ were playing.

I was not alone in this grand place. When night descended, the sky—whose heat and glare had been oppressive all day— sweetened to gray, and the gray sobered to the absence of all color, the tone of infinite space, deeper than black. The points of light that then began to shine in that space were so brilliant they illuminated the surface of the mesa: I moved about near my tent easily. I then appreciated as reality a proposition I had long debated—that stars are suns.

As the officer in charge of Sengwa, Ian Coulson was the sole representative of the central establishment in an institution served by people profoundly different from himself. He was their taskmaster, their confidant, their nurse, and the source of their income. There was pressure in Ian's responsibilities, because his employees were suffering from poverty that could not be easily relieved. Wisely, he did not try to know the details of their needs and complications. He knew that each of them was a member of a communal society, where what belongs to one—whether money, possessions, illness, or debt—belongs to all, and that is a lot to keep track of.

Ian had the institute running so smoothly that I ignored much of what he was doing, but every now and then an aspect of his strategy came to my attention. For instance, our project required three months of help from a reliable radio tracker on Ntaba Mangwe. Each tracking session would last roughly one hour and be flanked by two hours without responsibility; the effort must be repeated at three-hour intervals day and night. Realizing that the scouts would differ in their enjoyment of this way of life, Ian assigned them to it in pairs, each pair to do the full job for a ten-day stint. As a result, all of Sengwa's scouts got trained in the art of tracking, and all of them did the job for the same amount of time. He matched them up randomly, ignoring issues of culture and personal alliances, a procedure that had long been practiced in the assignment of transect crews. Since each scout was often paired with each of the others, they had developed a brotherhood that transcended tribal differences.

It happened that after a month or two, Andrew's assignment to tracking duty came around. For ten days he turned over his responsibilities in Rob's darting operation to Christmas, and came up on Ntaba Mangwe. I was observing and camping up there at the time. Andrew saw no reason why I should take my meals alone, and invited me to join the scouts at their campfire. This is how I came to know things that I never would have guessed about the scouts' sense of the spiritual structure and functioning of the universe.

But stay with me in the physical domain for another minute. As I have mentioned, a pronounced change in the structure of the atmosphere tends to occur just at sundown in dry savanna country. The temperature inversion that forms creates a ceiling that returns sound—especially low-frequency sound—back to the earth. At dusk you, as well as other listening animals, hear things from much farther away and get a sense of a much broader geography than appears to you at midday.

There were in Sengwa, as in Etosha, a great many lions. At dusk and dawn their roars echoed in certain crevices and ravines that cut between the sections of Ntaba Mangwe's crown: if you stood at the top of one of these a lion that was four hundred feet down would seem to be in front of you. I spent a few nights on a western outcropping where I could hear lions calling and answering one another all up and down the valleys. The way the crevices focused sound enabled me to assess the directions the calls were coming from. For each call I heard I noted the direction, and the time, and whether it was solo, group, or antiphonal. It seemed that another society organized by long-distance calling was also spread out below me. I soon gave up this project, however, because I was sharing the place with a leopard. I heard its rasping calls, and in the morning saw its footsteps beside my knapsack.

By the scouts' campfire we heard other sounds—drums beating in the distance. The men then talked among themselves about deaths or births or prayers. *Kure kwemeso nzeve dzinonzwa,* Andrew said. Where eyes cannot see, ears can still hear. The scouts speculated with each other about which village it was, and the nature of the occasion. The beat and the time of day told them that ancestral spirits were being invoked. That there had been a death. That the people were disturbed and surprised by their loss. That they were asking for an explanation.

"These ancestors," I asked, "what are they like?"

The answers to this question varied from night to night and from informer to informer. It seemed that ancestors might be in animal or human form, but the form made little difference, for animals, spirits, and living humans existed in a continuum and were in continual transformation. The drumming went on all night, its steady rhythm a heartbeat, evidence that ancestors as well as living people were present, insistent, and patient. I felt that the people were speaking through the drumming and the drumming was speaking through the people, and it was like the action of tides that flow back and forth, bringing sea to shore and shore to sea.

For a few days Andrew traded some of his daytime tracking sessions with a partner and helped me film the behavior of a collared elephant at close range. We climbed down to the base of the mesa and crept around in the bush. Andrew taught me to stay upwind of rhinos, and downwind of elephants and lions. One day this rule sent us around in circles, and I said to myself, this is what it is like to survive as a small animal. But few animals have as poor a sense of smell as ours. To compensate, we carried little bags containing ashes from the campfire. You shake the bag, smoke comes out, and you can assess the direction of air drift by looking at the smoke.

My efforts and the efforts of others to film the collared elephants were on the whole unsuccessful. In Sengwa, as Rowan had said, the elephants are just too shy. You can startle an elephant by startling any other animal in its vicinity. The impalas in the clearing, the baboons in the surrounding grove, the reedbuck on the floodplain, and the plovers and warthogs at the edge of the pool must all be unaware of your presence, for any of these alerted—by sound, or sight, or smell—will alert the others, in a chain reaction that will reach the elephant. This was a lesson in ecology.

For the scouts the ecology seemed to extend farther, to the possibility of ancestral spirits in certain animals we encountered while creeping around among them. With all these concerns at once, the scouts couldn't possibly teach us outsiders enough to make us safe without their help. We always needed their help and we always will.

At night, we told stories.

The master storyteller was Andrew. He could frighten you till every hair on your head rose up, or release pent-up laughter, or anger, or sympathies that you did not know you were withholding. He could get out of himself and sneak up behind and present his own absurdity with a mastery that made you laugh at him in spite of your polite impulses. He'd dart about in the light of the tree-hung lantern, acting out his own drama while we watched and listened, transfixed. A continually narrating reporter lived in his mind. Sometimes during the day he and I would watch animals through binoculars and he'd be telling their tale, finding cause for humor and pathos and suspense in the evidence before our eyes.

One evening Andrew recounted an experience that had led him to believe that the parts of nature work together as a deliberate system of checks and balances. I asked his permission to repeat it, and he wrote it for me, so I would get the details right.

In December 1984 I was at Ntaba Mangwe Camp walking transects. On the 16th of the same month I woke up early and went transect walking and finished transects around 1030 hours. When I got back to camp I found a squirrel trapped in a mosquito net in my hut. I caught the squirrel and tied it to one of the wall poles of my hut waiting for my friend John who had gone transect walking also but was doing a different set from the ones I walked.

The squirrel had been a problem, tearing our bags of mealie-meal and eating other foodstuffs. We had always tried hard to get rid of the squirrel but all plans had failed save for this day I found it trapped in a mosquito net.

John arrived around 1100 hours and I showed him the squirrel. He got the squirrel and wanted to kill it but I told him not to. I told him I had a better way to punish the squirrel and he agreed and handed the small animal to me. I took the squirrel into the kitchen and took a burning piece of wood and started burning its mouth and feet in such a way that it would not die from the burns and let it go. The squirrel ran back into my hut and climbed up to the thatched roof. Thinking that was enough punishment we let it up the roof and the squirrel stayed there for the whole day and part of the next morning.

During the afternoon John and I went to bathe in the Sengwa River feeling we had solved a problem which had been worrying us for days. When I finished bathing, I put on my patrol boots and tied the shoelaces firmly to avoid dust getting into my clean feet. John and I walked back to the camp and sat down telling stories.

When cooking time was near I decided to gather all the things I wanted for dinner. I went into the hut and collected mealie-meal and when I looked up to the roof I found the squirrel was very still but alive and I said, "At last we got you." A few minutes later I felt a very sharp pain inside my left boot and thought a burning coal had got into the boot without me noticing. I tried to take off the boot but before I managed I felt two more sharp pricks. When I took off the boot I did not see anything but the pain was increasing very fast and later on I realized I had been stung by a scorpion. I started yelling and twisting my face because the pain was just too much.

My friend John decided to take over the cooking and I sat thinking and trying to figure out how I could get rid of the pain. My friend was saying a lot of comforting words but I began thinking of how rude I had been to the squirrel. I thought the three scorpion bites were some form of punishment for what I had done to the squirrel. While I was thinking and getting convinced that I deserved it because I had also punished the squirrel, I felt a scratching movement, the feeling was like I was running sandpaper on top of my bare feet. When I looked at my feet I saw a small blackish snake moving over my feet and I jumped up shaking the small snake some two or more meters away from me. We decided not to kill the snake and we were all very sad thinking why such a thing had happened to me. We talked about it later and concluded that we had done a very bad thing to the squirrel.

I could not sleep all night because of the pain from the scorpion bites. The next morning I found I could hardly walk and so my friend John had to walk the transects for me. Around midday the pain cleared and we were all thinking about it.

When my friends went transect walking I remained at the camp lying on my straw bed. Sometimes I went out of the hut cleaning pots and plates with difficulty. The squirrel was still on the roof. I did not notice the squirrel climbing down the roof but only found he or she was not there at around 1050 hours on the 17th December 1984. The pain

on my leg cleared almost the same time the squirrel climbed
down and I've always wondered what kind of happening
that was.

"What do you think it was?" I asked.

"I think that scorpion and snake were helping the squirrel
by punishing me," said Andrew simply.

The behavior of lions was often interpreted as discipline directed at people. The same notion had occurred to me in
Etosha: whether it's true or not, if a lion looks you in the eye all
night, such an interpretation will occur to you. The scouts all
had experiences of this at one time or another. The senior scout
Zaccheus described for me an event that several of them often
mentioned. These are his written words:

It was during the night when I was at Ntaba Mangwe transect
camp that I had a marvellous dream.

I dreamed hearing a lion's roar on the eastern side of our
camp about 100 to 200 meters away.

I saw the lion in the dream. "I want peace in this place, I
don't want noise, go and tell the others," the lion said. On the
following morning I told my dream to my colleagues and also
saw the spoor of that lion.

That dream had followed a period of terrible quarreling
among the scouts, with an especially bad disagreement on the afternoon before the dream. When Zaccheus woke in the morning, he pondered the dream until his companions woke. Then he
asked whether anyone besides himself had heard anything in the
night. No, they had not. Then Zaccheus told about the lion's
voice and message and said, "Come outside!" And they did, and
there were lion tracks all around the hut. This marked the last argument the scouts ever had in the Ntaba Mangwe Camp.

"And elsewhere?" I asked.

"We have been peaceful."

On another evening, Andrew told a second story, and the next morning wrote it for me.

In the sixties and seventies people in the Mutoko used to grow crops in the mountains. The mountains are high and a lot of trees grow in them. In these mountains lived troops and troops of baboons. A lot of caves where leopards and hyenas lived are seen in almost every rock cluster in the mountains. The elder and young of Kasine respected these caves very much. Some of the caves are named after people or animals that once lived in them. Every bad incident that took place in the area was blamed to the elders who were responsible for telling the spirits what is required by the people and also thanking the spirits for anything good that happens, like after a good harvest, good rains. In some of the caves are some wells that have crystal clear water which is used by most of the people who have fields near them.

It is in these mountains where my father farmed. It is in these mountains where Paidamoyo's father used to farm. Paidamoyo was a man in his thirties but single. Being single he lived with his father. His father owned a muzzle-loader which Paidamoyo used to scare baboons with. This very gun is the one that left Paidamoyo with one hand because the left one had been amputated. It got burnt seriously when he was preparing gunpowder. From the time he lost his hand he stopped using a gun.

One day Paidamoyo was watching baboons in his father's field with his sister. Baboons came and got into the field. He and his sister chased the baboons but they did not go very far. They kept jumping from tree to tree. It was time to go home but the baboons did not go away. Paidamoyo knew if the baboons did not go far from the field it meant they would get into the field at first light the next day.

Paidamoyo decided not to go home so both of them slept in a small shelter. . . . The next day, the baboons came and Paidamoyo tried his best to chase them away but they did not go away. When the baboons had had enough they moved away leaving a huge male seated on a rock giving its back to Paida. Paidomoyo thinking he had a chance to sneak to the baboon, he grabbed an axe and advanced toward the baboon. He got as close as a meter but the baboon did not look back nor move. When he tried to use the axe the baboon turned and grabbed the axe and threw it away. It turned to Paida and started biting and kicking him. Paidamoyo tried his best tricks to kill the baboon but he missed all chances. The baboon tore Paida's flesh and left him unconscious. Paidamoyo's sister, having witnessed the fight, ran home to call the elders.

The elders came and found Paidamoyo still breathing weakly. They quickly rushed him to Hospital and he was made to stay in hospital for about two and a half months. While Paida was in Hospital his father consulted the spirits because this was the first time such a thing had happened. The spirits told Paida's father that he was being punished for what he had done. When asked what had taken place, the spirits said Paidamoyo had had sexual intercourse with his sister during the day and the night they had spent together in the shelter.

The baboons had come to let this thing come in the open. Paidamoyo's sister admitted that she had been forced into it by her brother and had been told not to say it to anyone. The sister had agreed not to say it because she had been promised death if she did.

When Paidamoyo came back from Hospital he was made to pay an ox and a few hundred dollars for his wrongdoing. He even admitted to having done it. This is how every-body in the community came to know about it.

Nowadays people have exhausted the soils of the moun-tains. Very few people like farming in the mountains because the crops are difficult to take home and also people are get-ting civilized. Paidamoyo no longer lives because he got killed during the war when the Freedom Fighters learned about his mischief and killed him.

This is a true story.

This story gave rise to a long, sober discussion in Shona. I excused myself and went away to sleep.

The results of our project in Sengwa, which have taken years to analyze (and much is still not fully examined), seem to confirm what we had guessed about elephants while underlining the com-plexity of what there is yet to learn. Individual elephants are linked or separated not only by immediate experience, including their calls, but also by varying degrees of genetic relationship. Watching their behavior was a continuous adventure, for I never knew enough to explain everything, even when I had the benefit of the radio-tracking data. Watching a male alone at a water hole, I sensed him as an individual but suspected he had a community. We knew too little about the communal dimension of males' ex-perience, and learned nothing in Sengwa, where we collared only females. Watching a family, I sensed each elephant in it as a node in a network of bonds. Watching the computer trace the simulta-neous movements of separated family groups, I sensed not only individuals but also groups as nodes. Comparing the areas the families were currently using with the areas where Rowan and the scouts had found them ten years earlier, we sensed elephants as history. As in people, there is more, much more, to each indi-vidual than meets the eye—or the ear, or even the mind.

My part of the project was scientifically simple. Such observations as we were able to make from Ntaba Mangwe, and from flights with Debbie twice a month, established that the tracking locations were trustworthy, and supplied information about the compositions and behaviors of the collared families. They revealed that there were many uncollared elephant herds in addition to those we had collared. Because of this, we couldn't claim to have documented long-distance communication, even though that often seemed the simplest explanation for the coordinated movements our tracking data were reporting between separated families.

In the early days on Ntaba Mangwe, the tracking scouts and I fell into a routine of relating their results to the map.[*] We mounted an exact map of Sengwa on a board and put two pins in it, at the sites of the tracking antennae. We tied a thread about two feet long to each pin. Taking one pin as center, we made a circle, and labeled five-degree intervals on the border of the map. Then we marked off another, outer circle whose center was the other pin—in both cases calling magnetic north 0°.

To track an elephant, a scout would stand at the base of a tall tower that had a directional antenna mounted on its top. The antenna was tuned to the sixteen frequencies that the elephants' collars were sending out. By selecting one of the frequencies he'd select a collared elephant to track. He'd put on headphones, which were connected, via a long cable, to the antenna. Now he'd slowly rotate a crank that turned both the antenna on top of the tower and a needle on a large horizontal compass in front of him. As the antenna started to point toward the elephant (out there somewhere, usually not visible) the scout would begin to hear beeping in his ears. Now he'd turn the crank very slowly. The closer he came to the exact direction of

[*] Laura and I had learned this technique from Rowan.

the elephant, the louder the beeps, and the needle named the direction from the tower to the beeping collar: 247°.

While he was doing this up on Ntaba Mangwe, somebody else was doing the same at the institute tracking station seven kilometers to the south, and getting a slightly different direction. Each tracker now knew the direction but not the distance to the elephant. Now they talked on the radio, exchanging results. Then we tightened the threads along the bearings to the chosen elephant from both antennae. The spot where the strings crossed gave us the elephant's location. It took us about an hour to locate all the elephants.

In time Russ created a computer program that located the elephants automatically when we typed in their bearings, and Bill created a matching program that plotted the positions on a map. This replaced the strings operation, but the spirit on Ntaba Mangwe was best when stretching strings was the only way. Then the tracking seemed vivid and fascinating, yielding timely answers to an ever-changing riddle. The scouts had many ideas about what was going on, and spent time between the tracking sessions climbing around to the edges of the mesa to search with binoculars to verify their guesses. Once the mapping was being done automatically at the station, the work on Ntaba Mangwe became just a routine. This seems worth mentioning these days, when primary experience is going out of style and being replaced by a secondary experience—mastery of the computer, which is only an analytic tool.

It was the computer, however, that gave us the power to relate the events of a day to larger patterns, and allowed us to think about those patterns in terms of the ties that bind elephants one to the other; and of geography; and of evolution. For instance, we learned a lot about the relationships among the three elephants we most often saw from Ntaba Mangwe—Babe, the collared Crooked Tusk, and Computer. All three families centered their activities on the Murere Pools. Babe and Crooked Tusk and their families were grouped together in about half of our visual sightings, but we never saw either of them with Computer and hers. And yet what do I mean by "together"?

To be exact: in five out of ten sightings we saw Babe and Crooked Tusk within a few elephants' lengths of each other. In four of the five cases when they were by this definition together, the group numbered thirty to thirty-five animals; on one occasion there were sixty. When only one of the two was seen, the group size was sixteen to twenty-one animals for Babe, and twelve to twenty-four animals for Crooked Tusk. When we saw both together, we noted the following: (1) when one of these large groups would separate, one collared female would accompany each subgroup; (2) the number of animals accompanying her was approximately the same each time; (3) even when the two groups were separate we often saw them at the same time or within a few minutes of each other; (4) when they appeared to be in the same group, they spent part of their time in two clusters with different behaviors; and (5) when they separated they did so with each family acting as a unit separate from the other.

These observations led us to conclude that Crooked Tusk and Babe were members of the same bond group but not of the same family.

The radio tracking enabled us to locate Babe 400 times, Crooked Tusk 463 times, and Computer 199 times. The three animals had almost exactly the same central home ranges, but Babe and Crooked Tusk were always within two kilometers of each other and moving together to the same places, while Computer's movements were random in relation to the others.

Rob's genetic data deepened the story. The mitochondrial DNA analysis showed that all three animals may have the same maternal inheritance. The nuclear DNA analysis showed that

Babe and Crooked Tusk were more closely related to each other than either of them was to Computer.

I conclude that there are, for elephants, several kinds of "we." There is the "we" in a family, whose members do everything together. There is the "we" in a bond group, whose members stay within close range of each other but maintain separate family behaviors—for example, the families of Crooked Tusk and Babe. Finally there is the "we" in a clan, whose members share the use of land but move about on it independently of each other. Computer's family belonged to the same clan as Crooked Tusk and Babe, but her family and bond group were different.

We took turns at the various tasks of the project. I spent several periods down at the station, radio-tracking from that antenna, entering the data into the computer, and copying data onto backup tapes. Part of the job was to check the quality of data coming in from Ntaba Mangwe. One day during a period when the trackers included an experienced older scout and an inexperienced younger one, I wasn't satisfied. The numbers the younger man was reading in over the radio were tending too often to end in 0 or in 5; I guessed that he was averaging instead of reading out precise bearings.

In the last radio communication of the day, I told him I was questioning his bearings, and why. He asked me to repeat my message for the benefit of the more experienced tracker. The experienced tracker retorted angrily, "Are you criticizing our work?"

I had made a serious mistake. The radio channel between the station and Ntaba Mangwe could be monitored by anyone in the national park system. My criticism, intended as a private correction, could be taken as material for disgrace. I was putting a man's employment in jeopardy.

I fretted all night, got up before dawn, and drove up to Ntaba Mangwe, to talk with the trackers before their 6:00 A.M. session. The moment I arrived on the crest of Ntaba Mangwe, I realized that the young scout who had been averaging numbers was no averager of human interactions. He came running out to greet me before the engine had stopped. "It's all right," he said, before I had said a word. It was transparent to him that I had made the hour's drive in order to apologize. I held out my hand and he took it and squeezed it in his two hands. The senior scout now emerged from the sleeping hut, wide awake and serious. After a brief exchange in Shona with his comrade, he forgave me as well. Then I turned around and drove back to the station.

After that day the younger scout took many unnecessary opportunities to help me, and introduced me to his family. His wife became one of my closest friends among the women. Following my departure from Sengwa, both the scout and his wife wrote me letters, addressing me as Ambuya, which means Honored Elderly Woman Relative, or Grandmother.

Shortly after that incident, while the same trackers were on duty, Rob, Laura, the scout named Zaccheus, and I had occasion to drive up to Ntaba Mangwe at night: we needed to check a solar panel that wasn't charging properly. I stood in the back of the open truck, holding onto a bar behind the cab to keep my balance. It was dark; I didn't notice a large overhanging branch, and as we lurched under it, it hit my head hard. No one noticed the accident, for we were all trying to hang on. I ran a free arm across my face in the dark and it came away wet, so I knew I was bleeding, but I was fairly sure the wound was superficial. Just for good measure, though, once the truck had reached the top and we'd greeted the scouts, I asked Rob, who had a flashlight, to shine it on my face. He did. The cut was superficial, Laura mopped me off, and we went on to other things.

But the scouts did not take my injury lightly. When they saw my condition they immediately, in one voice, moaned aloud.

I said, "Aw, it's not bad," but they moaned again and again, in a chorus. As we worked over the battery and solar panel, I heard them continuing to moan separately. After a while, we descended, to get back into place for the next day's work. As we went down, Zaccheus, riding with me in the back of the truck, moaned several times more.

I radioed to Ntaba Mangwe the next morning and spoke to the young scout. As he depressed his transmit button I heard a voice moaning in the background. It must have been the senior scout whom I had so recently offended.

When my wound healed there was no more moaning in my presence. But I kept thinking about what had happened. Clearly, it wasn't just I who had been hurt. It was we, the larger family of us, and we might have been worse hurt, and as we remembered our communal trouble, it was appropriate to make sounds that reminded us of our relationship.

And perhaps this response contained more than sympathy. Perhaps it contained fear, or even indignation, if my injury called into question my indigenous friends' communal luck and favor with their ancestors. Perhaps there could be no accident to any of us that would not cause the group to suffer and be in trouble together.

So I learned that my American way of experiencing people as separate from myself is by no means universal. I am bonded to the people who moaned when I was hurt. It was their inclusive response, not my injury, that made me weep later when, alone in my Americanness, I looked in the mirror and saw a small scar on my forehead.

We.

10

ZACCHEUS

THE FOURTH THURSDAY OF THE MONTH WAS PAYDAY IN Sengwa, for which all the Sengwa employees gathered at the institute. The trackers came down from Ntaba Mangwe the night before; people who had been walking transects or on anti-poaching duty returned to the station. The field emptied except for the few foreign researchers who went out to take over.

The scouts and the general hands, the pump man and tea boys, the accountant and general manager all showed up at the main institute building at 7:30, dressed in clean, pressed military uniforms with little khaki and green-plaid berets on their heads. They greeted each other and us officially, with little bows and serious faces. Mr. Coulson, in pressed khaki shorts, went to his office; except for one scout who manned the station radio, the scouts and general hands stood around thirty strong in the large, unfurnished "scouts' room." Our team moved about as usual, casually dressed, casually talking, casually working on the computers and collecting our tracking data, but taken aback by the sudden distance from our African friends. Payday was a scene out of an old Rhodesian pageant, in which we had no place.

The scouts waited anxiously through the first hours, the words "eight o'clock," "nine o'clock," "ten o'clock" embedded in the African languages flowing across the patio. Men stepped out of the employees' room to look up into the sky. Meanwhile, a great many people, most of whom I'd never seen, began to arrive from the communal lands beyond the compound and settled on the lawns: the remote place I had known as Sengwa was for this day spontaneously turning into a small city, like the ones you see when refugees gather for distribution of food. There were ragged women and children with a few clusters of bananas and baskets to sell, but most had come empty-handed. There were dozens of them, old as well as young, talking loudly among themselves and with the Sengwa employees, and looking at us suspiciously as if we didn't belong there at all. I felt uneasy. Where had they come from?

At ten thirty, a drone and a glint in the sky revealed an airplane bringing money from the city. Ian ran out of his office and drove off in his Land Rover—which he rarely brought to the station—in a cloud of dust. Half an hour later he arrived again with a visitor and the ceremony began. One at a time the employees were called into the library, where the officer-in-charge and the accountant from Harare sat. Something formal and official happened, including a reckoning of hours and the counting out of money. As each employee emerged his face showed evidence of an encounter with authority. One looked humbled, the next caught the eye of a waiting comrade. Each one looked awed, if not by the encounter, I thought, by the responsibility for the brown envelope he had just put in his pocket. I sat on the step outside our office, trying to take it in. Didn't this country belong to the Shona, the Ndebele, and the Tonga? Apparently not—not when the money was counted out.

Only one man among the dozens who went into the office emerged from it with perfect equanimity. This was the tall, very dark, very slender, very serious senior scout named Zaccheus. I think that everyone in our several cultures recognized a moral leader in Zaccheus, and figured that if there is ever such a thing as a last judgment, a reshuffling of authority along ultimate lines, we will wake up to see him in the front row.

Long before I met Zaccheus my curiosity was piqued by things I heard the parks ecologists and managers saying in Harare. It seems that as his father's herd boy he had taught himself botany, scrutinizing the plants near the grazing cattle and noticing their various forms and seasonal changes. Years later as a scout at Sengwa, he became the assistant of a Canadian botanist. What he learned—Latin names, to start with—went straight into his head without a detour into notebooks, and connected so clearly to what was already there that expert botanists in the country began to recognize him as a resource. "It's a shame he wasn't promoted," the ecologists were saying among themselves on the day I first heard his name. But Zaccheus hadn't wanted promotion. He had wanted to stay at Sengwa.

Zaccheus's personal qualities were as unusual as his qualities as a naturalist. He had an uncanny integrity, which was sometimes manifested as serenity and sometimes as stubbornness. One day he'd be working for the status quo in a starched khaki shirt, the next he'd be fire and brimstone. The principles preceded the man; it was not unusual for him to stop a process in its tracks. "He's a pain in the ass," Ian said one day to me as he emerged from a tiff with Zaccheus. I looked sharply at Ian, but what I saw in his expression was respect. Zaccheus was led by an inner light, and nothing would put it out. Through the diverse filters of our different cultures we all sensed that he was incorruptible.

Of all the scouts, only he had an office in the institute. This privilege came to him because of his expertise in botany. The office was a bare plastered room with a set of shelves and a huge wooden desk with a single drawer. On the shelves he kept a plant collection he was continually assembling. The desk's surface was always empty. The drawer, which he opened with a key, contained two books. One was the Bible, which he spent much time reading, and the other was a small book written about Zimbabwe by a woman visitor from Australia. These were Zaccheus's private possessions. The botanical books were locked in the library.

As we became friends, I sometimes visited Zaccheus in his office on days when we both had only intermittent obligations in the station. It was a brash thing to do, for I usually found him absorbed in thought or in a book. But he would welcome me. On several occasions he showed me what he was reading, and in time he selected and copied out for me several poems from the Australian book. For instance:

> Those who are dead have never gone away.
> They are in the shadows darkening around,
> They are in the shadows fading into day,
> The dead are not under the ground.
> They are in the trees that quiver,
> They are in the woods that weep,
> They are in the waters of the rivers,
> They are in the waters that sleep.
> They are in the crowds, they are in the homestead.
> The dead are never dead.
>
> Those who are dead are never gone away
> They are at the breast of the wife.
> They are in the child's cry of dismay
> And the firebrand bursting into life.
> The dead are not under the ground

They are in the fire that burns low,
They are in the grass with tears to shed,
In the rock where winds blow.
They are in the forest, they are in the homestead.
The dead are never dead.

"Is this true?" I asked Zaccheus.
"It is true."

I'd been thinking that the Ndebele and Shona people recognized ancestral spirit only in certain animals. But you can
never summarize another person's beliefs, for there is truth and
truth. My own beliefs define themselves differently on different
days. When I read poetry, I am astonished to discover what I
believe in.

I first met Zaccheus about a month after my arrival in Sengwa. As the driver of the flatbed truck, he had been busy in
other parts of the reserve, carrying road workers and gravel and
working on road maintenance. But near the middle of our field-
work, he was assigned one day to help us.

My pleasure at the prospect of working together turned to
anxiety as he arrived. He did not look well—his eyes were yellow and there were deep furrows between his brows. I took him
aside to ask whether he was all right, for I didn't want to put a
sick man to work. No, he was not all right, he said, for he had
had a nightmare. And since I had noticed his condition, the
dream was my business as well as his, and he would tell me
about it.

He'd dreamed he was in his family homestead in the communal lands beyond Bulawayo, desperately attempting to save
his second son from drowning. His efforts were in vain. When
he woke up he found himself in Sengwa, far from where he was
needed. He arose in full alarm and wrote by candlelight an anxious letter to his wife. In that morning's darkness—the hours

when lions make walking dangerous—he had walked the six kilometers to the nearest store and entrusted the letter to a bus driver. Then he'd walked eight kilometers to meet us at work, and arrived on time.

"When will you hear from your wife?" I asked.

"If we are lucky, in two months."

Was there no faster way to get news? I asked.

"There is no faster way," said Zaccheus.

Zaccheus said he was not ill. He, Laura, Rob, and I spent the day looking for elephants on the Matakenya Vlei. Vlei is pronounced "flay," a beautiful word for a broad meadow, or plain, covered with golden tall grass that waves in the faintest breeze. We used the peaks of anthills, as they are called (they're actually built by termites), for lookout stations. These are hard, peaked structures two to five meters tall with a broad base and an indestructible narrow top—a slender, slightly slanting finger about the girth and height of an adult human torso. Climbing to the top is a challenge and staying there is uncomfortable—you end up winding your legs around your pedestal so all your weight won't be on your rump. Most vleis offer a selection of anthills with a variety of views, and if you ever get lost you can count on the final quarter of the tip of the hill to tilt toward the north. Stationed individually on four hills within a hundred meters of one another, Zaccheus, Rob, Laura, and I enjoyed the passage of a large, slow elephant herd strung out along the vlei between us and the Sengwa floodplain. The view was slightly distorted by mirage. The day was an experiment: I wanted to find out what anthills would be like as viewing platforms.

After that day we didn't see Zaccheus for two months, but I kept thinking about him. Two months is a long time to feel the worry and powerlessness he must have been feeling. I asked Andrew, who would see him at night in the compound, whether he was all right. "Oh yes, he is working on the roads near the northern boundary." Then one morning I noticed the flatbed truck stopped down a side road, and a tall slender figure running toward us. "I have been wanting to tell you that my wife's letter has come," Zaccheus said as he arrived. "Our son has recovered from the accident that occurred on the day of the dream. He is home from the hospital and the danger has passed."

On the following Sunday afternoon, I had planned to look for the elephant named Lutya, who spent a good portion of her life in or near the Kove River. Since the junction of the Kove with the Sengwa lay close by the cottage where we Americans were staying, I figured I could do the search by myself with only a little risk. But I met Zaccheus in the station, and hearing of my plan, he offered to help me.

It was an exquisite afternoon. Although the Kove is a small, narrow stream, unlike the great rivers it flows all year long. At the confluence we saw five red ibises standing in a broad pool of inch-deep tepid water, waiting for inch-deep fish to dodge between their legs. Our path ran first on this and then on that side of a thin trickle, clear, warm, enchanting in its delicate movement over pale brown sugar-colored sand. Then Zaccheus led the way between the close, smooth, gray, lichen-covered gorge walls that rose above us, damp and cool. We paused to look respectfully at a milky green pool that extended under a rock wall, a crocodile's home, only slightly different from the adjacent shallows. After a time we climbed an earthen bank on the east side of the gorge and moved between fig and *Trichelia* trees, where warthogs and baboons and bush buck were also quietly moving, dark silhouettes in bright sun and light shapes against dark shadows. Tiny emerald-green birds called bee-eaters were flashing and disappearing in strips and patches of sunlight and shadow. Looking up the gorge we saw a fish eagle, a motionless sentry surveying the world from a high dead branch. Under the

eye of the eagle, Zaccheus, now tall, now crouched, brows knitted, lower jaw jutted out, moved along silently, attending to silhouettes and motions, and I scrambled along behind him.

We did not find the elephants. At the eastern boundary of
the reserve we decided our mission was accomplished, and
took a shortcut back to the station. We stopped along the way
to enjoy a shallow sandy-bottomed stream. It had low grassy
banks where ferns were growing in dappled shade under a row
of short, light green, willowlike trees. In the spirit of childhood
I sat down on one bank, took off my shoes, and put my feet into
the lukewarm flowing water.

I had forgotten that Zaccheus must get back, that the scouts
live in dark little huts with no water or electricity, that Sunday
afternoon is their only free time all week for washing laundry,
cleaning house, writing letters, preparing food, visiting with
friends beyond the station, and all their private affairs. I started
another conversation.

"That dream about your son—have you received other such
dreams in your life, dreams containing information about
something you need to know?"

"Oh yes," he said. "I receive such dreams often."

"This is wonderful!" I said.

"It is wonderful," he said.

I asked, "Where do dreams come from?"

"They are from God," said Zaccheus, and an unusual smile
filled his face. I felt the sentence continued "whom I know, because of the dreams."

We paused, enjoying the shadow patterns dancing on the
golden sand at the bottom of the stream. A meditation surrounded us, but a practical question was burning on my tongue.
Too soon, I spoke again.

"Zaccheus."

"I am here."

"When something happens that is far from the experience of your people, how do you speak to them of it?"

Now something extremely strange happened. Zaccheus answered me in a shout.

"YOU JUST TELL WHAT HAPPENED!"

I jumped—he had shouted as if his listener was far away, but I was not; and only the two of us were sitting there. I looked up cautiously, expecting to see I don't know what, something unearthly, or, if not, an angry man, but what I saw was neither. I saw a changed face, two intense burning eyes focused on me under knitted brows. *"YOU JUST TELL WHAT YOU SAW!"*

The voice echoed against something distant and my heart skipped a beat in my chest. Looking down as if into the water, I said, in a trembling voice, "Of course." After a long time I drew breath and looked up again.

"You must simply tell what happened," Zaccheus said in his normal quiet voice. His face was still severe. "Only God knows what it means." Then he spoke again, as himself, not an oracle. "Katypayne—could we go now?"

I came back to my senses. The afternoon had passed, we had used up all his free time, and night was coming on, dangerous with lions. Zaccheus waited while I pulled on my shoes, then set off walking very fast toward home, threading his way lithely, silently, and swiftly through the bushes. I ran clumsily and noisily in my effort to keep up.

My friendship with the elderly Ndebele man Sibanda had a different quality from my friendship with Zaccheus. Sibanda was a sociable fellow, exceptionally fond of foreigners. Seeing us trying to learn Shona, he insisted that we must learn Ndebele as well, and gave us assignments: there were daily lessons amid much laughter and perseverance on his part. As clever as he was friendly, he made all of us part of his community, gave us such help as was within his power, and used us for his own various purposes.

One day when he was sweeping in the library, I asked him to tell me something about a bird I'd found illustrated in a book. "No, I cannot see books anymore," he said. I offered him my glasses to try. By chance, they were a match to his disability—he told me excitedly what he saw. I said then, that if he would go to an eye doctor I would pay to have prescription glasses made for him.

This offer led to a complex set of arrangements within the institute—the officers looked sideways at me for my indulgence, and indeed, I had no idea of what I was getting us all in for. Sibanda took time off and traveled to the city of Gweru. He brought back an estimate signed by an optometrist: the glasses could be made for Z $110.

Z $110 (the equivalent of U.S. $55) would feed a household for several months; the price was out of proportion. Should I wait until our departure and give him my glasses to avoid the contradictions of money? But surely my glasses were not really adjusted to his eyes. So I gave Sibanda the money, and he took a leave of absence, and was ten days away from the station, during which time Joe Furunga did his job.

Gweru was about half a day's drive by private vehicle, a short trip, I thought. But in fact Sibanda's travels probably went about as follows: he walked home to pick up food, water, and clothing for the journey. As people heard of his plan to travel, many gave him commissions to do for them during the trip. He walked the six kilometers to the local store (Corner Store) by daylight, since there are lions at night. There he waited into the night for a bus and driver, which arrived at an unknown hour since there are many imponderables. While waiting he made himself comfortable amid a crowd of people with dogs, chickens, goats, and produce gathered on the concrete slab in front of the closed store. When the bus came everyone crowded into it, grabbed the back of the seat ahead of them, said a prayer—for bus accidents are the commonest kind and often fatal—and started a wild and dangerous ride at breakneck speed through the potholes on a dirt road. Maybe he changed buses and waited a second night. Once in the city, he looked for family, food, and rest in exchange for favors: the trip would add a fresh set of obligations to the long list already stored in his mind, and he would try to settle a few of them before coming home. As for the optometrist—but I could not imagine the problems with the optometrist.

Sibanda showed up at the station ten days after his second departure with a pair of glasses as evidence of the trip. He said that they enabled him to read. However, he used them only once in my presence. For a few weeks he carried them in his coveralls pocket, but they were liable to fall out, he said, when he leaned over to start the generator. He must keep them safe at home—whether in the tiny tin dome that was his house in the compound, or in his village in the communal lands not far away. I am sure, in any case, that the glasses were not wasted, even if they were used in barter.

In early October, it was time to leave Sengwa.

"When we return from transects we shall find you gone," Zaccheus said to me.

During their days on transect duty, the scouts returned at night to bush camps. They got their drinking and wash water from holes they dug in particular spots in the dry riverbeds. They slept in raised beds made of sticks laid parallel and bound together with vines, and softened on top with river grasses. Some of them did not like the indignities of life in the transect camps, but for others it was the best part of being in Sengwa. Zaccheus was one of those. He invited me to join his team for a survey.

I accepted the invitation on my last day. By this time Bill, Lillie, Rob, and Laura had already left Sengwa. Loki, Russ, and I had stayed on for a further three weeks, hoping to learn whether the elephants' movements would change after rain, should it rain. But it had not rained—it had not rained for six months. It had just gotten hotter and hotter. Our data had gotten worse and worse; something to do with the heat was corrupting our radio tracking so that the elephants were appearing in all kinds of impossible places. We ourselves were stunned and dazed with heat and drought, and we hardly had the energy to care. We just kept doing what we did as the time ran out. Suddenly, there were only four days left, and most of the scouts were out on transect.

I finished my personal packing a day early. Russ and Loki had organized the job of inventory and equipment packing, and early in the morning they were both asleep. So I drove out before dawn to the cluster of thatched huts under Ntaba Mangwe. Zaccheus, Joe Furunga, Mbanga, and Mariba greeted me warmly. They shared tea and hot milk with me and we walked out in two diverging teams from the base of the escarpment.

In the Manyoni valley, Joe, Zaccheus, and I encountered a large herd of impala eating beans that lay on the ground in great numbers. They were the fruit of the *acacia albida* tree (now named *Faidherbia albida*), a favorite food of many wild animals in Sengwa. A few days earlier, Andrew and I had watched two male elephants leaning against the bases of these same trees and shaking them until the beans showered down on their backs and heads. Hundreds of impala had been waiting nearby. When the elephants had moved on to shake other trees, the impalas had hurried to eat the beans they had left. We now found impalas again profiting from an elephant harvest.

On the western side of the river, we encountered a rhino fast asleep in a natural meadow. Her head was huge in proportion to her body, her legs short and fat; she was obviously very young. With her horn pointing to the sky, her huge chin lay on the path just where we would step. Zaccheus smiled in delight at the soundness of her youthful sleep, stepped quietly around her, no more than six feet from her nose. Joe and I followed in his footsteps, and we continued on our way.

As we returned to the field camp, we heard voices. Mbanga and Mariba were standing in the opening beside the thatched bungalows, craning their necks at the sky. It was strangely, thickly gray. Soon we heard a long rumble of thunder. One at a time, huge drops of water pelted the ground, with every drop making a dull thud and lifting a plume of dust. "God has heard your prayer," Zaccheus said to me. I thought, when did I mention that prayer to him?

No sooner had the drops begun to fall than a rainbow appeared in the western sky. Then the sound of men's laughter began to mix with the pelting drops. The rain grew stronger and so did the laughter. I had to leave hastily, for the roads would soon turn to soup and be impassable. The transect walkers would stay at Ntaba Mangwe Camp for several more days. Our farewells were quick—"God bless you and your family, stay well, and write letters"—and hardly interrupted the laughter. I made it to the station, where the rain continued off and on until early evening, filling the air with an extraordinary smell.

The next morning, I was awake before dawn. The sky had never seemed so clear or the earth so satisfied. I said to myself, I will go for one last walk alone before we leave. I jumped into the truck and drove down to the Sengwa crossing, a place where the river always flows, and elephants, and buffalo, and kudu, impalas, monkeys and baboons, warthogs and all manner of birds were likely to be drinking.

The light had not come when I reached the crossing but all was clarity, expecting light. I saw no living thing on the river—

everyone must be in the forest, I thought. I decided to walk up the river myself a bit and give thanks, then turn around and go. I stepped out of the truck and walked north on the compact rain-blessed sandy east side, bidding farewell to the trees and the sky, the sand, the river's central trickle, the hidden animals, and the predawn silence.

I was not looking carefully, so full was I of praise: the light that was filling and giving shape to the riverbed seemed to be an extension of the praise. I had gotten nearly a kilometer north of the crossing when a pair of storks in the shallow water in the middle of the riverbed caught my eye. Beyond them, I noticed motion on the west bank about a hundred meters away. A large lioness was getting to her feet. She stretched as if awakening from a nap, releasing as she stood a pile of younger lionesses who had been sleeping underneath her. A second, a third, and a fourth lioness stood up and stretched, one after another. They turned toward the river and looked at me.

I continued to walk north as if I had not noticed them. Looking out of the corner of my eye, I saw that the lionesses on the west bank had started to walk north just opposite me, at exactly my speed, which was for them quite slow.

I glanced at my watch in a pretense of minding my own business. "I'd better go back now," I said out loud, and turned around and started to retrace my steps. Out of the corner of my eye I saw the lionesses on the west bank stop, turn, and take a southward direction just like mine. For twenty minutes we walked at my pace, on opposite sides of the riverbed. As the choreographer of this dance I felt a certain awe. I felt anxious, too, not sure how we would end it, given that at the end I would have to cross to the lionesses' side to reach the truck.

About one hundred meters north of the crossing place, the lionesses came to a little rise that was the remains of an abandoned, much-trampled anthill. They crowded onto the top of it and stood there looking tall and holding their eyes and ears as high as possible. As if we were tied to each other by an imaginary string and they were the center of a circle, I pivoted in an arc one hundred meters long from the east side down across the river to the truck. The lionesses watched me from their spot. When I was safely in the truck, I saw each of them flick her tail. I waved out the window to them and drove away.

I arrived at the station at sunrise. Russ and Loki were already packing the other vehicle. I helped them finish and we hit the road.

Abake babonana baza bonana, I called to each mopane tree and each section of the road as we rattled and bumped past them, leaving them behind. Zaccheus had taught us this Ndebele proverb: The eye that has seen something will see it again.

11

WILDLIFE IS
THE ENGINE

SENGWA HAD FILLED ME TO THE BRIM: I FELT I HAD NO ROOM
for anything more. But this would have to change, for much of
what I'd savored in Sengwa had no counterpart in the outer
world to which I would now return. During all the Sengwa days,
I had known that troubles were brewing, relevant to what I was
savoring, and that one day I would meet those troubles head-on.

In the years preceding the Sengwa field season, an intense international controversy had flared up over how to keep African
elephants from extinction. The controversy touched on issues of
trade, and as a result 111 nations were involved in the decision-
making process by 1989. Scientists were turning from science to
politics in the service of their concerns; researchers who otherwise might have been collaborators were taking sides against one
another. Joyce Poole was a spokesperson for the point of view
endorsed in East Africa (Kenya, Uganda, Tanzania), which held
that African elephants, like Asian elephants, must be designated
an endangered species, making all international trade in ele-

phant products illegal. Rowan Martin was a spokesperson for the point of view endorsed in the southern African countries (Zimbabwe, South Africa, Namibia, Botswana, and others), which held that such trade must be encouraged and legal, carefully monitored and policed. The argument between the two factions came to a head in 1989 at a famous meeting in Lausanne, Switzerland. I was at home in Ithaca, listening to the radio.

The meeting occurred under the auspices of the Convention for International Trade in Endangered Species (CITES), the international body that names species for protection. Shortly before the meeting the Ivory Trade Review Group, an independent panel of experts, had released their finding that African elephants had declined, between 1979 and 1989, from an estimated 1.3 million to 625,000. Most of the losses were from poaching in East Africa. The poaching was supported by a thriving international market in ivory (the principal destinations were Japan and Hong Kong), by local corruption, and by a breakdown of control mechanisms all along the trade route. More ivory was leaving Africa each year, in the form of smaller tusks. This meant that younger elephants were being killed, which in turn suggested that most of the old elephants in the same populations were gone. Many people feared that the elephants in East Africa were heading for extinction.

The trade review group's announcement was followed by a public gesture by the Kenyan government: a televised bonfire, whose fuel was three million dollars' worth of elephant ivory that had been confiscated from poachers. A few weeks later the East African position in CITES won by a landslide. African elephants were added to the Endangered Species List, and all international trade in ivory became illegal. I heaved a sigh of relief.

But the Lausanne decision angered the southern African countries. Most of Africa's savannah elephants were living in those countries, relatively free from poaching and in populations that were increasingly compressed in habitats too small to support them. South Africa and Zimbabwe had developed an infrastructure that made possible the annual slaughtering and processing of thousands of elephants. Periodic elephant slaughters became an aspect of the mandate of national parks in those nations; elephant products brought in millions of dollars annually to be spent in part on parks maintenance. Wildlife can survive in developing countries, their CITES delegates said, only by paying its way in cash.

Furthermore, they argued that much of the elephant habitat in southern Africa was not in national parks but in "communal lands," the home of poor rural people. As the human population grew, people moved further into elephant terrain; they planted their crops where elephants raided them, and occasionally got killed defending them. This caused further problems that could not be remedied without money.

To counteract these problems, Zimbabwe had recently devised an innovative program that depended on income from the ivory trade. The proceeds from elephant "harvests"–culls and sport hunting–would be used in part to compensate rural people for their losses due to elephants' crop raiding. Those people would come to see elephants not just as a nuisance but also as a resource. Thus encouraged, they would resist opportunities to become involved in poaching, which, although not a current problem, was a problem to be anticipated. The leaders in Zimbabwe were dismayed by the ivory ban, for, without income, the local incentive that might otherwise develop would falter, the land between protected areas would become increasingly unsafe for elephants, and the viable elephant range increasingly fragmented.

I appreciated a certain logic in this argument, but I knew too much about elephants to endorse a plan that committed them to the recurring losses associated with culling. Like people, elephants live empathetically: the experiences of others become their own experiences, and there is no way to stop that. No matter how the pros and cons of trade in ivory were measured, to gather elephant ivory by culling was to inflict serious damage on the elephants that survived. No matter how the conflict between African elephants and human settlers was described, to control elephant population size by culling was to kill the spirit of the survivors. That, at least, was my impression. I do not believe that elephants have a way of ignoring the experiences of their friends and family.

This impression was shared by all who worked among elephants, particularly including those who had to manage the culling operations. In response, they modified the culling protocol over the years until it involved the destruction of all individuals that happened to be grouped together at the moment of shooting. But this, although a kind gesture, was not kind enough, for as our studies showed, elephants attend to relationships beyond the physical boundaries to which even the most sensitive culling program could be responsive.

My discomfort with Zimbabwe's relationship to its elephants was on my mind when we arrived in Sengwa for our field project. I decided to inform myself about the circumstances in which culling was called for, and how it was done. Hearing that a five-day workshop entitled "Management of the Hwange Ecosystem" was scheduled in the week before our elephant-collaring, and that almost all the participants would be ecologists and park managers, I asked if I might attend.

The meeting was held in a conference room in an elegant hotel, the Hwange Safari Lodge, which overlooked a half-wooded area in Hwange National Park. The sessions started with presentations on the interactions between soil, water, fire, frost, plants, and animals–from termites to elephants–in dry ecosystems. The speakers were well-known researchers and integrative thinkers. They described layers and layers of complexity: I scribbled as fast as I could. On the second day the focus turned to management. In a good-natured way, several Zimbabwean park managers expressed much frustration as they presented reports on their activities. Trained as scientists and charged with eleven lofty objectives, starting with "the preservation of ecosystem diversity," they lacked the time, personnel, and equipment to manage by their own scientific standards.

The notes I took as people spoke about matters bearing on calling are the source of the quotes that follow. Mr. M. L. Nchunga, the principal wildlife biologist from the Department of Wildlife and National Parks in Botswana, said his main objective was to make national parks pay for themselves. This was also one of Zimbabwe's goals, and Rowan Martin responded. "Two hundred U.S. dollars per square kilometer is what it costs annually to keep up national parks land, or four hundred dollars if there are black rhino on it. We have 45,000 square kilometers under protection in Zimbabwe. We have more elephants in the country than we have ever had before. How much and which areas should we keep as a baseline?" Embedded in Rowan's question was the implication of another: *how much and at what rate and where should we cull elephants to pay for all of this?* Nearly 25,000 elephants had been killed in Zimbabwe between 1981 and 1988, yielding more than thirteen million U.S. dollars.*

Was the need for money a driving force behind Zimbabwe's decisions to cull elephants? In Sengwa, I had gotten the impres-

* From *Elephant Management in Zimbabwe,* a review compiled by the Department of National Parks and Wild Life Management in 1989. I received a copy at the workshop, but quote here from the version updated in 1992.

sion from Rowan and Ian that the main considerations were ecological. I was glad that the schedule now announced a debate on the proposition "that management aimed at preventing large natural fluctuations in plant and animal communities is detrimental to the conservation of biological diversity." I sat on the edge of my chair, anticipating an informed argument about the ecological pros and cons of elephant culling. "It is expected," said the written instructions, "that the debate will look at the merits of conserving ecological processes as opposed to specific plant and animal communities; give an in-depth clarification of the concept of ecosystem resilience; examine the possible consequences of management by non-intervention in circumscribed protected areas; highlight the possible conflicts of a laissez-faire approach with policies and objectives for protected areas; and point out the dangers of holding numbers of any particular species constant in a dynamic environment."

The renowned savannah ecologist Dr. Brian Walker opened the debate. He wasted no time over other animals but headed straight for elephants, with a list of questions that must be addressed before culling is started. What evidence is there that irreversible habitat damage is occurring? What is the shape of the habitat recovery curve if you reduce elephant pressures? Are you sure culling will have the predicted effect? What other actions must be taken in conjunction with culling? How will you know whether culling was successful?

Walker reminded his colleagues of their earlier discussion of large-scale natural fluctuations—changes in abundance and rarity over periods lasting years and sometimes decades. The presence of such fluctuations argues against a static vision of nature, and against efforts to manage for a static impression. Walker said, "I believe the meeting has agreed that there is no ecological reason to cull."

I waited for someone to correct his impression and take up

the opposite side, but nobody did. In fact, Dr. David Cumming, of the World Wildlife Fund Multispecies Project, a careful, pragmatic, much-respected thinker, said quietly, "In the last fifteen years we [Zimbabwe] have culled for purely *aesthetic* reasons." Then Mr. Nchunga spoke again for Botswana. "Our plan to cull is for purely *economic* reasons and not aesthetic or ecological." Perhaps these confessions were disturbing to Rowan Martin, for he said, "We don't have an entrenched policy. . . . We are at a pause." He meant a pause in the middle of Zimbabwe's long history of culling. But the meeting had come to a pause as well. The debate was not resumed. Dr. Walker said, "The parks people must set their goals. We outsiders at the meeting can't do it for you. The floor should be closed to us."

When the general meeting reconvened, nothing had changed. "The basis for our decisions *is* aesthetic," Rowan announced. I think he was referring less to policy than to the practice of making local decisions spontaneously. In his book *The Fate of the Elephant,* Douglas Chadwick quotes Rowan as follows: "People are fed so many images of wild Africa, they don't realize we hardly have a truly pristine area left on the continent and certainly not in Zimbabwe. So we have to manage. But do we manage for what elephants need or for what pleases people? I myself prefer a nice acacia forest with a few elephants over an elephant-blasted landscape, and I'm prepared to knock a few elephants on the head to achieve it."

How then should Hwange be managed? The final session was devoted to an intellectual discussion of the principle of adaptive management. Respecting the uniqueness of every ecosystem, managers design their activities in such a way that they can learn from them. They monitor many aspects of the environment and the relationships it supports, and study their own interventions in relation to that baseline information. Adaptive management leads to the progressive accumulation of the information needed for the best management of particular ecosystems.

The Zimbabwean managers had been trying to do just this, but it's a complex and costly assignment. The parks administrators promised to try to increase their support, and the managers renewed their commitment to adaptive management so that decisions could be made on the basis of carefully examined information rather than spontaneous "aesthetic" impressions.

Rowan now announced a fifteen-minute break. After that, he said, we'd have a brief report on Zimbabwe's new wildlife utilization program, CAMPFIRE–the Communal Areas Management Programme for Indigenous Resources. Although this program had nothing to do with parks management, the report would end the meeting on a gracious note, since CAMPFIRE and the workshop had the same sponsor, the U.S. Agency for International Development.

It was exhausting to think we were about to start a whole new subject. I stepped outside and crossed a spacious lawn to the chain-link fence that protected us humans from the wild things on the other side. In the ten minutes that were my own, I saw nothing wild. I gave myself two minutes to pull against the fence, stretching my back, which was stiff from four days of sitting, and then returned to the meeting.

Brian Child, the young, energetic administrator of CAMPFIRE, explained the program as an attempt to better the health of two disadvantaged populations–wild animals and indigenous people–by assisting the latter to harvest the former in a sustainable way. Indigenous Zimbabweans have suffered since the time of European colonization, when they were driven off the fertile land and displaced to areas where the soil barely permits subsistence farming. They have survived marginally, sharing the land with wild animals that endanger them and destroy their crops, and which have been disallowed as a resource. With the blessing of the central government CAMPFIRE was now lifting this restriction for selected communities, promising them the opportunity to benefit from government-regulated harvesting of wild animals, particularly elephants.

Dr. Child was "brokering" this program in other countries, trying to gain allies for a proposal Zimbabwe would make at the 1992 CITES meeting to reopen international trade in elephant ivory. He argued that by managing elephant populations carefully, other African nations might also support their rural poor people and counteract the resentment many of them felt toward wildlife parks. In the context of improved relations, the people and the governments would never let African elephants go extinct.

Brian's report revived the spirit of the meeting. As drinks were passed out, his colleagues clapped him on the back, referring to him as the Golden Boy, and "the young Turk behind the winning idea." Everyone also knew that what he was promoting had been initiated by Rowan. Rowan accepted congratulations and said confidently, "Wildlife is the engine that is driving democratization in Zimbabwe."

Seven months later, at home following the Sengwa expedition, I found myself talking with six young conservation biologists— three of my four children, my daughter-in-law, and two visiting friends. All of them had heard CAMPFIRE presented, in their various American institutions, as a program with the potential to demonstrate that "wildlife utilization can support sustainable development," i.e., that the proceeds from wildlife farming can raise the standard of living for growing human populations, and keep them high without endangering the wildlife. This news made me dizzy. CAMPFIRE was only three years old, and in the few pilot communities where it was being tried out it was enjoying mixed success and failure. But the academic world loves an integrative idea and wasn't asking about reality.

I, for my part, was losing sleep over CAMPFIRE. Its runaway popularity meant that foreign agencies might sponsor it without looking deeply into its weaknesses. At the biological level the program offered the hope that free-ranging wild animal populations could be exploited and survive indefinitely as a human resource. I doubted this. I thought that if the ivory trade was reopened, poaching would increase in East Africa, supported by the same corruption as before, and culling would resume in southern Africa. I made up a slogan for the menu of the Wildlife Utilization and Sustainable Development Restaurant: "Would you like them poached or culled?"

The world's eye was on poaching, but I worried about culling. I distrusted the adequacy of the science that would be used to justify it. It takes a lot of time and money and work to assess the size and structure of a moving population, and, as I'd learned in Hwange, the priorities leading to culling are often economic rather than scientific. Culling would be practiced on "pockets of local abundance"–protected areas where elephants congregate, compressed by rapid human settlement in the surrounding landscape. What appears as abundance inside small pockets can be, on a larger scale, dearth. The supply populations might be dwindling, but because those populations are transient, you might think they were just somewhere else. Meanwhile, more people would be arriving to take advantage of the resource–"so the animals disappear into a black hole," said my son John, grimly. Even if I could endorse culling, this dimension of the plan would worry me.

At a political level CAMPFIRE appealed to foreigners because it seemed socially progressive, but there, too, I had my doubts. Only ten years earlier, at independence, the new government had promised a redistribution of land that would benefit the residents of communal lands. What had happened to that promise? The CAMPFIRE program, to be paid for by wildlife, would keep indigenous people on unfarmable land. I thought of American Indians.

Rowan's statement—"Wildlife is the engine that is driving democratization in Zimbabwe"—was ringing in my ears. What was he saying? In the spring, he lectured at Cornell on the wildlife utilization movement in Zimbabwe, again describing it as an advance toward democracy. With his permission, we made a videotape. The lecture contained a passage suggesting that the advance he had in mind was an advance in the thinking of landed white Zimbabweans.

> A number of people like myself and quite a large community in Zimbabwe, when Zimbabwe gained its independence in 1980, knew that something had to be done. We had a fantastic wildlife resource in the communal lands but it was going downhill very fast as human population numbers were rising. And I think a lot of us also felt very uncomfortable about what we had done during the colonial era. We had regarded communal land people as just a nuisance to our life. They were the people that did the illegal hunting within the national parks and it was quite all right to go into their houses in the middle of the night and drag them out of their houses and catch them in a wire snare or lash them with a piece of kudu skin. Because we had the holy grail there was no problem about that sort of thing. And we realized that a new era had been ushered in with the '80s and some of this behavior would be less than acceptable.

If the old attitude described here is a baseline, there is indeed important progress toward democracy. But should wild animals pay the price for the whole distance that that movement still has to travel?

My opinions were negative and reactive, bitter and confused. A colleague would say, "What a promising voice of the future this CAMPFIRE is." I would answer, "Oh no, something is terribly wrong with it." In fact something seemed wrong with all the proposed solutions to all the elephant problems. By depending on an ivory ban, the East Africans were depending on foreign wealth and foreign opinion to support their national heritage. Local people weren't involved enough, so the wildlife estate would always be corruptible, I thought. And what would the East African countries do about their own "pockets of elephant overpopulation" if the ban succeeded? No, we hadn't arrived at a satisfactory answer there either. There seemed to be no solution that respected all the realities.

I had anticipated, in Sengwa, that it was going to be like this. As our project had drawn to a close I'd begun to fear my return to America. I dreaded the conversations that would draw me into the economic perspective. I would be asked to defend or attack Zimbabwe's management strategies, and my inability to propose a good alternative would make me unhappy. I looked forward to my homecoming with a certain amount of spiritual grief.

12

DISTANT FRIENDS

Loki, Russ, and I drove both our vehicles to Harare and left the old Land Cruiser to be repaired and sent back to Sengwa as a gift. In the other vehicle we drove south, crossing the border from a slow, poor country into the fast lane that was South Africa. On the second day in that country we reached Johannesburg. There we had friends who welcomed us into their house and gave us baths and food and wine and listened to our stories. At the end of the evening we crawled under down quilts made by our hostess. Each in a separate room we lay down in safety, for the house was surrounded by a strong brick wall with broken glass embedded on its top edge, to keep us safe, as my hosts explained, from black-skinned intruders.

I was exhausted, but the glass in the wall kept me awake. My mind groped for Sengwa voices and faces, but they would not come. "You have left us," I imagined them saying: "We find you gone." I fell into a dull, despondent sleep.

In early morning, I woke suddenly with my heart pounding,

sobbing in the aftermath of a powerful dream: I had crouched all night by a mopane fire with Zaccheus and his wife. We had taken turns holding their infant son. Now he was in his mother's arms. I reached out my hands and the parents passed him to me. I saw their faces close to mine, serious. As I received the child, I suddenly had a powerful sensation that he was holy. So momentous was this impression that a sob exploded in my chest and woke me.

I cried strongly for a long time without words or meaning— it was like a silent tantrum. I cried as long as I could, but it was not long enough. I had to get up because my plane was leaving for America. It was too late to turn back, and besides, what would turning back accomplish?

My people at home greeted me with the warmest welcome imaginable, but for a long time I was racked by culture shock. I asked naive, rude questions like, "Where are all the cars going?" At the core of my disapproval lay the memory of the dream, as if it encapsulated my experiences in Sengwa, and I had, by coming home, rejected those experiences.

The dream sat uneasily in my heart. The child I dreamed about was poor; in comparison I was unutterably rich. He would grow up in the communal lands; I would be posting signs around my fourteen acres (once held communally by the Cayuga Indians): "PRIVATE PROPERTY: TRESPASSING FOR ANY PURPOSES IS STRICTLY PROHIBITED." He would be walking with other children behind their fathers' oxen; I would be driving in my private car to Quaker gatherings for the purpose of discussing the testimonies: simplicity, peace, community. He would be praying for rain, while my radio was announcing to people whose prayer was for entertainment, "Bad weather is expected tomorrow."

I gradually reunited with my friends and family, but remained divided from myself. I taught my people the Shona greeting "I am well if you are well," but I had forgotten how to be well in my own community.

Fearing other people's mysticism, I decided to keep my dream a secret. But it would not let me rest, and finally I told a friend. She asked, "What have you to lose by sending a message to the person it was intended for?" I had not thought of it that way. I sat down at once and wrote a letter to Zaccheus.

A letter of response arrived in just two months. Zaccheus's wife had given birth to a son at the time of my dream.

> I do not know what your dream means but the God knows
> and He will reveal the meaning to you one day. . . . You are
> the third person with a similar dream to the child–a holy
> child. Two people from my place dreamed before my wife
> gave birth, that she will give birth to a holy, or a powerful
> child. Let us wait and see what God will do, I hope He will
> give us the interpretation of the dream He revealed to you.

I wonder how often people get dreams like that in Ndebele villages. In my experience it was the only time.

Other letters also came from Sengwa in the months after our departure. The first contained the news that our friends were missing us and sending prayers and good wishes. Then several scouts wrote that armed poachers were sneaking into Sengwa and killing rhinos. Most were Zambians, who were ferried across the Zambese River, and were aided, as they walked the long way south, by local opportunists in a smuggling chain–for a single rhino horn was worth enough to make many people's efforts profitable. The timing of the incursions suggested an inside informer: the first rhinos were killed a month after our departure, just as the radio tracking ended, and all the observers came down from Ntaba Mangwe. Subsequent incursions occurred on the days of the month just following payday, when most Sengwa employees got time off.

A scout from the adjacent Chiriza Safari Area, the father

of several children and a close friend of many in Sengwa, was killed in a poaching confrontation. The remaining scouts in Chiriza and Sengwa were exhausting themselves in efforts to bring the situation under control, but without much hope. "We no longer know our houses," one scout wrote me. Dangerous and disheartening, the antipoaching maneuvers involved nights—sometimes two or three consecutively—in which the men silently huddled together in the thickets, without lights or fires that could give away their location. They suffered from the physical fear of dangerous mammals and snakes, and the mental fear that they'd catch a poacher whom they knew and be trapped by contradictory commitments. In time, I received a letter about a three-day search that culminated in this very situation.

> One of [the poachers got] frightened and threw away the bags he was carrying, also a pair of shoes, overalls and a pair of socks. Shortly it got dark and we went back to the station for a few minutes and then went patrol along the fence during the night. The next morning we checked for spoors along the fence and picked one spoor near Corner Store. [We scouts] backtracked the spoor back into the park. . . . The spoor took us to a place where the poachers splitted. One of them was now bare-footed. We tracked the bare-footed one and picked up some shoes. A few meters from where we picked up the shoes we found a bag, axe, a five-liter plastic container and a Parks hat. Protruding out of the bag were three big rhino horns. We opened the bag and saw the following:
>
> > 1 tent for camping
> > 1 home-made knife
> > 1 cup
> > 1 spoon
> > 1 rain coat
> > 22 bullets

> 1 set of flares
> 3 rhino horns

They unrolled the tent, and found it labeled with the name of a scout's brother. At his home they found both men, with a high-powered rifle and four rhino horns. The men, having confessed, were taken to the research station, presumably on the way to a seat of justice.

The scout's brother was now held captive by his former friends. Trust that has developed over many years doesn't evaporate all at once, and one of the captors unthinkingly set his rifle down on the base of the radio tower where the captive was sitting, and went into the institute for a minute. The poacher picked up the unguarded rifle and shot himself in the head.

In so doing he minimized the future humiliation to himself, his family, and friends. In a world that placed supreme value on relationships, he had failed many. I wondered whether he, like Paidamoyo, had envisioned punishment from the animal as well as the human community. But the world had failed in its relationship with him, too, for poverty is a failed relationship. And the inflated price of rhino horn in the Arab and Far Eastern countries, where it is made into dagger handles and aphrodisiacs, a sign of another failed relationship.

As if this were not enough to bear, soon Zimbabwe was struck by a severe drought that destroyed the crops and starved the domestic animals in the various parts of the communal lands where the scouts' families were trying to farm. "Oh what will we do?" one scout wrote me, enclosing a picture of his wife standing dejected in a field of dying maize.

Some people were able to harvest some crops, but they, too, had troubles to bear. Sibanda wrote me that he could not send me a picture of his family as he had intended, for an elephant had killed his wife. He was writing to ask a favor. Could I please send him seashells and rainbow beads?

This would be the third event in our history of exchanging gifts. The second event had occurred on the last day of the radio-collaring project. Sibanda had arrived at the station with a heavy burden, the only thing he could think of, he said, that I would appreciate as much as he appreciated his glasses. When I saw what he had brought, tears sprang into my eyes. He was giving me his drum.

To say that music was a strong bond between us is to use words that are not strong enough. I loved to see him dance, that little old man in his blue coveralls, and he loved to see me respond to drumming, dancing, and singing, and believed me when I told him that I hope to be a musician in my next incarnation.

The drum is a section of a hollow tree trunk. It is about two feet tall and one foot in diameter. All its parts show signs of much use. A piece of dirty kudu skin is stretched over the top and tightened against a series of pegs that are inserted into the high walls of the cylinder. The bottom of the drum, open but smaller than the top, narrows into a hollow stand about four inches high and six in diameter. In this section the remains of an old termite mound, witness to the drum's years on an earthen floor, make the drum excessively heavy. Its animality reminds me that some of the songs it accompanied were addressed to human ancestors, some of whom resided, if I understand correctly, in the bodies of animals.

Now I looked at the drum sadly, appreciating Sibanda's loss. I sought help from my friends. A friend named Elizabeth offered an assortment of periwinkles, conches, and scallops she had collected during a vacation in Florida; two others, both named Nancy, contributed necklaces made of beads of many colors, and I sent them off to Sengwa. My heart was heavy as I sent out these pretty things, thinking of Sibanda's family and of the failed relationship in which an elephant was the offender.

After six weeks a new letter came from Sibanda. After expressing thanks, he asked for more seashells, "specially those small round ones as those you sent me. I'm also asking for more beads, a couple of transparent without color and more of those rainbow-like, and really blue. I need these things for ancestral spirits. . . ."

In time I learned that the meaning of the shells went back to the time when the residents on the coast of South Africa were Ndebele. When they were driven away from the coast they were estranged from the relationships that had defined their universe. Their spirits still long for the sea. Shells help the ancestors, by reminding them of where they came from.

During the months when Sengwa's people were experiencing so many troubles, Bill, Russ, and I were working on the data we had brought home. Our thoughts were much on the intricacies of the Sengwa elephants' lives. One day a letter came from Rowan containing news of them. He had mounted an operation to remove the heavy radio collars, which were chafing the elephants' necks, and replace them with lighter marking collars. The operation was successful for fourteen of the elephants but unsuccessful for two—Computer, who could not be found, and Lutya, who died. Rowan wrote, "She failed to go under the first dart and we gave her a second dart after 20 minutes. She went down 5 minutes after the second dart but fell awkwardly with her head facing down a slope and her trunk was constricted under her left tusk. Mike Kock reversed the drug immediately after he detected her distress but it was too late."

This accident was unavoidable, as we say—nobody's fault. Yet I knew that it was our fault, for it was we who had collared Lutya, the shy matriarch who lived upstream from the institute in the beautiful Kove River.

13

SLAUGHTER IN
A SACRED PLACE

BILL, RUSS, AND I HAD FOR AN OFFICE AN ENORMOUS ROOM in an old barn next to the Cornell Laboratory of Ornithology. Each of us worked at home as well, and on different aspects of the data analysis, with the result that there were periods when nobody knew much about the status of the project as a whole. To remedy our ignorance we started meeting on Wednesday afternoons. On Wednesday, October 27, 1991, I was half an hour late; when I arrived, the men were leaning over Russ's computer, struggling with the issues surrounding the question of whether our data showed coordinated movement among the Sengwa elephants–coordinated, that is, to a greater extent than one would find were the movements random within overlapping home ranges. But as I entered they stopped, and looked up, and walked quickly to the door to greet me. I thought, "This is odd."

I said, "What's up?"

"Bad news," said Bill. "I got hold of Rowan by phone

yesterday to ask him to write a recommendation for me. And after we'd settled that, he said, 'I'm working on a difficult letter to Katy.' I said, 'Yeah, what's it about?' and he told me they've culled the elephants in Sengwa."

"CULLED?"

We moved to a corner of the room where there were chairs. The spaciousness of the big barn room usually made me feel comfortable; now I felt cold.

The Department of National Parks and Wildlife Management had performed a cull in early September in which one-third of the Sengwa population was destroyed. "They got two hundred forty-nine elephants, including four of ours and their families."

"Who?"

"Jabula, Miss Piggy, Friday, and one more. Mufambo, I think he said, but maybe it was Munyama. The bush was thick, they had to make decisions fast, they were shooting from a helicopter, they'd get some members of a family and then see the collar, and after that it was too late to not finish off the family."

We all drew breath and sat quietly. Then I asked Bill and Russ how they felt about this news. Bill said that he was not surprised, for Rowan had culled in Sengwa before, and he'd talked about culling again. It was a poor way to treat colleagues, he thought, not consulting or informing us, but Rowan wouldn't have altered his plan for anyone. Zimbabwe was a poor country, a country with problems we could hardly imagine. And Rowan was smart, really smart. And there was nothing we could do about his decisions anyway. The Sengwa elephants were his business and none of ours.

"I disagree," I said.

There was a pause. "I know how you feel," said Russ.

"Hell, so do I," said Bill. "I feel bad, too."

"What are your thoughts, Russ?" I asked.

Russ said he didn't have anything to add to what Bill said, at the moment. He thought he agreed with Bill.

A gulf had opened up between us. On one side they sat, my friends of twenty years, looking at our work, their computers full of data, a university, a tradition, a pyramid of supporting institutions at hand to help them with their minute and specialized problems in data analysis. On the other side I sat, stunned by the news of the many deaths.

Russ spoke again, saying he couldn't think of an alternative to culling, and so once again he guessed he agreed with Bill.

We pushed our chairs aside. Embracing one another for reassurance, we separated, I heading toward the door, they to Russ's computer. We must try to get through this, everyone's respectful gestures said. We've known each other since my children were little, I said to myself. We've got to get through this; we're like family. But halfway across the room Bill added a hesitant afterthought. "This will make working in Sengwa a lot easier. If there's a cull of the same size next year, the Sengwa population will be small enough so we can collar every family."

No! shouted a furious voice in me as I groped my way out of the barn, for although it was the middle of the morning, no light seemed to be entering the windows over the great doors. I let myself out the small side door onto the grassy hillside.

In brilliant sunlight the grass was green and fresh, the day was high with autumn energy, but I threw myself down and sobbed out loud in grief and rage for wasted blood, aborted lives, and desecrated holiness—pounded and kicked the ground and cried out loud.

When I made my way back into the barn my friends stood up as if from one impulse, offering to help. Russ drove me home in his car. Bill followed in mine so I would have it at home when I needed it.

As we drove across the seven miles of hills and valleys I felt

Russ glancing at me, a glance brimming with compassion, and I rejected it. *Your pity is for a person out of touch with the real world. I am grieving for the real world and I will not be consoled.* Entering my house I pulled the door shut and made my way through the two front rooms to the bedroom in back. Even before I fell onto my bed I saw the lower Sengwa floodplain. Here lay Jabula by her pool, a massive, still heap streaked and spattered with blood, and the pool was red. Here lay heaped against her other elephants of all ages; some were corpses, others were lying on their sides, raising and shifting weak legs, flopping trunks, trying to stand, falling, groaning. Here was a lunging, battering, stinking helicopter; men aiming, shooting, and shouting while around them elephants not yet crippled or killed screamed and ran in circles, charging into the dust-filled bush only to charge out again. Drawn back and back by their imperative to help; with each emergence giving fresh bellows of grief, horror, fear, and disbelief—their eyes wide and white, and temporin streaming down their cheeks as with tender trunks they freshly explored heads and bodies, reaching into ears, mouths, eye sockets, vulvas, hovering over pools of blood, dung, and urine, and awaiting their own death, as dictated by the mercy of the culling protocol . . .

I stood by helpless, and gave a great bellow of distress; emerging from my throat, it filled my bedroom with an eerie crackly woman's voice: "Mercy!"

Mercy! My bellow changed the scene, transported me to a reeking room up many flights of stairs in a distant city, late in a tired day. The smell was of sweat and old smoke, of unresolved conflict, of fatigue, labor, necessity. I stood in the room, twice my normal size. In silence I demanded mercy. Three tired, gray-faced men whom I knew but did not know turned toward me from where they sat in worn yellow leather chairs. They looked through me, for I was transparent to them. "You have come at a particularly difficult time," said one. "Don't talk. We understand your concerns. They would be our own, if we had the luxury—but good afternoon." I backed out, silently so as not to disturb them further. Archetypes, all of us, we had nothing to discuss.

I fell asleep and slept into the middle of the night, opening my eyes to find myself—with relief—at home in my bed. I closed my eyes and dreamed once more, and woke to write in my notebook:

> In the wee hours a waking hallucination: I reached into my womb (as a vet would reach into a cow's birth canal)—my sleeve rolled up—I'm both people—painlessly—& pulled out a pair of testes, healthy, egg-sized and shaped, no blood; & flung them into the scrap basket in my living room thinking "this probably isn't the best place for them: they'll soon rot." . . . The operation was matter-of-fact: I was doing something that had to be done.

I slept again.

In the morning, strangely, I woke feeling refreshed. It seemed my psyche had taken matters into its own hands during the troubled night. Sensing danger to itself, it had made a hasty adjustment. It had separated its adversarial parts, and so preserved itself until dawn.

A dreamer often has some grasp of what his or her dream did and did not mean. I believe my "testes" did not represent people, or rather, even if there were people as referents on the surface, there were more important referents deeper down where I am peopled only by myself. I believe the testes and womb represented conflicting attitudes in my own mind, one of which was, at that time, blocking the other. It was not so much my male colleagues I cast out, as a feeling of obligation to tolerate what they were tolerating.

In another era and through the mercy of another psyche, a

similar struggle was represented as a noble one in Gluck's glorious opera about the priestess Iphigenia. With the dagger raised over her appointed victim (and the shuddering audience knows, as she does not, that he is her own brother, Orestes), she pauses. A cohort of lesser priestesses rushes forward, exhorting her to do the violent deed, to complete the task the king has decreed. "Stay, Barbarians!" Iphigenia cries to the priestesses—"Respect my weakness!"

For whatever the rules are on this king's island, something in her will not tolerate the sacrifice.

Isolated by sorrow and disagreement, I stayed at home for several months, visiting the lab only when Bill and Russ had specific questions for me. They carried the bulk of our work, respecting and forgiving my absence.

On the day we received news of the cull, we had been preparing a presentation for a conference on animal behavior. The presentation was a poster entitled "Vocalizations and Movements in Free-Ranging African Elephants." Illustrated with my photographs, the poster showed the methods and preliminary results of our Zimbabwean work. There was a handsome graph showing when each of the collared elephants had made powerful calls during our three months of data collection. There was a spectrogram depicting one particularly eloquent elephant's vocalizations, which we believed were estrus calls. Sitting beside the poster, Bill would give a computer demonstration on a large video screen, showing how two elephant families had coordinated their movements with each other. A pink and an orange dot on an outline map of the Sengwa Wildlife Research Area represented the collared elephants. By poking a key one could move the elephants on the map to their next locations, three hours later. In a few exciting minutes one could get a condensed view of months of animal movements over the land, could see two elephant families making the synchronous adjustments of direction that had enabled them to browse through a large area while neither competing for the same bushes nor getting out of each other's acoustic range.

The urgently calling elephant was Jabula. The coordinating elephant herds were those of Miss Piggy and Lutya. Lutya had died in the uncollaring maneuver. Miss Piggy and Jabula had died in the cull, and their families with them. Of the animals who illustrated our ideas about elephant communication none was now alive. Dots on a screen and a set of half-tested hypotheses were all that was left of them.

During my night of dreams, Bill and Russ were driving to the conference. Two mornings after I had cast out my testes they were sitting by our poster showing colleagues how we had collected our data, discussing our findings and the extent to which they did and did not prove anything. They came home satisfied, for a number of people had been interested and some truly excited. They brought me business cards of professional friends who were sorry I had not been there.

I had spent that weekend wandering around in the swamp behind my house, looking at the signs of oncoming winter. I could see it in the sky, in the colors of the leaves, in the changing behaviors of deer and birds, squirrels, chipmunks, and honey bees. I was splitting wood and carrying it by wheelbarrow out to my thinking cabin, and building a fire in the woodstove and smelling the sweet smoke and the pine walls of the cabin, which give off a special fragrance with the first fire of winter. Sitting by the stove in the Morris chair that my father used to sit in, I was searching through books on my shelves for company, and a strange assortment of voices reached me. In particular I remember a set of poems about whales, written by young children.

A baby whale is come
Seeks through the world
And finds a home
What beautiful is born.

                    by William Lopez

The freeliness of swimming on the bottom
of the sea was nice from the inside out.

                    by Karen Marcotte

The men kill the whale
They do not waste the great whale
Except its beauty.

                    by Margaret Rakas

I enjoyed other writers, too, especially the innocent and the bitter. I enjoyed the words of the soldier-poet Wilfred Owen, as he quoted a corpse in the underworld: "You are the enemy I killed, my friend."

I sympathized with the poet Hölderlin in his lament:

Oh friend, we arrived too late. The divine energies
    Are still alive, but isolated above us, in the archtypal
        world . . .
What is living now? Night dreams of them. But craziness
    Helps, so does sleep. Grief and Night toughen us,
Until people capable of sacrifice once more rock
    In the iron cradle. . . .

You mean on the grass beds, I said, *the beds laid out on sticks in the thatched huts with clay walls. I know the people you mean.*

A little herd of deer lived near my writing cabin, habituated to my presence and I to theirs. On some days they slept close up against the building. This seemed a great honor and comfort in those days.

Weeks passed and Rowan's difficult letter did not come. I called his parks office in Harare repeatedly, and learned each time that he was away. Finally I sent a brusque note asking to hear from him. It was not that he could have said anything to make a difference. The cull had occurred. My desire for further communication was an inappropriate gesture when I couldn't have what I wanted.

The letter arrived just before Christmas. In relation to the four collared elephants who were killed in the culling operation, Rowan wrote:

> I realize that you are upset at the loss of these animals (I have received several telephone calls to that effect). All of us here regret their inclusion in the cull. However, it is not the first time this has happened—I guess we have probably killed by now more than 75% of all the animals which have ever been tagged at Sengwa—and it certainly won't be the last.

It would have been prohibitively difficult, Rowan wrote, to exclude or include any particular animals in a cull. But it was "preferable that there had been minimal selection among herds—our motives would not stand up to inspection if we demanded that certain herds should be protected preferentially above others."

The 250 elephants killed were one-third of a population that had been growing fast. There was evidence that much of the growth was due to immigration from the surrounding area. Therefore 1992 would almost certainly see another cull "to bring the population closer to 300 animals."

> The cull stemmed from our concern for habitats at Sengwa, particularly the regenerating *Acacia tortilis* woodland. We are anxious to keep densities low enough to permit the *tortilis* to form a canopy again.

On a larger scale, we now have over 70,000 elephants in Zimbabwe and it is doubtful if we can sustainably carry more than 40,000. The maximum number we can cull annually is limited by practical considerations to about 5,000. With an annual population growth rate of 5% this means that some 70,000 animals will have to be removed over the next 14 years.

Those paragraphs made up about a third of the letter. The rest were like them. I received them as if they were blows being struck in a fight. In the spirit of a sporting event, Rowan ended with very best wishes from himself, his wife, and daughter, and with an additional request for me to convey their best regards also to Bill, Lillie, Russell, Loki, Rob, and Laura.

In the early spring a letter arrived from Andrew. Carefully, respectfully, he summarized what happened to "our friends the elephants" during and after the cull. They had been driven onto the floodplains and killed by professional marksmen. A few scouts, Zaccheus and himself among them, had been sent to measure the corpses. The bodies had been cut apart, the tusks cut and pulled out, measured, weighed, and driven away for storage in a safe. The skulls had been loaded onto the big trucks and transported to a pit near the station for later study of teeth. The leg bones and ribs had been dumped in a huge pile in the mopane forest near the Sengwa North Road. The vertebrae and other bones had been hauled to ditches and gullies in many parts of the road system to help check erosion during the rains. All of this had taken more than a few days.

When later I returned to Sengwa, I learned that the smell of rotting, especially bad at nighttime, had lasted throughout the rains and for several months into the dry season. The nights had been eerie with the voices of angry hyenas and lions fighting over the skulls heaped near the compound. A year after the cull, I saw vultures and storks still squabbling and flapping on the bones of the elephants we had known.

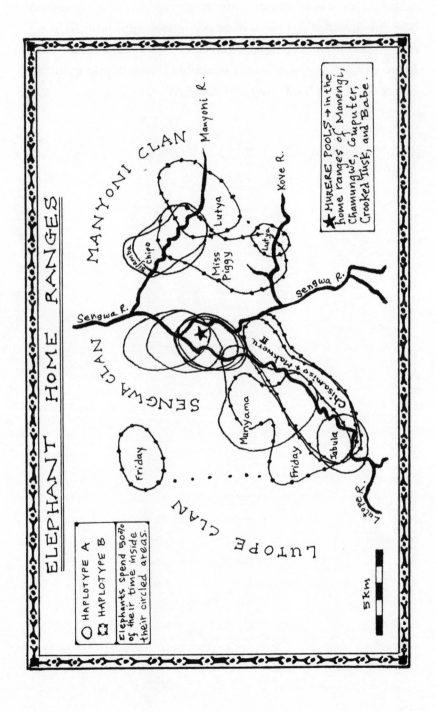

ELEPHANT HOME RANGES

MANYONI CLAN

Manyoni R.

Chipo

Chamba

Lutya

Miss Piggy

Lutya

Kove R.

Sengwa R.

Sengwa R.

SENGWA CLAN

Chisamisa + Mkwelu

Munyama

Friday

Friday

Jabula

LUTOPE CLAN

Lutope R.

★ MURERE POOLS → in the home ranges of Manengi, Chamungwe, Computer, Crooked Tusk, and Babe.

○ HAPLOTYPE A
⬡ HAPLOTYPE B

Elephants spend 50% of their time inside their circled areas.

5 km

14

PASSING BELLS

"What passing-bells for these who die as cattle?

"Only the monstrous anger of the guns."

Those words went home to England from the First World War; the soldier who wrote them did not return. You have heard at times funeral bells for somebody you never knew, and have thought to yourself that they rang for someone who, like yourself, loved the familiar ways of life. I decided to assemble the information that existed about the elephants whose lives had been cut short by the Sengwa cull. This started as a desire for them to have passing bells, and for myself to ring them in the face of the grand indifference. Perhaps it was only for my own sake that I wanted to do this, but there is value in doing things for oneself in a time of grief. It would be restorative to imagine again the acacia groves as they were when I watched my gray friends there placidly stripping and chewing bark; to walk again in the deep cool shade under the dense, formal *Trichelia* tree, trimmed to pastoral perfection by kudu, where one afternoon I suddenly became aware in the darkness of an enormous fabric, larger and heavier than a curtain, quietly waving over my shoulder, and looking up saw that it was an elephant's ear. I would visit again the pungent, delicate, small-leaved *Combretum* bushes on the Lutope and remember a day when I saw drunken elephants reeling contentedly after feeding on them. It was not loud bells that I wanted, but memories of normal tranquillity.

In time that desire took me bodily back to Sengwa. There Ian Coulson gave me a copy of the parks report he had prepared on the culled elephants. Pleased with the report, he hoped it would contribute to our understanding of the collared elephants. It contained the measurements the scouts had taken on the corpses, organized into columns, with one column for each kind of measurement and one line for each elephant. Elephants that were shot in the same group were recorded together on the same page.

Since all the elephants died prematurely and were shy and seldom seen, the cull information complemented my behavioral notes in several dimensions, and became one of the sources of my accounts. Perhaps you will be surprised, as I was, that so much was known about the animals' economic value and so little about their lives.

JABULA

On her collaring day in 1990 the helicopter lurched, swerved, and battered its way down the light gray sands of the Lutope floodplain. Elephants were sighted, a dart was shot from an air rifle held out the window, a large elephant swaggered, staggered, and fell. The helicopter landed and three men bailed out of its belly and ran as best they could across the soft sand to the elephant. One of them was Rowan, overjoyed, for he recognized one of his old collars on the animal, and she was Jabula.

Jabula and Rowan had met here in this relationship three times before. She was by now so old that she might die naturally within a few years, for she was on her last set of teeth, and when the seventh falls out it is not replaced. Rowan and his team of scouts had collared Jabula in 1980, 1982, and 1984, and had located her hundreds of times. She was "a member of the southern clan," true to a very small home range just north of the southern boundary of the research area. We had refound her in her traditional place, ten years after her first collaring. "She's a grand old matriarch," Rowan had said as he showed me the traces of her movements on his computer, during my first visit to Harare in 1986. Now as we stood beside the darted animal he said the same words again.

During the following months we located Jabula 413 times by radio tracking. Of all the elephants we studied she confined herself to the smallest range, spending nine-tenths of her time within twenty-three square kilometers. The center of her activity was a permanent muddy water hole that elephants had gouged out of clay on the Lutope floodplain, just big enough for an adult elephant to bathe in. Close by it stood some fine patches of young *Acacia tortilis,* a delicious-barked spiny tree that is a favorite food of elephants.

Most of our sightings showed Jabula in a family of about twelve, browsing and bathing. Their faithfulness to the tiny area surrounding the muddy pool suggests that it contained all they needed. But the behavior of their neighbors, Makweru II and Chisamiso, whose movements we also followed, showed that sufficiency is not the whole story. These families spent half their time in an area the size of Jabula's entire home range, and the other half in an area six times its size. What explains these elephants' different relation to the same habitat? From the genetic analyses Rob had done on the blood samples, we knew that they belonged to different matrilines. Was Jabula sharing her resources with her family and defending them from her neighbors?

Jabula was a prolific mother. The 192 mothers killed in the cull had on average three placental scars, but Jabula had seven. Only five of the slaughtered females had mothered as many calves as she. She was nursing a calf when she was collared in 1980, again in 1982, and again or still in 1984. In 1990, she had a large juvenile calf. Three weeks after her fourth collaring, Bill saw evidence that she was ready to mate again. While Debbie and he were flying an air census, he searched in Jabula's usual area for the sound of her location beacon in his earphones. He heard the beacon but saw only an aggregation of bulls on the Lutope floodplain—nineteen bulls, most of them big. Debbie flew across the dry river again with the same results, searching in the trees beyond the bulls and finding nobody. On the third pass Debbie flew low, and there in the middle of the aggregation she and Bill spotted Jabula's orange collar.

She must be in estrus, Bill said. He came home to the station and looked in the data-storing computer for any loud calls Jabula might have made while he was out flying. Sure enough, there was a long sequence of calls like the calls I'd recorded in Amboseli from Zita while she was being pursued by a crowd of young males during the early days of her estrus.

If Jabula's sequential calls did result in impregnation, she lost the calf, for the parks personnel found no fetus ten months later when they dismembered her body. She was, however, lactating again. Perhaps she was already pregnant on the day when Bill saw her surrounded by prospective mates, and gave birth shortly afterward. But if so, why was she making estrous calls? The calf she was nursing on the day of the cull would have been around one year old. There were in fact several small calves near Jabula on that day. Two were killed and five were taken captive, for what fate I do not know.

Jabula seems to have been a prolific homebody in a small,

sufficient place. On the day she and her family were killed, September 4, 1991, they appeared to have been in the middle of another reproductive event. A short distance from their pool, in a gully called the Kamashaboya River, thirteen individuals including Jabula were killed together. Five were adult females—four nursing mothers and one pregnant. Two other elephant groups, each containing seven individuals, were slaughtered at the pool, and one of these groups contained only young males. The other contained, in addition to several females, a huge attendant male—the second largest animal in the cull. Probably the females at the pool were members of Jabula's bond group and one of them was in estrus, guarded by the very large bull, while the cohort of wishfully thinking young males waited in the wings.

One out of the fifteen pages of the parks report was devoted to the thirty-two animals culled and captured from Jabula's home range. There were four measurements on each dead animal's body, seven on its tusks, two on each unborn fetus or baby, three on each live-captured baby, and two expressions of each animal's dollar value. Each page concluded with a financial summary. The body measurements were converted to a standard, the "adult equivalent," to which the size of each elephant body was compared for purposes of estimating its value. I assume that the dollars referred to were Zimbabwean, about half the value of American dollars at the time. The value of the ivory is based on weight in kilograms.

The summary for Jabula's extended family was as follows:

adult equivalents shot:	20.911 @ $1,330 = $27,812
adult equivalents caught	0.587 @ $1,330 = $781
total adult equivalents	21.498 @ $1,330 = $28,592
total ivory	146.088 @ $200 = $29,218

One-seventh of the ivory came from the huge bull who had made the mistake of courting a female in Jabula's bond group.

FRIDAY THE THIRTEENTH

Friday the Thirteenth was named by Rowan and Laura for the day of her collaring and her collar number.

She was the smallest elephant we collared and all the animals with whom she was killed were small: only one female approached the size of an average adult female. We know very little about Friday. We sighted her only four times after the collaring, and each time her group was of a different size and composition, so that I imagine her as an animal like Flavia in Amboseli, who had no family. We never saw her among enough others to suspect the presence of a bond group. Between her movement patterns and those of any other collared group we found no evidence of coordination.

Like Makweru II and Chisamiso, Friday had a very large home range. She moved from spring to spring along the walls of the western escarpment called Samapakwa, a precipitous area much frequented by rhinos, and in the Kamashaboya gully and along the dry middle Lutope floodplain where browsing was good but water was scarce.

The youth and instability of Friday's herd, her apparent lack of core or extended family, and her wide wanderings lead me to fancy that these animals might be survivors of an earlier cull, and that what we were recording of their movements might reflect the diminished status of a fragmented herd, a shifting group of leaderless, displaced animals. While this is speculative, it reminds me not to present the Sengwa elephants as an undisturbed elephant population. The population had, in fact, been culled every couple of years from 1978 on. Tattered elephant populations are not abnormal these days. They are like remnants of human populations in warring areas; what is remarkable is the semblance of order that the survivors superimpose on the wreckage of their former communities.

On the day of the cull, Friday was lactating and pregnant, carrying a male fetus weighing 54 kilograms (about 120 pounds). If my guess about the status of her family is correct, I would have wished for her rather a daughter, had she lived, to keep her company during her years of reconstruction.

Ian summed up the economic value of Friday's family as follows:

adult equivalents shot	5.709 @ \$1,330 = \$7,593
adult equivalents caught	0.174 @ \$1,330 = \$231
total adult equivalents	5.883 @ \$1,330 = \$7,824
total ivory	35.68 @ \$200 = \$7,136

MUNYAMA

We wanted to know about the elephants' relatedness for a number of reasons. If close relationships exist among groups, will they be the same groups who coordinate their movements with each other, remaining in hearing distance for the benefit of kin who might need help, yet sharing the resources they visit in such a way that they don't use them up? How will relatedness be reflected in the locations and sharing of home ranges? And will animals in bond groups, as revealed by their loud greeting calls, turn out to be closer relatives with each other than with elephant families they do not greet?

Genetic analyses of tissue samples are fraught with ambiguities. But such conclusions as Rob was able to draw suggest a link between relatedness and home range behavior. The most interesting elephant in this part of the study was Munyama.

Munyama's home range behavior was similar to Friday's: both families, separately, moved extensively in the west, visiting the scattered Samapakwa springs. Just to the north of Munyama's and Friday's home ranges lived six other collared elephant families who might easily have reached the Sama-pakwa springs but did not visit them during the months of our tracking project. These were the elephants who lived near the Murere Pools, the large and abundant pools in an old oxbow left behind by the Sengwa River when it changed its course years ago. The Murere Pools (except the one that is full of croc-odiles) are the most popular elephant waters in central Sengwa, as I discovered when I later spent part of a field season quanti-fying elephants' presence at all sources of water visible from the top of Ntaba Mangwe.

The Sengwa-Murere elephants had small home ranges, cen-tering and extensively overlapping on the pools. Somewhat dis-tant from these animals, Jabula also had a small home range centering on a different pool. Two other distant elephants had small ranges centering on a small watery area in the Manyoni floodplain: these were Sijamba and Chipo. All the rest of the collared elephants had large home ranges with more than one center. Seeing on the map how the different home ranges are distributed, you might form the opinion that the smallest ones center on places where both food and water are abundant, while the larger ones reflect the necessity of traveling in order to find everything one needs. Then you begin to wonder whether the frequenters of the best resources "own" them and defend them from the others. During my later survey of water use, I did see a little evidence of this kind of defense and exclusion.

Now it becomes interesting to look at the genetic data. Rob did two tests on the blood samples he collected. One was a test for relatedness as passed down maternally and revealed by sim-ilarities in the elephants' mitochondrial DNA. The other is re-latedness on the whole, both maternal and paternal, as revealed by similarities in the elephants' nuclear DNA.

On the basis of the mitochondrial DNA, Rob divided all the collared elephants into two genetic groups, which were mutually exclusive although females in the same group were not necessarily closely related to each other. Group A turned out to include all the elephants who had small home ranges with single centers on local water sources. Group B included all the animals with large, many-centered home ranges, which were distributed in various parts of the research area but did not include the principal floodplain pools. Two or three clans contained families from both genetic groups.

I surmised that the closely related A female elephants who shared the smallest and, by my standards, best home ranges, were to some extent excluding others from "their" property, leaving the Bs to follow a different strategy that involved opportunistic foraging instead of territorial defense. The Bs were the animals whose far-flung movements required coordination if the animals were not to lose touch with each other. Miss Piggy and Lutya, both B animals, had provided our most interesting examples of prolonged coordination.

There was one exception: Munyama. Like a B animal, she had a large, several-centered home range, and it overlapped extensively with those of Friday, Makweru II, and Chisamiso: all B-group animals. It was puzzling that her mitochondrial DNA declared her a member of the A group.

In Rob's second set of tests, the nuclear DNA tests, relatedness was expressed not in terms of groupings but in a gradation that included the members of all possible pairs. For a standard Rob had used a set of samples from pairs of elephants sure to be closely related—mothers and calves.

So much variability showed up in these samples that he felt confident labeling only five pairs of collared elephants as significantly closely related to each other. Three of these pairs were from animals in the same mitochondrial groups, and were individuals we had repeatedly seen together as members of the same families or bond group. But the other two pairs came, surprisingly, from animals of different families belonging to different matrilines. Munyama was a member of both of these pairs. She turned out to be closely related to both Makweru II and Chisamiso—B animals. Her mitochondrial DNA showed her to be unrelated to group B through her mother, but her nuclear DNA showed a B-relatedness after all—through her father, for nuclear DNA tells about maternal and paternal inheritance, while mitochondrial DNA tells only about matrilines.

You can't draw a valid conclusion from a sample of one, so I offer the story of Munyama simply as a teaser. She seems to offer a special case, a female who shows home range behavior like that of a father from a different matriline. What she was doing would not have been learned from her father, since bulls live mostly separately from females in bull areas, nor from the mother, whose home range behavior was different. Did the elephants near her, through some inherited sensibility, recognize her as kin? There was only one Munyama and she is dead now, but her home range behavior was quite interesting because it posed that question.

I was a member of the foot crew on the very hot day that Munyama was collared. The amount of time that passes before the tranquilizing drug takes effect varies from animal to animal. After being darted, Munyama ran for a long time through a thorny thicket up a rather steep hill. The foot crew, including myself, burdened with heavy knapsacks in increasing heat, ran after her, but slowly. Eventually we found her, fully drugged and looking sick, with closed eyes, sitting up on her breastbones, or "brisket." As tranquilized animals have sometimes suffocated in this position, we—roughly a dozen people—hastened to push her over onto her side. She fell heavily, and in the fall her left tusk broke off, about half a meter below the tip.

The scouts stood over her solemnly, their faces and voices sad with the same sadness they later extended to me on the

night when the tree hit my head. "Ah," they exclaimed all together, and "ah," and "mm," and "uh!" and "arrhh!" to themselves over and again as they stood near the unfortunate animal,
and throughout the rest of the day as they remembered. They
named her Munyama, or Bad Luck.

On the day we collared Munyama, the plane circling overhead spotted ten other elephants with her. We saw her several
times later, in groups of twelve or thirteen. She was a large,
healthy lactating female with a small calf. She had four placental scars. On the day of the cull, her group included fifteen animals. Eleven of them including Munyama were shot. Four
calves were captured alive.

The value of Munyama's family to the Parks department
was summarized in Ian's report as follows:

adult equivalents shot	9.063 @ $1,330 = $12,054
adult equivalents caught	0.580 @ $1,330 = $771
total adult equivalents	9.641 @ $1,330 = $12,823
total ivory	56.217 @ $200 = $11,243

MISS PIGGY

Rowan gave Miss Piggy her name. He was charmed by her
pretty, symmetrically broken outsplayed stubs of tusks, and by
her long eyelashes.

She was one of several collared elephants whom we sighted
a number of times, finding them equally likely to be in small or
in large groups. In its small configuration Miss Piggy's family
group always included at least eleven animals; in its large configuration twenty-three.

One of my happiest memories is of a long, quiet August afternoon I spent with Andrew, watching Miss Piggy and her family graze in a grassy meadow on the Manyoni floodplain. We sat

comfortably on the riverbank in the deep shade of a huge tree, leaning against its trunk, far enough from the elephants so we could whisper without bothering them, but near enough to see what they were doing. There was a gentle breeze, we were downwind of them and they weren't aware of our presence. I set up a video camera and let it run on its own. It made a record of a long, placid, undisturbed afternoon.

We had decided to find Miss Piggy that afternoon because our tracking data were showing an interesting relation between her herd and Lutya's. For more than a week the two families had been making long excursions back and forth between the Kove and the Manyoni rivers, excursions that required them to cross a rugged waterless bushy ridge called Ncherera. They were moving more or less simultaneously but not together, separated by a kilometer or more, and seldom meeting at either end of their excursions. We imagined they were keeping track of each other's locations by listening, and I hoped to learn something about this by accompanying Miss Piggy for a day.

But nothing happened to suggest that her family was attending to anything beyond the enclosed meadow where we found them. We lay languidly against our trees, watching until the sun went down, and then, still unperceived by the elephants, slipped away.

The records of the two families' movements are wonderful to watch on a computer screen, where one can advance time and see the elephants making simultaneous changes in direction, and other apparent adjustments to each other's whims over distances of one, two, sometimes three kilometers. There were such large distances between Miss Piggy and Lutya during this period that neither family could have been receiving a direct benefit from their proximity. The indirect benefits probably included undisturbed access to food or water, and the knowledge that relatives were close by in case a need for group support should arise. The adjustments the elephants were making reminded me of how human friends and relations go out of their way to be available to each other.

Although we had intended to collar the largest elephant in each of our subject families, Miss Piggy was the smallest of the four adult females in her group. The parks document recorded no placental scars, which is surprising considering that she had a nursing calf. On the day of her death two young calves from her group were captured and then shot—one at the cull site and one at the station. The rest were shot directly. Three of the adult females were pregnant; among them was Miss Piggy. She was carrying a male fetus weighing 1.5 kilograms.

The parks report evaluated Miss Piggy's family as follows:

total animals shot	13
total calves caught	0
total adult equivalents	9.455 @ $1,330 = $12,575
total ivory	56.963 @ $200 = $11,393

RUNYANGA

Runyanga, like Nyanga, is Shona for crooked; among themselves the scouts called the real Crooked Tusk by this name. I did not know at first that she was among the elephants destroyed in the cull. She was not on Rowan's list, since we had no scientific investment in her, but in Andrew's letter I read: "and our old friend the real Crooked Tusk." In some ways this was the hardest loss to bear. I considered her a great elephant, an opinion based partly on her appearance, partly on her behavior, partly on the way her companions seemed to regard her leadership, and partly on pure fantasy.

My information about her life up until the day of her death comes from direct observations—of which there were many, for the people who had encountered her had stories, many quite dramatic. She'd chased people on foot countless times; she chased us, too, one day when she was foraging under Ntaba Mangwe. Russ, Laura, and I had spent an afternoon watching her and her family (most of the adults had strangely oriented and asymmetrical tusks) from the heights. As we prepared to descend, Laura said, "Wonder if she's going to ambush us." Just as we reached level ground below the mesa, out she came all alone, trumpeting with her trunk stretched out in front, ears and eyes wide, feet thundering toward our truck. Laura, at the wheel of the pickup truck (I was in the open back), said, "Let's see how fast she's running": 20 kilometers per hour, over a dirt road on which we could go no faster. After a quarter kilometer she wheeled around and disappeared into the forest she'd come from. "She was hell-bent on scaring us," said Laura afterward. She succeeded.

It was easy to identify this Crooked Tusk, with that wild heaven-pointing tusk, her immense size, and thirty-seven family members. But as she was never collared we have only visual sightings as evidence of her home range. These, such as they are, do not support my conjecture that dominant families have small home ranges. We saw her on the south side of Ntaba Mangwe, on the east side in Chipo II and Sijamba's domain; on the west side in the thickets where she, Friday, and Munyama were culled; and Rowan reported having found her far to the north, outside of Sengwa altogether, on the back side of Samapakwa. "She has two home ranges," he said. Who knows to whom she was related? Nothing about her fits anybody else's pattern, and her blood, although spilled, was not collected for analysis.

The real Crooked Tusk's experience must have been different from that of a small leaderless animal like Friday, and different from that of a mother with a tiny home range like Jabula.

She was impressive to her followers. Thirty-seven and some-times more elephants waited for her every decision. She carried the burden and the status of matriarch and, I suspect, a con-comitant accumulated experience. Presumably this had some-thing to do with her unique opinion of people, which she acted out, convincingly but without harm, over and over again.

She was huge and old and without a young calf. She carried more ivory than all but one other female killed in the cull. There is a saying among Shona women that shows sympathy with elephants, who have to hold their heads up through the day. "Aren't you tired," one woman says to another, "carrying such a heavy child and such heavy breasts?" The other re-sponds, *"Nzou haire merwi nenyanga dzayo"*–The elephant does not find her tusks heavy.

When I returned to Sengwa after the cull, the first person I met was the scout named Timothy Chifamba Dube, a serious, sensitive young man whose observations and insights had been particularly astute during a few days when he had helped me observe elephants on Ntaba Mangwe. Timothy wanted at once to speak of the cull. While telling me about it he lowered his eyes. Remembering that Timothy's wife had been badly injured by a buffalo that had gotten into the compound, I said, "But at least it must be a relief for you to know that the real Crooked Tusk is gone."

"Oh no," said Timothy. "No. No. Crooked Tusk was won-derful. We liked her. We are not at all glad that she is gone, no, not at all. No–we are sorry. She was a great elephant." He looked up at me then and our eyes met, and his had a pained expression, as if to ask what sort of person I was, after all.

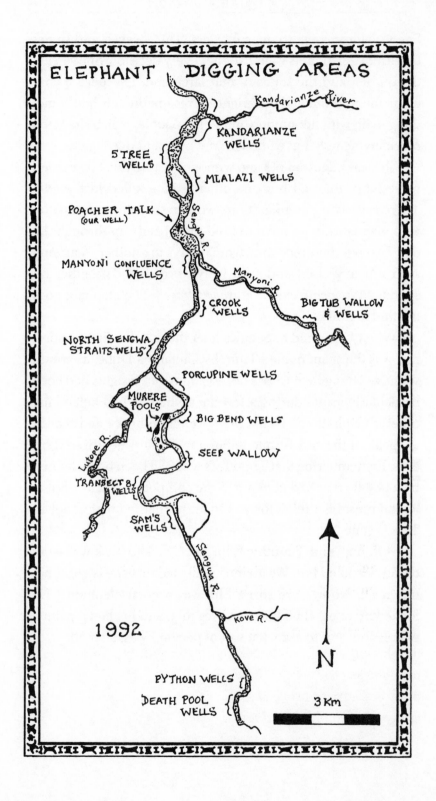

ELEPHANT DIGGING AREAS

Kandarianze River

KANDARIANZE WELLS

5 TREE WELLS

MIALAZI WELLS

POACHER TALK (OUR WELL)

Sengwa R.

MANYONI CONFLUENCE WELLS

Manyoni R.

CROOK WELLS

BIG TUB WALLOW & WELLS

NORTH SENGWA STRAITS WELLS

PORCUPINE WELLS

MURERE POOLS

BIG BEND WELLS

Lutope R.

SEEP WALLOW

TRANSECT 8 WELLS

SAM'S WELLS

Sengwa R.

1992

Kove R.

N

PYTHON WELLS

DEATH POOL WELLS

3 Km

15

DELVING AND
DIGGING

What sort of person was I, after all? I no sooner
record the question as a thought of Timothy's than I recognize it
as one of my own questions that had brought me back to Sengwa.

It was not a conscious, but an organic, question. Uncon-
sciously, I knew that I was not well because Sengwa wasn't well.
We were of one blood and some of it had been spilled. Sengwa
had moaned for me when I was injured: now it was Sengwa
who was injured. I'd better get back.

It is strange to be driven by unconscious motivation. All
your conscious behavior slips into conformity with something
you cannot exactly explain to yourself or others. To justify a return to Sengwa I needed a new scientific project, but what
mattered to me most about this project was the quality of relationships it would engender. It must not disturb the animals; it
must respect the people. Few projects are designed with these
priorities uppermost: I found my search narrowed to a descriptive natural-history project, which I'd have to support by

spending my savings. Okay, I said to myself, this is the experience that I am having. One day in a Quaker meeting I heard a young man say, "Maybe if I let go of the complicated parts, simplicity will grow." In the wake of the cull, I was like him. All I wanted was for simplicity to grow.

I searched my mind, and found a memory. I was on Ntaba Mangwe with Andrew on a late afternoon toward the end of our stay in Sengwa. The sun was sinking over Samapakwa and everything that still received its rays was beginning to glow orange. For more than an hour nothing moved except sun, shadow, and color, although Andrew and I, sitting side by side with our elbows anchored on our knees, were watching living animals. Our binoculars were focused on a motionless congregation of elephants about three kilometers to our north. Thirty elephants were standing as if rooted in the sand. What an unlikely place to rest, I thought. The sun's reflection is making of the place a broiling pan, it's four months since the river's last flowing, and the sand offers nothing to eat or drink. I strained my eyes for details, but each elephant was only a small dark spot made blurry by heat waves. What I was sure of was that they weren't moving in relation to each other. Gradually I recalled other afternoons when I'd had the same impression of elephants on this and other patches of sand. Finally it occurred to me to ask Andrew if he knew what was going on.

"Oh, yes," said Andrew. "Would you like me to show you?" An hour later we arrived at the spot. The elephants had departed, so we walked directly to the grassy bank and peered over . . .

Beneath us, in an area twenty or thirty meters wide running half a kilometer down the river, lay several hundred empty cylindrical holes, ten to twenty centimeters in diameter, the smallest only slightly larger than the tip of an adult elephant's trunk. Around and among and between them was a great deal of elephant dung, some dry and shredded, some fresh, and many large, middle-sized, and small elephant footprints. Facing each hole were four very deep cylindrical prints: a large elephant had stood there for a long time, slowly sinking down. Some of the holes slumped into themselves and were half filled with sand. Others were crisp-edged with fresh dribbles on the adjacent sand, reminding me of the "dribble castles" that children make on the seashore. We could see straight down into one hole close to the bank: I guessed it was half a meter deep. I climbed down and, lying beside it, reached my arm in to the shoulder. I could barely touch the bottom, where I felt damp sand covered with a very thin layer—half a centimeter—of coolish water.

Years earlier I'd seen six holes like these in the upper reaches of the dry Hoaruseb River in the Damaraland desert in Namibia. Fed by rains in the mountains far inland, that river flows above the sand only a few days of the year, and even then it doesn't always reach the sea. Under the surface, however, it flows, as you can tell because all the vegetation that the local elephants and rhinos eat grows in these riverbeds, and, for the animals that know how to find it, there is plenty. Garth Owen-Smith, our guide in Damaraland, told us that the holes in the river were wells dug by elephants. No animal except an elephant can replace them when they collapse, but several species depend on them.

Five years earlier Garth had observed the disappearance of all elephants from the Hoaruseb; the wells and the dependent animals had also disappeared. But shortly before our visit he'd been surprised to encounter an elephant family in the same old place. "They walked down to that spot, dug a well, drank, and left." By the time we saw them, this well was surrounded by others, and by the tracks of birds and small animals.

Was it through memory or some trick of perception that the

elephants had twice found the shallow water table under the upper Hoaruseb? In either case I admired their ability. After ten
days the desert had so desiccated me that although I longed for
water, I was never able to quench my thirst. If I could have
shrunk myself to the size of a meercat, I would have crawled
down into an elephant well and stayed there.

But what were two hundred elephant wells doing in Sengwa, within two kilometers of a large complex of open pools?

There was my project. Volumes had been written on what
elephants eat but nothing on what they drink; volumes on what
they destroy but nothing on what they build. Now the project
left the domain of the unconscious and became an intellectual
challenge. I sent a letter to the Department of National Parks
and Wildlife Management in Zimbabwe proposing

> . . . to learn when, where, and under what circumstances
> elephants in the Sengwa Research Area in Zimbabwe dig
> temporary wells, how they choose well sites, which
> elephants do and do not dig and (or) use the wells, whether
> well sharing is a function of relatedness, and how and to
> what extent these things change as the dry season
> progresses.
>
> Observations from the top of a high mesa which
> overlooks three traditional elephant well digging areas will
> enable us to compare the elephants' use of surface and
> underground water at various points in the season. With the
> hypothesis that elephants dig when available surface water
> becomes scarce or contaminated or both, we will
> periodically measure the depth and collect samples of water
> in open pools near the digging sites, later testing these at
> Cornell for mineral and organic content. With the
> hypothesis that elephants choose sites where the water table
> is closest to the surface, we will periodically measure the

depth of the water table under the river sand in a set of areas
where elephants do and do not drink. We will monitor
animal tracks at well areas. We will record sightings of
known individual elephants in order to correlate digging
and sharing of wells with genetic or social relationship and
home range as determined in our 1990 study. When
possible, we will video film elephants digging wells.

It was a happy day for me when permission arrived in the
mail, and to double my happiness, my son Sam and his friend
Matt Irinaga offered themselves as my coresearchers. They
were seasoned field-workers. They had spent the spring together on the Arctic ice shelf in Barrow, Alaska, participating in
a census of bowhead whales. From the freezer they would fly
directly into the oven of central Africa. We would be joined
midseason by Lysa Leland, an old family friend who had recently been studying monkeys in Uganda. For one week, Lisa
Naughton, a visiting wildlife conservation student from Florida,
would give us the benefit of her keen mind. Ian Coulson had
written me that one or two Sengwa scouts would also be available to help intermittently. There was no room in the field station, but how would we feel about making a camp on top of
Ntaba Mangwe?

It was twilight on June 24, 1992, when Sam, Matt, and I
rumbled down the road near the compound in our dusty, battered old Land Cruiser. Friends were out walking on the road.
As we gathered to talk, I was so overwhelmed with feeling that
I retained little of what I heard. I think I was like a female elephant greeting members of her bond group after a long separation. In the very moment of joy I had to discharge a burden of
fear, as if I had been thinking when we were apart that I might
never enjoy the company of my endangered friends again.

I quickly recovered from this state of mind, for the truth was all around me. The people were resilient. They had survived the drought, although they had lost cattle, goats, and maize. The death of Sibanda's wife, the cull, the poaching, the suicide, and further hardships had torn the fabric of individual hopes but drawn the community closer. "And you," said one woman, "we heard you were in the hospital after they told you about the elephants." The losses had not been as extraordinary as I had imagined. I learned a new proverb—*Usiku umwe hahodzi nyemba*—"a single night does not rot the cow peas." And now that you are here, my friends said, we shall have happy times again. It was to their liking that I had returned with family.

A visitors' cottage was, after all, available for us at the station, and Ian assured us of whatever help the institute could give; Ntaba Mangwe would remain our central workplace. Ian and his wife, Smolly, were happy in the birth of their second child, a son. Everyone was in Sengwa, and each greeting with old friends was emotional. "I have lost cattle," said Zaccheus, "but God spared me the family." Without rancor toward the elephant that had killed his wife, Sibanda told us about the circumstances—she was harvesting pumpkins, and so was the elephant. Sibanda's relations with the ancestral spirits had healed in the aftermath of the ceremonies with which my gifts had helped him, and so had his heart. He had gotten a new wife, who took care of his farm and children and whom he loved very much.

At the workshop, seven strong men helped us lift and lash a gigantic barrel onto the flatbed truck. The old Lister generator pumped subterranean Sengwa River water up to the overhead tanks, which released the water into a hose that ran into our barrel. By midafternoon, the barrel was half full. Then, slowly, Zaccheus drove the truck up the steep track to the top of Ntaba Mangwe. Following behind, Sam, Matt, and I admired an ancient baobab. Its fat, fleshy trunk was scarred at many heights

by the tusks of elephants: its sap had quenched the thirst of generations. As we passed through the mopane grove whose fallen
branches would supply our firewood, I tried to explain about
this wood, in which a single large branch or trunk acts like a fur-
nace full of fuel that you never have to stoke. Matt, who was
making his home in Alaska, listened without believing. We
mounted the escarpment, rounded the last bend, and there was
the view that can never be described . . .

Within a few days, we started our survey of the Sengwa
floodplain from the western outlooks on Ntaba Mangwe. We
would compare the amount of time elephants were spending at
wells and at open pools. Our 1990 radio tracking had shown
that the home ranges of several elephant families (members of
the Sengwa clan) were visible from Ntaba Mangwe; the Murere
Pools, in the center of our view, were common property to them
all. All those families had survived the cull, and from Rowan's
old tracking project we knew that elephants' home ranges are
stable over more than two years.

It's strangely difficult to count animals at midday from a
high platform. The landscape seems still, empty, and bleached:
you have to discipline yourself to recognize tiny movements as
evidence of life. You have to search equally in equal-sized areas,
realizing that a scope's width at two kilometers deserves as
much attention as a close view that requires you to sweep your
binoculars in and out and from one side to the other.

Toward midafternoon it becomes easier; as color comes into
the broad sand valley, you see that it is cutting through hills and
lumps and sandstone-walled mesas and escarpments, which are
flanked by darker forest. The cliff walls change from pale red to
purple as the view recedes, and from purple to the ineffable
gray-blue that distance imparts to all things. The dry mopane
leaves, tan to olive green at midday, become blue and brown.
Against this changing mosaic we learned to identify the colors

and shapes of warthogs, baboons, impalas, buffalo, kudu, reedbuck, waterbuck, elephants, leopards, lions, hyenas, jackals, porcupines, cranes, herons, and more. As the season heated up we spent increasing amounts of time looking at mirages as well—sometimes distant vleis took on the appearance of a vast still ocean, and one day I saw whales . . .

Buffalo appeared at a distance as dense, dark, equal-sized spots moving in herds containing hundreds. Distant elephant herds contained animals of many sizes. Buffalo drank at any time of day, but the elephants, as in Amboseli and Etosha, moved toward water in the afternoon. Closer in we counted impalas and baboons, and wondered why the two species so often moved together. Impala fawns are occasionally eaten by baboons, but baboons climb trees and give alarms: perhaps we were seeing some kind of imperfect mutualism, like that between human nations that sell arms to each other.

After ten days we descended to the floodplain to examine the wells and pools the elephants had been using. Large and shallow, the pools lay in the grooves left by old meander bends or oxbows of the river. These lazy loops bore witness to a time when the river had flowed less urgently than in recent years. They had contained the river's main channel until it broke through, digging deeper shortcut channels. Even the main channel changed from year to year, as Sam found when he created an accurate map of the floodplain.

In the dry season everything from cranes to crocs lived in the oxbow pools or made frequent visits to them. The Murere Pools lay in the groove left by a once western oxbow within two kilometers of our outlook on Ntaba Mangwe. Southward from Murere lay another set of pools in the groove left by a once eastern oxbow. Sam named this place the Seep-Wallow.

There were also sources of water that we couldn't see from Ntaba Mangwe: had we studied other elephant herds, it would have been important to monitor these as well. They were the springs under the escarpment called Samapakwa, and sections of the Sengwa River where water flowed in a thin, warm, clear layer above the surface sand. It was my impression that only one area of river flow was much used by elephants. This was a place near the mouth of the Kove where we saw seven elephant bulls nearly every day. That water was less salty than the water in the Sengwa, if piles of crystallized salt beside the flow is a fair indication. Were the bulls monopolizing the fresh water that was easiest to get?

Come close! Afternoon sun is shining down on the wide bend of the Sengwa called Mlalazi. We'll climb this anthill on the west side, and a steady breeze will keep us downwind of the diggers. Inattentive when their trunks are in wells, they probably won't notice us at all if we're quiet. Six large elephants—a still life. Minutes go by and nobody moves except one small calf who wanders among the rooted adults. One trunk comes free, slowly lifts, loops up, delivers a small amount of water to the mouth, flops down, shaking out sand from side to side, and inserts itself into the hole again. We've timed the rate of trunk lifting—this and everything else about well drinking is slow. Sam, Andrew, and Matt have rigged up a well-pump to establish the rate at which emptied wells refill. In one minute an elephant could get a hundred times as much from an open pool as it gets from a well. What's in these wells? Brandy?

Early and late in the season, we walked the twenty kilometers of the Sengwa floodplain inside the boundaries of the research area with a team of volunteer scouts, locating and describing all the elephant wells and well areas. The river twice changed character within this range. From a gorge a few meters wide it became a floodplain half a kilometer wide, only to shrink down again as it passed through a narrows at the northern boundary.

In wide areas we spread out and walked parallel, each person collecting data in a predefined strip. We counted every well and set of animal tracks in each kilometer-long section, and noted which tracks went into the wells. We photographed and noted the condition in which different animal species left the wells. Andrew carried a topographic map, which he scrutinized as we walked; at one-kilometer intervals he called us together to consolidate our data.

By the end of the third day we'd covered the twenty kilometers and found fourteen separate well clusters, occupying together less than 1 percent of the surface of the floodplain. The smallest cluster included only six active wells, the largest two hundred. Most clusters were close to the entrances of tributaries and/or were on the outer edges of broad curves, where fast-flowing water had scoured the bottom of the channel during the last flood, lowering it. But as there were also two mid-channel well clusters, we realized that in their search for the water table, elephants do not confine themselves to edges.

The depths of wells varied from very shallow to as deep as an adult elephant's trunk can reach and still make a cup at the bottom—1.10 meters. Within each cluster of wells we also found pits, apparently abandoned digging efforts, but between well areas there were stretches of sand half a kilometer wide and a kilometer or more long, with no pits. On what evidence had the elephants decided not to dig in those areas? Sam, Matt, and Andrew dug pits in seven unexploited areas and found the water table always deeper than the length of a trunk. How had the elephants known?

Zaccheus, who had known Sengwa for twenty-seven years, told us that in every dry season the areas of the floodplain near the large confluences were pockmarked with elephant wells. Our surveys told a more detailed story: the preferred wells and well areas changed from early to late in the season, following changes in the water table. To my surprise, this rose in some places as the season progressed, even though no rain had fallen. An ecologist explained to me that this occurs when deciduous trees (especially mopane, in Sengwa) drop their leaves; less subterranean water is then lost to transpiration. There must be a deep aquafer as well, replenishing some of the water that has been lost. To study elephants properly, one should know about all these things.

Were the locations of well sites traditional, with younger elephants learning from older? Were they selected logically, by going to confluences? Or the result of daily visits within the season, to the areas where standing water had lasted the longest as the river went dry? Each explanation seemed reasonable, but one day I saw a herd of elephants initiate a new well area that was neither traditional nor damp on the surface. An old female stepped off the bank of the floodplain, took a couple of steps, and started shoveling sand with her front feet. Pretty soon she was scooping out the core of a well with her trunk, and half an hour later she'd started the delicate business of lifting sand out of the final vertical tube. By this time three others were also working. An hour into the job, all the diggers struck water at forty centimeters.

I don't know how they'd assessed the depth of the water table. Bernie Hutchins, a Cornell engineer who has helped us a lot with the elephant study, suggested that elephants' low-frequency acoustic sensitivity might enable them to use a sonar system based on echoes from their footfalls. But on the day the new well area was opened, I saw no evidence that the elephants were doing anything but digging.

Among several hundred wells, a few that had clay bottoms always contained a small amount of standing water: these tended to be large-mouthed and hollowed out under the surface. During our clifftop surveys we saw competition for them among elephants, and among baboons, and concluded that for these species, water-holding wells are a coveted resource.

Late in the season, when things were exceedingly hot and dry, we also saw what may have been competition at the oxbow pools. Not that the Murere water gave out, but greater numbers of elephants wanted to use it more of the time, and they started arriving earlier in the day. We'd see three or four families waiting in the nearby forest—one day they waited in a line—while others were drinking and bathing. I guessed these were all families in the "A" genetic group, and their patience with each other was an aspect of clan behavior, but other explanations are also possible.

In most of the well areas, the wells were deep and ephemeral. Digging was very slow, and so was drinking, and there was no sign of competition. I was especially interested in the behaviors in these places, where mother elephants took their time creating wells, and trained their infants (with a kick, a shove, or a trunk hug) to be patient around the fragile resource. I sat one afternoon watching a matriarch with a tiny bull calf who insisted on noodling his trunk next to his mother's, breaking down the walls of the well she was trying to dig. She kicked him a couple of times, but he wouldn't be discouraged. Then she drew him aside to an empty spot about ten meters from the well and scuffed open a deep, wide, cool, damp wallow. She pushed him into the wallow and scooped damp sand over him until he was engaged in the wallow as his own playful project. Then she withdrew to her well and finished it, free of distraction.

I once heard about an area with wells too deep for calves, where adult female elephants were seen drawing up water in their trunks and pouring it into their youngsters' mouths. On several occasions I myself saw mothers and calves together on their knees drinking from deep wells.

Buffalo and every species of antelope ruined elephants'

wells without apparent concern, but a few species of smaller mammals seemed to appreciate certain wells and maintain them as a future resource. These wells survived the visits of hyenas and jackals, wildcats, leopards, lions, civets, servals, and porcupines. I once saw a porcupine back out of a broad, slanted well, combing the inner walls of the well and the ground with its quills. On another day when I was looking down on the Manyoni floodplain from a height, I noticed a dark rope lashing back and forth out of a cavernous elephant well. After about two minutes, a leopard carefully backed out of the well, keeping its head well down. I'd been watching the tail, sweeping back and forth as the forward end drank.

Warthogs destroyed the wells of elephants and dug their own in places where the water table was very shallow. Their well areas were messy, peppered with hoof prints and evidence of wallowing as well as drinking. We couldn't quantify the elephants' work in the areas they shared with warthogs.

Baboons dug their own wells, sturdy and reusable, at the edge of the riverbank in places where clay was mixed with sand: elephants may have been the original dowsers. Baboons also made extensive use of the wells that elephants had dug in dry sand, and here is the remarkable thing: not only did they avoid destroying the wells, but they regularly maintained them. They patted the walls with their hands as children do with their sand castles, pressing the grains of damp sand together and making the walls firmer. When you came to a well area where baboons had drunk, its elephant origins were manifest in the dung spread all through it, but every well was hand packed, and little delicate prints of baboon hands and feet were all around. The wells visited by baboons thus became a collaborative effort of elephants and baboons.

A myriad fluttering butterflies and other insects also made use of the elephants' wells. The story grew more and more complex, yet as we took the time to enjoy it I felt increasingly peaceful, as if simplicity was growing.

One day I asked Andrew about the Shamwe people who had lived in Sengwa until it was declared a reserve. Had the move to the adjacent communal lands displaced them from their spiritual as well as their physical roots? Andrew said, "I think the lion named Matakenya moved with the people. I will take you to meet Siamanja, the Shamwe head man, and we will ask him."

Visiting anybody with Andrew was the deepest pleasure you can imagine. Kind attentions spread in all directions from where he stood and suffused every gathering of which he was a part, so he was a favorite friend of many people. Children knew him as a child, young adults knew him as a young adult, foolish people knew him as a playmate, and wise people knew him as a philosopher. He seemed to be all ages at once, a creative and respectful equal of each person he met.

We left our vehicle by a narrowing path not far outside the reserve and walked between bushes to a circle of cylindrical clay huts with thatched roofs, each one about four meters in diameter, shaded by tall trees. Around and between them the ground was swept clean. Several small orange and black chickens were clucking and pecking at insects on the ground between the huts. Two little girls and a slightly older boy of perhaps five were playing with a sleek long-legged puppy.

Andrew stood outside the circle, which, although unwalled, was the family's living room, and there being no door to knock on, clapped his hands together. The boy jumped up and ran to us. Quietly Andrew greeted him in Shona, "Good afternoon; how are you?"

"I am well if you are well," replied the boy.

"I am well, so we are well," said Andrew, and asked him whether he knew the whereabouts of Uncle Siamanja.

The boy ran into a hut and emerged with an old man dressed in clean ragged clothes, smoking a pipe. Andrew bowed, pressing his hands together; the two men took each other's hands and greeted one another warmly and seriously, repeating the ritual exchange, and more, inquiring about other members of each other's families, and gravely smiling from time to time. After a few minutes Andrew introduced me, and said that Siamanja would be pleased to answer my questions.

Siamanja clapped his hands. The boy ran quickly to bring two chairs, onto which Siamanja and I settled ourselves, while Andrew crouched between us. My chair only had three of its original four legs but the boy propped its unsupported side on a platform carved out of the wall of the hut.

Siamanja said he would like me to take notes, so I pulled a little notebook out of my hip pocket.

I asked my questions one at a time. Andrew and Siamanja got a long conversation out of each one, turning away from me and chatting, chewing on the pipe, frowning, commenting, telling a story, laughing–only a very small part of what they said was translated for me. At the end of an hour's interview, I checked my notes with Andrew, and he said, "Yes, that is right."

Matakenya was the Shamwe head man who used to live beside the Sengwa river near the double baobab tree. The people would take a concern to Matakenya. Matakenya would take it to Simutenga, a spirit medium. Simutenga would clap his hands to show respect and Matakenya would then be possessed by a spirit. Simutenga would speak to spirits when they were manifested in his presence, and tell them what the people wanted.

Now there is a lion with black and white spots who is called Matakenya. This lion is easy to recognize. He is here now, when they are asking for rain. So the ancestral spirits have come along, intact with the moved family.

The ceremonies used to take place under the Matakenya baobab, with much beer brewing, drumming, dancing, and drinking. One container of special beer was reserved for Simutenga.

In the present village the lion Matakenya sometimes roars all night in front of one or another house and the people wonder why. In the morning they ask the person who slept there what he has done that they haven't known about, and what happened in his dreams.

The same spirits protect the people, and protect the land.

As we finished I asked, "Is it all right for me to have asked about these things?"

Siamanja answered me seriously. "You *must* know, so you won't offend the spirits."

Two of Siamanja's statements have become a part of my further thinking. He told me that the same spirits protect the land and the people, and that you must know the spirits so you won't offend them.

I don't know exactly what Siamanja and Andrew meant by "spirits." In Shona the two English words "god" and "nature" are both translated as "mwari." I take this as a sign that the Shona people regard the universe as one fabric. The developed Western world has paid dearly for its rejection of such a philosophy until now, when, in a sudden outcry for the preservation of biodiversity, the philosophy is being restored. We say that the same principles protect the people and the land. With increasing dismay, we are realizing that to understand and not offend those principles is no small assignment.

*   *   *

Most of Zimbabwe was experiencing a drought while we were studying the elephants' wells. Sengwa was not badly affected, but in surrounding areas the trouble was severe, and had attracted attention in the American news. On the day I left for Zimbabwe a friend at home had pressed into my hand a check for one hundred American dollars. "Use this," he had said, "to help a hungry family."

As I accepted the assignment, I knew that it would be difficult. If one family was hungry all would be hungry; it would be an offense if one family was helped beyond its neighbors. When I got to Sengwa I asked Andrew and Zaccheus for advice. Two days later Andrew brought me a message from Zaccheus. We must buy forty kilos of mealie-meal and get it to Joe Furunga's brother. This man was blind, he could not work, the government was giving no help, and he had a wife and two children. I noted that my advisers, from the Shona and Ndebele cultures, had selected a Tonga family to help.

Within a month the institute truck made a trip to Gokwe; the driver obtained for me forty kilos of mealie-meal. News passes quickly through the bush, and on the following Sunday, when I was up on Ntaba Mangwe, I received a radio message from Ian Coulson that a strange-looking couple was asking for me at the station.

"Who?"

"Party by the name of Furunga." I asked Ian to urge the party to wait while I drove down, but while he was on the radio they disappeared. Barefoot and blind, they had walked twenty kilometers to the station in the heat of the day, and returned twenty kilometers to their village empty-handed.

I let everyone know that I would be spending the following Sunday in our cottage. That morning I baked sourdough bread in a cast-iron pot set on the coals of a fire. Just before noon I noticed a strange-looking threesome walking toward the house.

Tall, erect, light-footed, Joe Furunga was in the lead. Behind him walked a small woman in a clean ragged dress, looking down and placing her bare feet carefully on the path. In her right hand she held the end of a peeled stick about eight feet long. Behind her, lightly holding the other end of the stick, walked a blind man as tall, erect, and light-footed as Joe and with the same round cheerful face. Joe left quickly after introducing us, for he was on duty at the station. The couple and I drank tea and ate hot bread with jam, spilling it all over the place, for my bread didn't hold together like the sadza they would make from the mealie. But with no language in common except the food, we enjoyed ourselves. Then we crowded into the vehicle with the bags of meal; Lysa and the institute's accountant, Chowa, who lived not far from the Furungas, joined us. Half an hour later the road became impassible near a prosperous homestead on a hill—a village with a dug well. Chowa dodged into one of the huts and emerged with his wife and seven children. Expecting us, they had killed a chicken and prepared a fine sadza and stew. I thanked the family for killing a chicken, but at this everyone laughed—"We love it when guests come, for then we eat meat."

Toward the end of the feast Chowa said he was sorry he did not have an mbira. This is a small traditional instrument, with metal keys that make a buzzy tonal sound, resonated by a half gourd: you pluck the keys with your forefingers and thumbs. You sit or crouch while playing, the roundness of the gourd rests in your lap, and you attend to it with your hands close together. Now Chowa asked in a reverent voice whether we knew that the skill to play the mbira is inherited, not learned, and that Furunga is an mbira player. No—I was amazed that nobody had mentioned this to us before—we had not known.

Beyond Chowa's village the footpath was too narrow and uneven for a vehicle. We watched as the Furungas lifted the twenty-kilo bags onto their heads and started off, foot ahead of foot, each person with one hand on the bag and one on the stick that joined them. After a while they stopped and each one turned around carefully so as not to uncenter the load. Furunga called back to Chowa. Chowa responded and waved, and Mrs. Furunga waved back.

"He says, 'Let me know when you need music,'" said Chowa.

Quiet friendships had developed among the members of the team up on Ntaba Mangwe. Andrew, Sam, and Matt often spent evenings in the cookhouse writing letters, Andrew to his wife and Sam and Matt to their girlfriends. When they began to fall asleep, Matt and Sam would retire to a large tent down the hill from a metal bungalow that had been built in association with the old tracking station. Andrew would retire to the bungalow, as would Zaccheus when he was with us, rolling a barrel against its door lest a leopard come in the night. Lysa and I would go out onto a little north-facing peninsula not far away, spread out our sleeping bags, and listen to the natural voices of the night. Lysa had put up a tent on a flattened bit of the ridge. Protected by her presence above me and by the promontory's vertical walls, I slept a little farther out under the stars. In the morning I would creep to the cliff's edge and watch the valley fill with light. Lysa, from her spot, could see the sun rise over a dip in a long ridge that joined the main body of the mesa to a separate vertical-walled lump to its west. On some mornings I joined her just before sunrise and we watched the dip together, waiting for the sun.

A few minutes before dawn one morning, Lysa pointed out a movement on the ridge that she had noticed before. The better part of a kilometer away from us, a tiny human figure was carefully moving westward. Silhouetted for a moment against the horizon, it disappeared into the dark shape of a cliff and reappeared on top, making its way to a huge flat rock on the highest point of the lump. There it stood, a stick figure of a man, facing east.

Suddenly the man's legs and arms began flinging out in all directions, spinning and whirling and stamping. We heard a sharp click just after each time we saw a thin leg strike the rock.

The sun rose over the ridge, huge and tulip red, asymmetrical and wobbly. The dance stopped. The figure traced its earlier steps in reverse and turned into an ordinary man. When the camp came to life there was Zaccheus as if he had just gotten up, poking the fire and preparing tea.

The drought continued for two months more, and then it broke. Rain fell in Sengwa and all over Zimbabwe.

16

BE PATIENT WITH
YOUR DRUMMING

ONE DAY WHILE SAM WAS MONITORING THE MURERE FOR
visits of animals, he noticed two barefoot men wearing gray
shirts, carrying rifles and handmade knapsacks, and suspected
that they were poachers. They crossed the sandy riverbed by
crouching and taking flying leaps, swishing their feet to the sides
as they landed, as if to disguise the humanness of their footprints.

Sam radioed Ian Coulson at the institute, who deployed a
team of scouts with rifles to apprehend the men. Andrew was
sent out to Samapakwa with the team. Zaccheus was planted in
the radio room as the central coordinator of information. All
day long then for many days he stood with a map on his desk
and a radio in his hand, like a general in some army, while on
Ntaba Mangwe we Americans, the only people with an overview, assigned ourselves a responsibility that we hadn't anticipated. While surveying the movements of elephants we kept an
eye on the movement of people as well. Every now and then we

heard a volley of shots and cried to one another, "Who shot? Was somebody shot?"

Occasionally, we noticed a new suspicious movement or finding. One day, Sam reported some bundles of grasses tucked into a rock wall near the road at the bottom of the mesa. Excitedly, Ian and a helper drove out to investigate. Zaccheus laughed when he heard about this. He had collected and stashed those grasses one day several months earlier while waiting for the road-building crew to shovel stones into a sandy area in the road. He was going to use them to freshen the beds in the Ntaba Mangwe Transect Camp.

But the angry, confused spirit of war was in the air. It was absurd, as I have always thought war must be. You don't know what is going on, you can't protect the people you love, you can't catch the people you are meant to catch, the people you are meant to catch are not personal enemies, and anybody might be killed at any time.

Two rhinos were killed during that incursion. The scouts caught the poachers, who were taken to justice. In view of what I had heard about justice, I wasn't sure whether I was glad they were caught or not. I wasn't even glad Sam had reported them, as the report placed our friends, who were hell-bent to protect the rhinos, in ultimate danger. It was unnerving to hover on top of the world looking down and listening, like Olympian gods, to life-threatening affairs for which we ourselves were partially responsible.

This was the first of several successive incursions. Every day became more precious than the one before, as none of the scouts died. But in spite of all their efforts, they could not win the battle. The poachers were always ahead, already having killed one or more rhinos. Several poachers got caught, but the number of rhinos plummeted. Our aerial censuses during the previous research season had revealed dozens of rhinos. Now, two years later, we were watching the process of extinction. It doesn't take much.

We talked among ourselves about Rowan's scheme to save the species. He wanted to tranquilize all of Zimbabwe's rhinos, saw off their horns, and sell the horns on a legal market. The horns would grow back in, to be sawed off again, a renewable resource. If local communities could profit from having rhinos in their midst, Rowan predicted, they would break rather than support the smuggling chains. We thought he might be right in Zimbabwe, but how about places where local communities are less cohesive? And for what experience of life would the de-horned rhinos survive?

During the days of shooting we saw signs that the elephants below us were nervous. One day we documented a stampede that involved ten families and lasted six hours. Sam saw the first family start running from a spot north of the Mlalazi Pools—as far north as he could see. That family's panic was apparently spread by sound, because before they arrived the next family south on the floodplain was running. The stampede spread from one to the next till it affected elephants as far south as we could see. No elephants drank from their wells on that day: I assume that there wasn't time. Only at the open pools could they grab quick gulps and keep running, and some that were drinking at those pools were far from their ordinary ranges.

The incident and several others like it occurred on days when the sound of shooting was in the air, for poachers had just been sighted near the northern boundary and a team of scouts was closing in on them. Perhaps the guns terrified the northern elephants, we thought, by reminding them of the culling they had experienced a year earlier. The panic that accompanied their flight must have been debilitating. We speculated about the impact of culls on the survivors. People who survive human culls often suffer from spiritual injuries. In humans, erosion of spirit is considered a real phenomenon, for it has measurable manifestations. We will probably find the same when we come to studying other species in adequate detail. It is not in the evolutionary scheme of things to have to put up with mass killing.

The repeated disturbances during the end of the season reminded me of a disagreeable piece of unfinished business. I had intended to talk with Rowan, face-to-face, about culling. He had been unavailable when we arrived in the country, for he was caught in a political crisis that threatened his position in the government. The crisis had prevailed throughout our stay; now I must try for a conversation during our final week in Harare.

Recently I have found in Wendell Berry's essay "A Practical Harmony" an encapsulation of the sort of thing I wanted to consider with Rowan:

> The goal is a harmony between human economy and nature that will preserve both nature and humanity, and this is a traditional goal. The world is now divided between those who adhere to this ancient purpose and those who by intention do not—a division that is of far more portent for the future of the world than any of the presently recognized national or political or economic divisions.
>
> The remarkable thing about this division is its relative newness. The idea that we should obey nature's laws and live harmoniously with her as good husbanders and stewards of her gifts is old. And I believe that until fairly recently our destructions of nature were more or less unwitting—the by-products, so to speak, of our ignorance or weakness or depravity. It is our present principled and elaborately rationalized rape and plunder of the natural world that is a new thing under the sun.

"Principled and elaborately rationalized" because we know what we are doing; while doing it we are measuring the depletions and acknowledging the unfairnesses for which we are responsible. I wanted to ask Rowan how he reconciled his plan for continuous elephant culling with what he, an elephant biologist, knew about the lives of elephants, and with what he, a Zimbabwean, knew about the traditional relation between indigenous Zimbabwean people and wild animals.

I thought about these things as Sam, Matt, Lysa, Andrew, and I drove precariously up the Charama escarpment and travelled the length of the scrubby, overexploited Mafungabusi Plateau, heading back toward Harare. I was aware, as we met the pavement on the eastern side of Gokwe, that it was transporting us from the indigenous world into the world of fountains that arch like diamond necklaces over enormous, productive fields.

But I was on a fool's errand. Only in my last week in Zimbabwe was I granted a few minutes of consultation in Rowan's office. Halfway into my first sentence Rowan held up his hand. Quietly, with a stern half smile that could have been that of an authoritarian father reprimanding a child, he said, "Katy, you are talking to a stone."

I stopped talking and looked at my colleague. I thought, "For crying out loud, Rowan." But Rowan's expression said, "You are in a subordinate position here, and it would not be wise for you to keep talking." At the same time it said, "You know I have struggled with this for a long time, and my mind is made up."

I didn't finish my sentence, for I wasn't a zealot. Now I see that my silence preserved my status as something different—an adversary. And that, for better or for worse, was the outcome of the conversation for which I'd traveled so far and waited so long.

I think we both appreciated the complexity of the situation, appreciated that the one of us who might have been permanently silenced was not, and the one who claimed to be a stone was not. My recollection is in fact of something intensely human, of two people engaged in different levels of the same problem, energized by different convictions, answerable to different human contingencies, valuing differently the experiences we'd had among wild animals, living in a different sense of what is possible, and so espousing different views.

When I stepped outside, the air was lovely. I looked up into the crowns of blooming trees—for October here is spring, and Harare is a beautiful city—and felt a surge of relief, although my work was unfinished. "I'll be back," I thought to myself, looking at the building I was leaving.

A few days later, a Sunday morning, was my last morning in Harare. The other members of the team had departed before me. I dropped by Rowan's house to leave off some data, for we were coauthors on publications from the previous field season. Rowan, alone in the house where in previous years I had repeatedly been a family guest, received me cordially. We sat on the broad porch of the spacious colonial house looking out at flowering jacaranda and bougainvillea, pale rich purple and brilliant red orange against a blue blue sky. One small and two big dogs, including fat old Portia with her graying nose, lay at our feet, moaning, scratching, and sleeping.

I said that Sengwa had been wonderful, and I was grateful to have been there. Rowan said that he was sorry his affairs had not permitted him time to join us for a visit. I told him a few details about the elephants, their preference for their wells over other sources of water, and the use the other Sengwa animals were making of the wells. Rowan listened with interest and pleasure, remembering Sengwa and her living inhabitants. I said I'd enjoyed crouching beside the elephants' wells, examining each one the way you examine a spider's web or a whale song, as a unique and useful masterpiece. Some were large, some small, some old, some new, some tilted, some erect, some deep, some shallow, some made mostly with trunk work, others with much foot work—all made by members of a single species, and designed on a common theme. I described the elephants' uncanny selection of digging places where the water table was within a trunk's length of the surface, and Rowan was interested in the mystery.

I told what it was like to examine the animal tracks near the wells with the scouts, and learn from them whose tracks they were. Baboons, hyenas, warthogs, impalas, porcupines, jackals, buffalo, lions, leopards, civet or serval cats, and many birds, as well as elephants, were drinking from the wells regularly.

I said that without the scouts' intricate understanding of the bush animals we couldn't have done the project. We'd used several field guides in identifying animal tracks, but the scouts had had further criteria. They had noticed how the gestures of animals differently affected their foot movement and placement and distribution of weight; the combination and placement of tracks on the sand had told them stories that they had relayed to us.

It was a shame the scouts' reservoir of knowledge about Sengwa's wildlife was not available to others, I said—a shame that in these days, when 40 percent of rural Zimbabweans could read, all existing field guides were written by foreigners in foreign languages for foreign tourists and hunters. Why not engage Andrew and Zaccheus—good writers, naturalists trained in Sengwa—to make field guides in Shona and Ndebele for the use of the people who should ultimately be responsible for the fate of the local wildlife?

I had taken the liberty of suggesting this idea to Andrew and Zaccheus. Both had said that they would like to do work of this sort. If allowed to return again, I said, I would like to make it possible for them to write field guides in their languages. It might be a valuable thing for future generations of Shona and Ndebele people to have a record of this generation's intimacy with wild animals. The loss of such intimacy struck me as one of the problems of Western-educated people.

After a moment of careful thought Rowan, who was Western educated, said he liked the sound of that project, and a proposal for it would probably receive his support. With that gesture he waived a chance to get rid of an adversary; and I the adversary felt a burst of gratitude and respect.

We said not a word about each other's wrongheadedness toward elephants. Not that we forgave the wrongheadedness, but something else was going on, something that set us adversaries suddenly into the same world with each other. After all, preservation of community is a first principle in all cultures. *Pfavira ngoma, usiku urefu,* the Shona say: Be patient with your drumming, the night is long.

Five years have now passed since that day in Rowan's garden. There has been no further culling in Zimbabwe, but this does not signify a change of heart. It is because the wildlife estate ran out of money, and culling is expensive. The Sengwa cull was the last the Department of National Parks and Wildlife Management could afford, even though it had a stockpile of ivory worth tens of millions of dollars.

This contradiction frustrated Zimbabwean officials intensely and drew them into cooperation with leaders from several other southern African nations that also had growing elephant populations. The meetings of the Convention on International Trade in Endangered Species (CITES) provided a spectacular forum. There, at two-year intervals, representatives from more than a hundred countries, most of which had neither elephants nor the desire for ivory, found themselves listening to escalating reports about elephant populations that were out-

growing their limited habitats and raiding the crops of indigenous farmers. They heard complaint after complaint that costly
management procedures were needed while unspendable
money was sitting in storerooms. The urgency of the complain-
ing intensified with time, until in June 1997 the convention
voted for a partial ban on the ivory trade.

The New York Times reported the decision as follows:

> JOHANNESBURG, June 1997–A worldwide ban on the
> sale of ivory was eased today to give three southern
> African countries, all of which have healthy and
> growing elephant populations but little money to take
> care of them, the right to sell their stockpiles of ivory.
>
> The Convention on International Trade in En-
> dangered Species (CITES) backed a deal that would
> allow the countries, Botswana, Namibia and Zim-
> babwe, to make a one-time sale to Japan next
> year. . . . The decision came after almost two weeks
> of debate over whether sales of any sort would en-
> courage the kind of poaching that was a factor in the
> decline of Africa's elephant population from 1.3 mil-
> lion in 1979 to an estimated 500,000 today.
>
> But the southern countries and their supporters
> argued that the ban was punishing those countries
> that had made great progress in protecting their ele-
> phant herds. . . . The revenue from the ivory sales
> [nearly 60 tons of ivory, is] estimated at more than
> $30 million. . . . "This is a triumph for sanity, objec-
> tivity and for recognizing developing countries' abil-
> ity to take their own decisions on natural resource
> management," said Dick Pittman, the president of
> the Zambesi Society. . . . "It's a major, major achieve-
> ment."

The ivory sales would be permitted if two conditions were met. First, all ivory-producing and ivory-buying nations must demonstrate, within a twenty-one-month period, that the partial reopening of the ivory market would not lead to a resurgence of poaching. That such a thing could be demonstrated seemed to many CITES representatives, including those from the U.S.A., an absurd impossibility. Much effort had been devoted to a search for ways to make every population of elephants, Asian as well as African, safe from poaching. No solution had been found that could be readily implemented, even though much attention was given to the fact that there are measurable differences in ivory from geographically different elephant populations.

Second, the money from ivory sales must be plowed back into wildlife management. Recalling what management means in Zimbabwe, I found little comfort in this stipulation. For eight years Zimbabwe's plan to cull five thousand elephants a year had been thwarted by lack of money. If renewed trade in ivory enabled Zimbabwe to revitalize its culling program, each decade would see the destruction in Zimbabwe alone of fifty thousand African elephants. Zimbabwe's ivory stockroom would instantly refill—would the new ivory be sold as well? Would further trading be proposed in subsequent years, to support further culling?

The goals of wildlife management and commercial farming are becoming indistinguishable, I said to myself. I began to feel bitter and depressed. But then I started hearing from friends who had attended the CITES meeting. Strange things had happened there, suggesting corruption of the CITES process. In time, I put their several stories together into the following:

The circumstances of the vote, taken in the last evening of the meeting at the insistence of Japan, Norway, and Zimbabwe, were unusual. For the first time ever in CITES, the voting was secret. The secrecy was in itself a controversial decision, also pressed by the delegates from Japan and Norway. The outcome of the vote surprised many participants, suggesting that under the cover of secrecy some representatives had cast their votes contrary to their openly stated positions and to their mandates from their home constituencies. This apparently allowed several countries with no elephants and no trade in or industry using ivory–Norway, for instance, and a group of Caribbean states that receive the benefit of Japanese "development aid" programs for fisheries–to support resumption of the ivory trade.

In what seemed to be a reciprocal action, several southern African nations with no trade in or industry using whale products then supported Japan in trying (again by secret vote) to reverse the protected status of the northeast Atlantic population of minke whales. The status of whales is initially determined by the International Whaling Commission; after the CITES meeting, Japan and Norway tried to introduce secret voting there, too.

Japan, Norway, and Zimbabwe have made many attempts to legalize the exploitation of endangered species in the past, but on this occasion they had unprecedented success in gaining allies. The political collusion has created a dangerous situation for both whales and elephants. My informants speculated that this new development was made possible by the secret vote.

I suppose that the Convention in International Trade in Endangered Species and the International Whaling Commission were founded as mechanisms to curb the greed and dishonesty of individual nations, and that the founders are now rolling over in their graves.

Propose an alternative, I say to myself.

The best alternative is no ivory trade at all.

But in case the decision is made to reopen trade in ivory, I will propose an alternate form of the trade. CITES has appointed a committee to study the risk of partially reopening the market for the proposed ivory sales. Can poaching be curbed if it rears its ugly head again? If the committee decides that it can, I will recommend that "legal ivory" be redefined to exclude ivory from culling or sport hunting. Otherwise, legalization of the trade will result in the *legal* deaths of vast numbers of elephants, through government-regulated culling and sport hunting, without a blink from the international community.

For those who want to harvest ivory and save elephants, it is worth noting that it is possible to harvest ivory without harvesting elephants. Left to their own devices, elephants die of old age. Elephants' tusks grow all their lives, so that the oldest animals carry the most ivory. A healthy elephant population free from poaching, culling, and sport hunting would produce more ivory than a managed population. Iain Douglas-Hamilton pointed this out long ago, and Rowan Martin confirmed the observation when he used a mathematical model to explore a series of alternative culling schedules with "ivory production" as their goal.

Local people who know the terrain, its wild animals, and the hazards of walking among them could collect the ivory from randomly aging and dying elephants. Most of these people live in communal societies, which are self-regulated for honesty when the situation is such that they can communally benefit from it. The greatest challenge would lie not in the means of harvesting—for that could be accomplished on foot, slowly, in the old manner of gatherers—but in the many levels of human relations surrounding the harvest.

This way of doing things need not disturb the ivory-producing elephants. The oldest females in the population, the ones with the longest geographical and social memory, would live to old age and the families would have their leadership to the end. The biggest males in the population would transmit their fitness to the next generation for as long as they possibly could. The families and bond groups and bull groups and populations would remain intact: In short, elephants could produce marketable ivory while living natural lives.

Or almost natural—some form of birth control would be needed for populations in confined areas. During the first year of an experiment in South Africa, an immunovaccine called pZP seems to be working as a contraceptive for elephants, with little disturbance to the treated families.* Perhaps it would take some time to get it right, but I doubt that contraception would, in the end, pose an insuperable problem.

In its focus on the elephants and rural people, the program I would propose would resemble Zimbabwe's CAMPFIRE. But while CAMPFIRE recommends that one of the vulnerable parties be harvested for the benefit of the other, I would propose that both be allowed to live.

The program's weakness would be the same as that of all other ivory-trading programs: it requires honesty. In an honest context, my plan would be preferable to any that involves destroying the lives of elephants. But in the absence of honesty, it is better that there be no ivory market at all. Better for the elephants, and that means better for all of us. For the community that includes us all is larger than any of us knows, and its health reflects the quality of the relations between all of its parts. I am well if you are well. I am well *only* if you are well, too.

* As reported in *Bioscience* (February 1998).

17

EVERYTHING
CHANGES

DURING THE LONG JOURNEY HOME FROM ZIMBABWE IN the first days of October 1992, I entertained myself by thinking about the Shona and Ndebele field guides that Andrew and Zaccheus would write. That work would expose future generations to the scouts' intense sensitivity to wild creatures—a sensitivity I regarded as a cultural treasure. Within a few days, an awareness of my role as facilitator in the scheme to preserve the treasure brought me a dream, which arrived with a title, as if it were a theatrical performance.

TAKING BACK THE CHILD

SCENE I: A filthy passenger car in an old African steam train, which is heading west through sunstruck bush country. Except for myself, the only woman and the only white person, the passengers are African men, anonymous, exhausted, preoccupied, silent, and without joy.

I am present to keep one of the men company. He is engaged on a dark mission: carrying a small baby to the end of the line, where he will put it up for adoption. The baby is in a basket, at the man's side. I am going along not because I believe in the mission but out of compassion, to make a hard day bearable.

The train windows are so dirty that I can hardly see out. But suddenly a flash of light shoots obliquely through the window beside me and strikes my head. In that instant I decide, without forethought, that I myself will adopt the baby—never mind that I do not know how to care for him nor how to bring him up.

A half second later, the father lifts the baby out of the basket and clasps him to his chest. He looks at me with the first sign of life in his eyes, saying, "I have changed my mind. I will keep the child." He does not know that I had the same impulse in the same moment, nor will I tell him. The coincidence of our decisions to keep the baby fills me with wonder.

SCENE II. We are the same people in the same car of the same train, traveling rapidly east, as I know because sunlight is streaming through the windows on the other side of the train. Every man is on his feet dancing, drumming, singing, and laughing: I, an invisible observer, hear exuberant voices over the din of the wheels on the tracks, see dust raised by the dancing streaming out of open windows, and feel that everything is charged with energy.

SCENE III. I am moving among serene, long-skirted African women with babies on their backs and buckets on their heads, in a grove of large gray-green acacia trees under a blue sky. Walking gracefully along a pinkish footpath toward a spring, the other women are talking among themselves in a language I don't understand. In mid-conversation one of them gestures to me, and points to a baby in a shawl on a stout woman's back. It is the baby who was on the train.

The baby was the people's culture, as I knew in the moment of waking. They had taken it back, and in so doing, had turned away from the West. As they turned back toward home they celebrated, and I became an outsider. I had known I wouldn't know how to take care of the child: now I realized that I didn't even know his language.

In Ithaca I found a Zimbabwean Shona teacher, Mabel Hungwe, the wife of a Cornell graduate student. She was sophisticated, having grown up in cities and received a fine education, but in her childhood she had often visited the communal lands where her grandmother lived. Mabel taught me in her apartment, with her year-old son, Mukudzeyi–"God's blessing"– crawling at our feet, nursing, or resting against her pregnant belly.

I chose to learn as a child would learn, through conversation. "How shall I congratulate you when your new baby is born?" I asked.

"Oh, you can say *'Makorokoto'*: that means 'congratulations.' And I will say, *'Tese.'* That means 'all of us.' The baby is for all of us."

One day, I arrived just as Mabel was returning from a visit to a local hospital, where a Shona friend lay dying. That day we talked almost entirely in Shona. Mabel expressed her feelings for the dying man and his wife, so far from their larger family, saying, *"Ndine urombo, ehoi"*–"I have sorrow, alas"–words of compassionate grief. Spoken in a heartbroken voice, they seemed the saddest words I had ever heard.

Mabel did not spare me from aspects of the Shona experience that she found disturbing–for instance, a belief in witchcraft that is still prevalent in many rural areas. At the time of a death people look about at the women in their village, searching for a witch to blame even if another cause for the death is obvious. Once suspected, a woman may be thought of as a witch for the rest of her life. Life is difficult and unfair for rural Shona women, Mabel told me. It is better that you are American.

In June 1994, the International Fund for Animal Welfare paid my way to Johannesburg for a conference on elephant translocation. This seemed a marvelous coincidence, for the trip would enable me to visit Andrew and Zaccheus in Zimbabwe and to advance the plans for our field-guide project.

Just as I left my house to drive to the airport and catch the plane, I heard the phone ringing. Uncharacteristically, I ran back in haste and answered it. It was Loki's father, calling with a message from Loki in Zimbabwe. A single-engine plane carrying Ian Coulson, Andrew Masarirevhu, and Timothy Chifamba Dube on an aerial wildlife census had crashed in the Bumi Hills. Timothy and the pilot had been killed in the impact; Andrew and Ian, terribly burned and heroic in their assistance to one another, had been flown to an intensive burn unit in Pretoria, South Africa. Both were now conscious, but neither was expected to live through the week.

By the time I landed in Johannesburg, they were both dead.

I'm that faraway figure in the small valley halfway down the long hill—I'm the one wearing the blue canvas hat like Sibanda's. Men, not women, wear such hats: they are sold to laborers at the rural bus stop stores, but in Sengwa we all wore them. I'm wearing a skirt, but it, too, is inappropriate, for it is a wraparound skirt that would fly in the hot wind were I not pinning its wings against the crooked trunk of a mopane tree. Backed up against the crooked tree I am an awkward, lost human figure, surrounded by many other people.

The valley is flanked by high hills, foothills of the eastern highlands. Looking northward, I see against a hazy sky the wild and crazy profile of the blue mountain range called Nyanga, or Crooked. The people near me are Andrew's relatives, about whom he'd told me fond and descriptive stories; he wanted us to meet. The women are wearing sun-bleached cotton dresses or skirts and blouses, with sun-bleached scarves on their heads. A few men are wearing black suits, some are wearing National Parks uniforms, some rags. The rags and the khaki and black suits alike are streaked with earth for the men have been digging. Some are in shoes but as many are barefoot, nor would many of the bare feet fit into shoes, so spread are they and so cracked. They are moving, skirts and shirts and neckties flying in the wind, between the northern hillside where the funeral service was held and the fresh grave in the valley to which the wind carries the sound of their vigorous wailing and singing.

Andrew lies in the grave. You can see his death in the faces of more than a hundred people flowing toward it down the hill. His uncles, brothers, father, grandfather, sons, and male friends surround the grave, where something is happening. Ringing the men and unable to see anything through the wall of them are women—his wife, mother, aunts, great-aunts, grandmothers, cousins, sisters, and daughters. I stand among the women, weeping, and they are weeping but we are separate. *"Ndine urombo, ehoi,"* I say, but this causes one of them to glance fearfully toward me. I sense in her eyes the fear of a witch.

A young Christian minister stands on the rubble pile beside the grave. From the dust in the air we women know that the men are shoveling dry earth and dust into the pit. When it is full they continue to shovel, building a rock wall around the new earth as they add it. The shape is that of a bier, such as I have seen in pictures of Egypt. When only a single layer of rocks remains to be set in place, the men speak to one another and disperse. Then for the first time the women see it, a symmetrical, solid structure beautifully built, almost a meter high, on all sides smaller at the top than at its base. Beside it, facing the pale blue mountains, stands the small cookhouse in which Andrew's wife and four children have been living for nearly a year. It is unfinished; his salary was slowly providing enough money to finish it, a few bricks after each paycheck. His family will continue to live there indefinitely, a responsibility for Andrew's father and uncles and part of their property.

As the men, Loki and Rowan among them, disperse, each makes his way up the gently sloping face of a small southern hill overlooking the grave. They look down at their feet as they climb, as if searching for something. In a few minutes they return, each with a field rock, a rock warmed by the sun and cleaned by the wind, in his right hand. In single file they parade around the bier, fitting their rocks together carefully to make the top surface.

The women do not show the same composure as the men. The last ten days of continuous grieving has so exhausted them that they seem hardly alive. Everything is mixing into a new order. Things could have been worse: he is here and buried, not lost or rotting, not abandoned in South Africa, not becoming a restless, resentful spirit that, unable to join his family members, would haunt them. The women take turns contributing verses to an unending song. Translated, its words are, "Andrew, did you remember to say good-bye to your mother? Did you remember to say good-bye to your sister? Did you remember to say good-bye to your grandmother?" as each one cries out, in turn, for a lost relationship.

Before the physical ceremony at the grave, there was a spoken ceremony under the sky on the hill. Rowan was one of several who spoke. Carefully and formally he honored Andrew for his work, explaining exactly what had happened, as far as anyone could say, to cause the plane to crash. His words were translated in detail. Andrew's mind and spirit had qualified him for the task that had killed him: therein lay the irony of the situation, but it was nothing to be superstitious about.

I had driven to the funeral in the backseat of Rowan's car, next to Andrew's brother. In the course of our hours together, I asked Rowan to permit me to make a brief, informal visit to Sengwa. I wanted to talk with Zaccheus. Zaccheus was not able to attend Andrew's burial, for he had to drive other scouts to the south for Timothy's burial, because there were two diverging teams going to the funerals of Sengwa staff. Zaccheus would be grieving and I wanted to grieve with him. Besides, we needed to decide the fate of our field-guide project. On top of that, I had a small piece of research to do, if Rowan would grant me permission.

Rowan arranged a ride for me on the following day. The timing was such that I missed the service for Ian in Harare on the following Friday, and I deeply regretted not being there. So did several of the Sengwa scouts, as I learned when I was in their midst. "We have lost three of ourselves," they said.

I greeted Zaccheus in his office. Very glad to see each other, we agreed at once that we could not do our project without Andrew. I asked Zaccheus to accompany me back to the eastern highlands to talk with Andrew's wife and four children about their needs. He said that he would very much like to do that, and a few nights after my arrival in Sengwa, we set out in each other's company under a full moon. After resting on the cement step at Marapira for several hours with other travelers, goats, chickens, and the mailbag, we boarded the bus that Andrew had taken so often. That is how I came to know what the ride is like, and to think about the many journeys that the moon witnesses.

But my story finds its natural end in the days before that journey. In the absence of its leaders, the Wildlife Research Institute is proceeding with its formal schedule. The station flag goes up, the pump generator turns on, and the scouts gather,

as usual, at seven. Tea is ready to be served at ten whether anyone is there to drink it or not; the lawns in the institute's two
courtyards are watered at eleven forty-five; the men dismiss
themselves at noon and gather again at two; tea is served at
three; the men disperse in the evening. Aside from these ap-
pearances and the manning of the radio room, I do not know
what everyone is doing—perhaps they themselves do not
know. Toward the end of the first day, a small gathering occurs
spontaneously in Zaccheus's office, where he and I have spent
several hours in conversation, trying to come to terms with the
great shift in the universe that snatched Andrew, Timothy,
Ian, and the pilot away from us.

One of the entering scouts asks me whether I've come with
work to do. I say that I have. My request would be for a small
team to walk the length of the river over the course of the next
three days, just as we did two years ago with Andrew. I'd like to
know what the elephants' well digging is like in a subsequent
year.

A cloud lifts in the room and all voices answer at once.
Work will bring relief to us all.

As we walk the river we regain balance. The floodplain is
alive and fascinating. We dedicate our walk to Andrew, who,
the last time we made it, was the master of ceremonies, calling
us all together at the end of each kilometer's survey and entering our findings on a map that he made with the help of the
topographic map. This time Zaccheus, holding Andrew's map,
takes that responsibility.

At sundown on the first day we reach the same place we had
reached at the end of the first day when we did the river walk
with Andrew. But Zaccheus is looking unhappy. We examine
his map and find an error. We shall have to start the second day
by backtracking to the place called Poacher Talk. I say, "Oh my
goodness, this happened last time as well. We are feeling An-

drew's presence so intensely, we are even making his mistakes."

Poacher Talk is a nondescript spot in a broad expanse of hot, gray sand north of the Sengwa-Manyoni confluence. It's the most desolate portion of the whole twenty kilometers, and the longest section of those we'd found two years earlier that had no wells or attempts to dig wells. We had dug seven wells of our own in such areas, to find out why the elephants had eschewed them. That is to say, Andrew, Matt, and Sam dug them, taking turns digging and making fun of each other. In each well-less area we had found the water table deeper beneath the sand than an elephant trunk could reach. Somehow the elephants knew.

Poacher Talk was the deepest pit we'd dug. At more than two meters down, the digging hadn't produced even damp sand. When Matt, the tallest of us, was out of sight at the bottom of the pit, the sand that his shovel was sending up to us was bone dry. All the way down the sand had no sticking power, so the pit had to be considerably wider than deep, and the longer the men had dug the stupider their effort had seemed. Finally, they stopped, by which time we were all in a silly mood.

There was no shade nor water anywhere near the pit; it was midday: none but fools would have spent the morning as we had spent it. Matt got out and we all collapsed with laughter at our enterprise. Sitting on the sand piles with our feet hanging into the pointless pit, we stayed right where we were and fell into a long conversation about poachers. Andrew got into a storytelling reverie in which he imagined the experience of a pair of poachers trying to get away with murder in Sengwa. He got us inside the heads of poachers so vividly and in so many dimensions that we all forgot everything else for a whole hour. When, later, we placed the pit formally on Sam's map, we named it Poacher Talk. Now I tell the scouts about all of this, and they laugh, remembering Andrew.

But our error means that many wells will have to be counted

again at the confluence: we will lose time by starting tomorrow so far north of our intended starting place. Our second day will be a long one. At best we will reach Croc Pool by noon. Each of us looks forward to Croc Pool, for it is the scouts' favorite spot in Sengwa: the crocodiles are scary and interesting.

But when noon comes on the morrow, we can't find Croc Pool. In fact, we can't find any of the Murere Pools. Are we hallucinating, all of us together? We fan out in all directions and search. We hold the topographic map this way and that way, lining up notches and lumps on distant hills. This is absurd, though. The face of Ntaba Mangwe is looming over us and we all know that this is what it looks like from the Croc and Murere Pools. We are standing where they should be.

We look at each other. The river has flowed since any of us was last here. A river can pull sand down and change the contours of the land. It can flatten out the land until there are no pools left.

Those pools were the biggest source of water for all the wildlife in Sengwa.

We wait for Zaccheus to speak.

"Ah," he says, finally, an expression of extreme puzzlement on his face. "Everything changes."

I turn away to hide my sudden tears. Even Sengwa changes. Alone and weeping, I walk east along the flat, high, barren plain covering the place where the Murere Pools used to be.

On the far side of it I come to a vertical drop; below it lies a new channel. My hands fly up. I shout for joy!

For although the channel is dry, of course, there is water underneath, if someone knows how to find it. And elephants, who know, have been here. In the new channel elephants have dug wells.

"Zaccheus! Joseph! Engson! Christmas!" The scouts come over to join me. We count the wells and there are one thousand.

ACKNOWLEDGMENTS

I AM GRATEFUL TO EVERYONE WHO APPEARS IN THESE STO-
ries. All the events I report really happened and all the elephants and people are real. Even so, my reporting must be
taken with a grain of salt, for no two people ever see quite the
same thing, and there's no such thing as the last word. I myself
would describe us all differently if the experiences we shared
had been different.

The scientific research that brought us together was initially
sponsored by John S. McIlhenny, who, though shut in by ill
health, expressed his passion for natural history by supporting
studies of wild animals and the restoration of endangered
species. I am sad that this book was not ready in his lifetime, for
I wrote it in part for him.

The Cornell Laboratory of Ornithology offered a home to
our elephant studies before the founding of the Bioacoustic Research Program. Many thanks to Charles Walcott, the director
who took the risk of putting us on the laboratory's map before

our studies were an obvious part of its mandate. I am also grateful to the present director, John Fitzpatrick, and to Christopher Clark and Kurt Fristrup of the Bioacoustic Research Program, for my ongoing association with the research program and Cornell. Many members of the lab helped with the technical aspects of the expeditions I've summarized here, and with the analysis and archiving of the sounds we brought back: I thank them all. I won't attempt to thank all my associates in the field, for we were like family—too close for thanking. I just hope they enjoy the book.

Our African expeditions were supported by the National Geographic Society, the World Wildlife Fund, and the National Science Foundation. In 1990 I also received a Guggenheim fellowship. In January though March of 1985 and 1986 I was a guest of the Amboseli Elephant Research Project in Kenya. In June through October of 1986 and 1987 we were guests of the Department of National Parks and Tourism in Etosha National Park, Namibia. In June through October 1990 and 1992, the Department of National Parks and Wildlife Management in Zimbabwe welcomed us in the Sengwa Research Institute and provided the infrastructure that made our radio collaring, tracking, and air flights possible.

Then, too, there were friends who contributed personally to the work. Jack McIlhenny I have already mentioned. Caroline Getty sponsored the genetic research that was an aspect of the Zimbabwean project and included me in the journey into the Namibian desert with herself and Russ and Aileen Train. Another journey, in which I joined Bess Tonachel and four other women for a week of elephant-watching in Tanzania, was a gift from Bess, matriarch. Frank Baldwin, Rozalind Kenworthy, and Elizabeth Bixler made private contributions from home in the belief that our work would help elephants. I hope they were right and I wish they'd been with us. Without all this help and the adventures, friendships, and discoveries to which it led, my story would not be the same.

I am deeply grateful to the friends in Sengwa who shared their experiences with me, at greater risk than they realized: I am aware that my attempt to write about their views of the world is fraught with possibilities for misunderstanding. Andrew Masarirevhu and Zaccheus Mahlangu gave me permission to reprint their written words. Zaccheus has corrected the errors in my reports of events in which he participated, but others probably remain in the larger text. I hope that they are harmless and will be forgiven.

When it occurred to me to try to write a book, I asked for advice from two friends whose writing I admire. Scott Elledge took a look at an early outline and wrote me: "The conclusion will come clear as you keep forcing yourself to put into words all you feel sure of after long study." Jim McConkey read my first effort to tell about the elephant cull and responded, "Maybe you are writing this book, in some unconscious way at least, to resolve these crucial problems; maybe the answer to them, however ambivalent or uncertain it may be, is what underlies everything that follows." Clearly, what I most needed was time to figure out what I felt sure of.

In this dimension I received help from Elizabeth Marshall Thomas, Sy Montgomery, and the literary agent Sarah Jane Freymann. Their combined efforts eventually brought *Silent Thunder* to the attention of Rebecca Saletan of Simon & Schuster. There is no way I can express adequate appreciation to Becky for her confidence in the project at its outset—for that confidence won me the wherewithal to live while I worked out "everything that follows"—and for her wise and sensitive professional guidance in the years of our work together.

The book was nearly done when Becky accepted the position of editor in chief of North Point Press. At Simon & Schuster, in a style very different from Becky's, Bob Mecoy then shook me out of my involvement with the final draft, encouraged me to admit some stridency in the end of chapter 16, and hit the bull's-eye by giving words to an idea that was in my mind but not on my tongue. "If they want to save elephants and harvest ivory," he said, "they should harvest the ivory without harvesting the elephants." The text delivers some words roughly like those as if they were mine: here I gratefully acknowledge them as Bob's.

Back home, my family and friends had long sustained an interest in my project. I won't forget countless forms of practical and moral support that we all received from Nancy Gabriel. I won't forget the biweekly Wednesday breakfasts with Mike Yarrow and Steve Holmes. Mike, a sociologist, was working on a book about coal miners in Kentucky; Steve, a Harvard graduate student, was writing from a psychological perspective about John Muir's early life. Many were the pointed questions we fired at each other, and many the waffles consumed.

Joyce Poole, Russ Charif, Bill Langbauer, Laura Brown, David Larom, Sam Payne, Lysa Leland, and Tom Engelsing read versions of the manuscript for scientific as well as personal integrity. Nancy Dyer, Holly Payne, Laura Payne, John Payne, Ann Edwards, Howard Nelson, Elizabeth Marshall Thomas, Roz Kenworthy, John Kennedy, Carey McIntosh, Joan Ferranti, Richard Hendrick, Bob Lloyd, Sue Lloyd, Ruth Yarrow, Carol Kimball, Margaret Kennedy, Peggy Lawler, Joyce Morgenroth, Ann Silsbee, Paul Berliner, and Sidney Holt all gave me insights from their various perspectives as writers, conservationists, humanists, family, and friends. My daughter Laura made the maps and dedication drawing. Ruth Lee, the book's designer, and Edith Baltazar, its production editor, saw me through many transformations. Michael Accordino designed the jacket, and Pete Fornatale kept us working toward a single goal. The book reflects the contributions of all these people, and probably of others I will remember after it is too late for formality.

Finally, I wish to acknowledge the compassionate animals in whose remembrance I have written all these words. All these greeting rumbles, and all these cries for help.